SEYCHELLES SINCE 1770

D1263044

DERYCK SCARR

Seychelles since 1770

History of a Slave and
Post-Slavery Society

Africa World Press, Inc.

P.O. Box 1892
Trenton, NJ 08607

P.O. Box 48
Asmara, ERITREA

Africa World Press, Inc.

P.O. Box 1892
Trenton, NJ 08607

P.O. Box 48
Asmara, ERITREA

Copyright © Deryck Scarr 1999

First Africa World Press, Inc. Edition 1999

Library of Congress Cataloging-in-Publication Data

Scarr, Deryck.
    Seychelles since 1770 : history of a slave and post-slavery
society / Deryck Scarr.
        p.   cm.
    Includes bibliographical references and index.
    ISBN 0-86543-736-X (hardbound). -- ISBN 0-86543-737-8 (pbk.)
    1. Seychelles--History.   I. Title.
DT469.S457S33   1999
969.6--dc21
                                                                99-20019
                                                                       CIP

Published in England by:

C. Hurst & Co. (Publishers) Ltd.
38 King Street, Covent Garden
London WC2E 8JZ

PREFACE

Slave and post-slavery societies of the Americas and West Indies are today uncommonly heavily and often very well studied historically; those of the Indian Ocean in Île de France or Mauritius, Île Bourbon or Île de la Réunion, and particularly in Seychelles, are very much less so. Small size along with relative remoteness until an international airport opened in 1971 may have something to do with this in the case of the subject of the present book, Seychelles. And perhaps the fairly widespread image of Seychelles as a latter day Eden – if not indeed the site of the Biblical Eden itself, as General 'Chinese' Gordon once solemnly proposed – went to encourage the, for the most part, relatively superficial inquiry that has taken place into these Islands' past, even though the archival record is very rich, and can be strange.

With its fundamental dependence on the original record in Seychelles especially, but also on the Seychelles records in Mauritius, La Réunion, London, Paris and Rome as well, this book could not have been written without sustained and long-suffering help in particular from the then national archivist of Seychelles, Mr Henry MacGaw, and the Carnegie librarian, Mrs Flavie Jackson. Their enthusiasm, willingness to make introductions, and general kindness were essential. Ms D.J.F. Griffiths was my valued research assistant. For access to private archives, personal experience and first-hand opinion in Seychelles, I am greatly obliged to M. France Morel du Boil, Monseigneur Felix Paul, M. Gustave de Comarmond, Archbishop French Chang Him, Mme Maryse Eichler, Dr Maxime Ferrari, the Nageon de l'Estang and Chesnard de Giraudais families, Lady Bonnetard, Mr Kantilal Jivan Shah, Mr Maxime Fayon, M. Guy Lionnet.

I acknowledge with a very strong sense of obligation the value of conversations with, additionally, Mr and Mrs Georges Balthide, M. Alexandre Deltel, M. Henri Dauban, the Arissol family, M. Harry Savy, M. Henri Gontier, Dr M.H. Stevenson-Delhomme, Mr Javad Hadee, Mr R.S. Rassool, Mr Suleiman Adam, Mrs Douglas Bailey, Mr Joseph Stravens, Mr Nicholson Stravens, M. Maxime Jumeau, M. A. de Charmoy Lablache, M. Davidson

Laporte, Inspector Antoine Low Tee, Mr Joseph Lablache, Count Godwin Spanni, Bishop Briggs, Sir George Souyave, Frère Louis Augustin, Mr and Mrs A.W. Bentley-Buckle, Mr Justice Sauzier, Mr and Mrs David Dale, Dr Guy Ah Moye, Dr Brian Barbier, Mr J.A.M. Lousteau-Lalanne, Mr A.C. Mackellar, Mr and Mrs Marcel Fayon, Mr Georges Payet, Mr C.D. Collet, Mr A. O'Brien Quin, Mr Bernard Lousteau-Lalanne, Mr Tony Hayman, Mr and Mrs John McQueen, Mr Bill Jackson, Mr Patrick Nanti, Mr Bernard Sham Laye, Mme Paule Lanier, Mme Renée Troian, Miss Nadine Camish, Miss Fiona Nicholson, Mr Bernard Verlaque, Mr Albert Gendron, Miss Paule Hoareau, Mr and Mrs Roger Wilson, Mr Ed Palfrey, M. and Mme M.R.M. D'Offay de Rieux, Mr and Mrs Bernard Jorre de St Jorre, Mme René Michel, Mrs S.J. Oliaji, Mme Bryan Georges, Mr Ali Parkar, Mr Serge Savy, Jacques Hodoul, James Michel, Yvon Ogilvie Berlouis.

I am indebted to former President J.R.M. Mancham for an instructive interview, as well as to then Prime Minister and later revolutionary and in the end democratically-elected President F.A. René for a number of conversations as well as for hospitality at his home. Sir Colin Allan, last Governor of Seychelles, was a supportive friend from the Western Pacific who had opened my way there to archives of the old Anglo-French Condominium of the New Hebrides (Vanuatu of today) and performed a similar service in Seychelles. Outside Seychelles, I was and am very grateful to Mr James Cameron for his conversation and for lending me his unpublished newspaper despatches and private correspondence on the Collet *règne de terreur*, to Mr W.W.E. Giles, Mrs Hilda Giles and Sir F.D. and Lady Jakeway for their own reminiscences of the 1940s; to Dr Mary Seed, daughter of Sir P.S. Selwyn Clarke, and to his executor, Mrs Molly Barger, for access to Sir Selwyn's private papers. In Rome Brother Ethelred Fergusson smoothed my path to the Marist Brothers' archives. In London Mr Jeffrey Ide, then Keeper of Public Records, very kindly asked his staff in Portugal Street to suffer and succour a necessarily importunate visitor. In so many of these cases I can, alas, thank only the shades. And I am grateful again to the Archives of Mauritius, the British Library, Rhodes House, the Church Missionary Society, the Society for the Propagation of the Gospel, the Archives Nationales and its dependencies in Paris, as well as to the model Archives Départementales de la Réunion and the Bibliothèque

Municipale de Caen. The Institute of Commonwealth Studies in London provided a base.

So, in Seychelles for some months, did Anse à la Mouche, Beau Vallon, Praslin, La Digue and even for a time remote Frégate Island. There or anywhere else, nothing but the historical record coupled with the author's own perception is responsible for the pages that follow.

Canberra,   DERYCK SCARR
March 1998

CONTENTS

MAPS

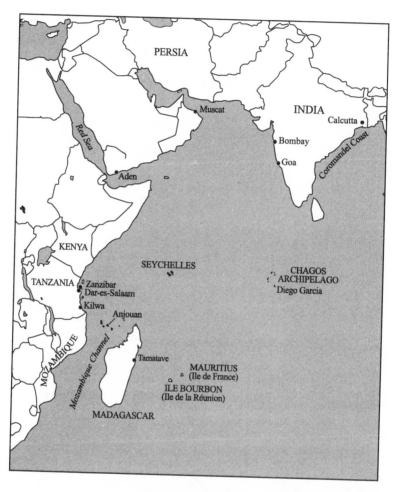

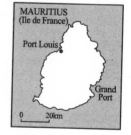

The Indian Ocean

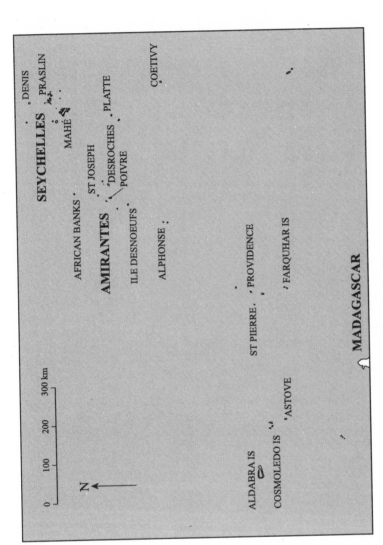

Seychelles

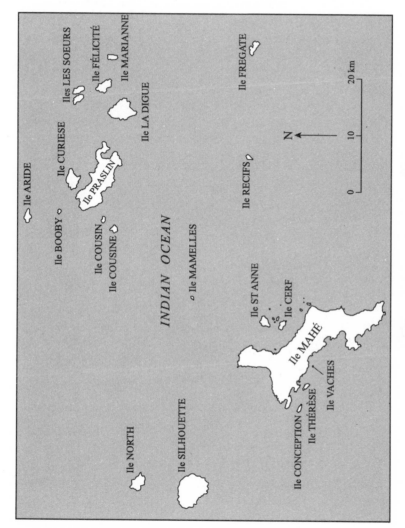

The Granitic Islands

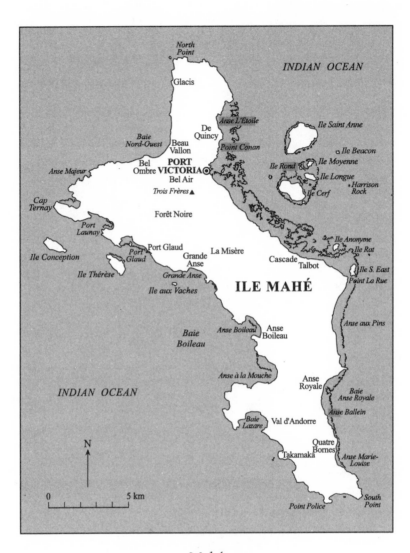

Mahé

1

A KEY TO AN OCEAN
1770-1811

Human history in Seychelles has often been made very much by the geographical position across thousands of miles of sea between 4 and 10 degrees south and 46 to 56 east that gives these Islands an air of strategic importance, without there ever having been more than half the apparent substance. Variously counted at between ninety-two and 115 islands depending on the definition of 'island', the archipelago which acquired both its name and many of its enduring social characteristics in the late eighteenth century totals around 107 square miles of land for birds, giant tortoises, crocodiles at one time, turtles and man to form societies in the midst of the Indian Ocean.

In 1976, having in effect no choice because Britain was leaving and would not contemplate the assimilationist option which France offered successfully to neighbouring La Réunion, the people of Seychelles declared themselves a state. Seychellois of Mahé, the principal island – all of 17 miles long by 5 wide at its broadest – gathered on 29 June to hear their President and Prime Minister address them at independence celebrations in English, French and Créole. Their history was as much encapsulated in the fact that these three languages had to be spoken as in the range of skin colours among the crowd who heard President J.R.M. Mancham launch into his personal poetic evocation of his people:

> *This unique blend of races*
> *Ambassador of all cultures*
> *Mirror resplendent of all colours*
> *The melting pot of ethnical prejudices*
> *The fusion-spot of every civilisation*
> *You are a sample of the world to come....*

At least the forty-two islands that stand on the Seychelles Bank
–Mahé itself along with the other main islands of settlement Praslin,
La Digue and their satellites – are unique geologically. They are
the only mid-oceanic islands of granite in the world. Typically a
continental rock, granite is here found in the midst of the sea
almost 600 miles from Madagascar, the nearest landmass, rising
with much memorable erosion to 3,000 feet at Morne Seychellois,
the highest peak of Mahé. They are understood to be part of the
huge palaeozoic landmass of Gondwanaland which included modern
South America, Africa, Antarctica, Australia and peninsular India;
and were left on their own when Gondwanaland broke up and
dispersed. These granite massifs, islands of great beauty, probably
reached their present form a million years ago. Human beings
have inhabited and for the most part despoiled Seychelles for a
mere eight generations.

Mankind did of course sight them long before the first houses
of timber and thatch went up on St Anne Island at the mouth
of Mahé's fine harbour in 1770. The East Indiamen *Ascension* and
Good Hope were there in January 1609 riding as in a pond close
under St Anne's lee. Their crews watered with the utmost security,
but for the crocodiles. They were in no fear of their fellow man,
'for you cannot discerne that ever any people had bene there
before us'. The Indiamen's people called their find the 'dezert'
or 'Desolate llands', but only in the sense that they were uninhabited.
As the *Ascension*'s bosun put it, 'these islands seemed to us an
Earthly Paradise.' Another of the shipborne diarists wrote:

> We found heere good store of cocos, some fresh fyshe (whereof
> most part were skates), lande turtles of so huge a bigness which
> men will think incredible; of which our company had small lust
> to eate of, being such huge deformed creatures and footed with five
> claws lyke a beare. Wee kylled also many doves with poles of
> wood, which was a sygne of the small frequentation of this place;
> yet for those that are forced and stand in neede of water and such
> things as afforenamed it is an excellent place and comfortabell ....[1]

These paradisial land-specks had been sighted by Portuguese a
century before – grey-green peaks jutting randomly out of an empty
sea. Portuguese charts of the early sixteenth century show land-
specks in the approximate position of the granitic as well as some
of the coralline islands; but the promise that the biggest is rich

in gold, silver, silk, sulphur or amber surely indicates the wrong latitude, or a leg-pulling seaman. A map of 1517 names the main granitic group the Seven Sisters. It gives the name which serves the coral Amirantes to this day: *ilhas que achou da segunda rez o almyrante dom Vasco*, islands sighted by Vasco da Gama on his second voyage in 1502. The charts were not good enough to warn one mid-sixteenth century Portuguese seaman that he was approaching what is now called Boudeuse, a particularly treacherous low-lying cay. His ship's bones lie there still, fathoms down. And it would have been remarkable if those excellent Indian Ocean pilots, the Arabs, had not preceded the Portuguese by many years. Aldabra, the great atoll famous for its giant tortoises, may derive its name from the Arabic al-Dabaran, the Five Stars in Taurus. In the early sixteenth-century text of the pilot Sulaiman bin Ahmad bin Sulaiman al-Mahri, Seychelles themselves appeared as the Zarin Islands. Sulaiman had not sighted them himself, but on the word of seamen who had done so, he reported the existence of the granitic group. He had also heard that there were other low, sandy cays running down towards the African coast – later to be known as the Amirantes. The certainty, with him, was that every-thing about the Zarin Islands was unknown, for they were shunned as a danger to navigators.

There was no Arab settlement, then, unless by a shipwrecked crew whose story died with its last members. And the feathery casuarinas are likely to have been brought by birds. For centuries, the islands made their existence apparent to the world only by the fruit of the extraordinary palm which is unique to some of them, the coco-de-mer. The fabulous nut was washed up on surrounding shores from India to Indonesia. It became the object of the goldsmith's embellishing art and the storyteller's invention. According to tales collected by Antonio Pigafetta for his account of Magellan's circumnavigation, the coco-de-mer shared its homeland with the legendary roc and, one would like to imagine, with somewhat less legendary pirates too as they moved on from their haunts in Madagascar during the 1720s. In the 1830s foun-dations of buildings, graves and cannonballs were spoken of as being found on Frigate Island. Treasure was also much spoken of – although it should be remembered that the Indian Ocean pirates were not interested in burying their booty; in the 1720s they were negotiating with the Tsar to pass it through his port of Archangel.[2]

Until archaeology passes judgement on local conviction that certain stones on Silhouette's shore mark ancient Arab graves, or until skeletons are found with the treasure of the 1720s pirate Le Vasseur for which intensive search was made at Bel Ombre on Mahé for thirty years in vain, we must be content with the written record. This says that the first man to be buried in Seychelles was Laurens Verdier, from that great source of seafarers St Malo. He was laid to rest at St Anne on 4 August 1771, without immediate benefit of the rites of his church. On 1 December, happily, the first parish church was inaugurated, to the honour of St Anthony of Padua; and on the third the *habitants* – fifteen of them originally, with seven slaves – held a form of mass for his soul '*pour qu'il plaise à dieu lui accorder place parmi les predestinés*'.[3]

The church had other uses. On 17 March 1772 the widower Dominique Sicard from Antibes, sea-officer in the service of Louis XV, married Marie-Joseph Darrae – just in time, for their son Louis, the first recorded '*creole de lisle Sechelle*', was born the next day. So one tradition was established in Seychelles, but only one, for men and women living together there have not always troubled St Anthony or his heirs to marry them. Nor do men always concern themselves at all about the children they may scatter out of wedlock. Nearly eight generations' experience was behind the lawyer who interjected, when paternity laws were discussed in Seychelles Legislative Council in March 1965, 'Bulls don't look after their young – cows do!' Strictly, St Anthony had no direct heirs on St Anne. The parish books close on 13 October 1772, when they record the baptism of Joseph-Benoit Marie, ten-year-old slave of Commandant Antoine Nicolas Benoit Gillot. The fact that the black boy's baptism is recorded in the same book as that of the white Sicard child may be one pointer to the origin of the idea, much propagated locally, that Seychelles never had a colour question.

If it were true, the credit would lie with France, and the outcome would be unique in French as in British colonial experience. As recently as 1766 Paris had decreed that all blacks were slaves, their progeny indelibly tainted and forever barred from entering the ruling white class.[4] The same registers were sometimes used in Île de France also – and there the taint was recognised too. Proponents of the view that Seychelles uniquely differed would have had to explain how white people of the Mascareigne Islands came to identify themselves as '*Seychellois*' and call blacks '*Créoles*', a name more frequently applied impartially to all those locally born in French colonial societies, and in the Mascareigne islands proper – Île de Fance and Île de la Réunion – often held to be a mark of distinction for whites locally born. The first two generations of settled life in Seychelles were at any rate conducted under France. Expeditions from Île de France – 'Mauritius' to the Dutch and British – explored the islands in 1742 and 1744. In 1756 another expedition annexed them to France, leaving a stone of possession on Mahé – so named by Lazare Picault, commander of the first two expeditions, for his patron the great governor-general of the Mascarenes, Bertrand-François Mahé de la Bourdonnais, who was soon afterwards distracted from these relatively insignificant discoveries by his struggle for India with that eternal enemy, the British.

Awesomely beautiful, the islands declared themselves when Lazare Picault anchored in 1742 on the south-west coast of Mahé – originally named Île d'Abondance by him for its ranks of coconut palms along the shore, and its streams falling from granite heights rich in magnificent timber. These islands had probably been cut off from landmasses longer than any other islands; evolution had produced 190-foot trees. Beaches of white sand were revealed; coves where small craft could be safely careened; a harbour where fifty first-rate sail of the line could ride in perfect security, however hard the south-east monsoon blew between May and October. In the ravines, or among the *bois de natte*, played grey parrots, turtledoves, guineafowl; 'unknown' species like the magpie-robin and black paradise flycatcher appeared. There were giant land tortoises, green turtle for eating and *caret* or hawksbill turtle for shell. There were crocodiles up to fourteen feet long; a weary exploring party sent inland by the commander of the 1756 expedition, Corneille Nicolas Morphey, frigate *Le Cerf*, said that they found crocodiles on the mountain tops.[5]

These and the expeditions that followed them left the Islands scattered on the map with place-names. Morphey named the whole group Séchelles in compliment to the Vicomte Moreau des Séchelles, then controller of finance; he added Cerf Island so that his own ship should not be forgotten. *La Digue* and *La Curieuse*, which came for timber in 1768, are similarly enshrined now in granite. Their commander Marion du Fresne changed the name of Picault's Île des Palmes to Praslin, so that the Duc de Praslin, Minister of Marine, should not go unremembered. Du Fresne himself sailed on to his explorer's death in New Zealand without a memorial in Seychelles. These expeditions left little apart from names, and a feeling of uneasiness in the councils of France. In theory the strategic value of Seychelles was obvious. They were out of the hurricane track, as Île de France and Bourbon were not. And they had easy access to legitimate areas of France's ambition in Madagascar and Africa, from which slaves came to aid the civilising mission, and to Arabia and India, centres of the wealth indispensable to the spread of culture. Seychelles, sea-officers believed, were the most important *point d'appui* France had in the Indian Ocean. They would admirably serve, say, a frigate preying on the eternal enemy's Bombay trade; she could send her prizes back to Seychelles, and take advantage of the prevailing winds to rejoin them there and escort them to Île de France next January; and she could still count on having a crew so revived by fresh fish and green turtle that they could carry her on at once to ravage British shipping off the Cape of Good Hope.[6] The trouble was that Seychelles could equally well serve the British, and some of their adventurers in India threatened to put the Islands to use. When the Chevalier Grenier published an account of his Indian Ocean voyages made in the late 1760s, he suppressed descriptions which would give any idea of the strategic advantage of Seychelles, lest the British should occupy them before France got round to it.[7]

France could do this at a cost of 200,000 livres a year, one of the many memorialists in Paris reckoned. Used economically, the money would send a ship from Europe with supplies every year, as well as a small vessel several times to Île de France.[8] Seychelles might be used as an experiment in controlled colonisation, another advised after talking with seamen who knew the islands. France's great misfortune overseas was that Frenchmen who went to the colonies did so only to make money and come home quickly. Let Seychelles be a new departure: people them with young found-lings on six acres apiece and have them work hard at agriculture as peasant proprietors in the tropics not relying on slaves, for it was essential, to a healthy colony to have many inhabitants actively employed in a small way, said this visionary, rather than a few in opulence and idleness.[9]

Perhaps he had talked with the second-generation *grand blanc* of Martinique, Médéric-Louis-Elie Moreau de Saint-Méry, who would discourse temptingly about his Antillean neighbours there and on Santo-Domingo. It was easy to believe that by the mere fact of being on the island white people were ennobled, he said, yet they felt they were birds of passage, camping on a fortune, always about to go home to Paris. Gambling became a passion, and they agreed that the climate and the ready availability of nubile girls – black, coloured or even white – made sexual restraint not worth attempting. Whites indulged their children beyond measure, giving them slave children to whom even in play they would be tyrants; on growing up the slaves would, according to their sex, become either instruments of, or ministers to, the master's pleasure. White créoles were hospitable to a fault, and impetuous, alternating between lethargy and impatience. Women were pampered, and had a tendency both to melancholy and to extreme jealousy of others of their sex, which they nonetheless covered by effusive demonstrations of affection. They could brook no obstacles because these were so remote from their experience; they married young and would rapidly replace a defunct husband with a new one.[10] Or perhaps the designer of colonies in Paris simply had a crystal ball. If so, nobody else looked into it. Society in Seychelles acquired many of these characteristics. And the Islands were colonised at first because a great botanist joined hands with an entrepreneur who might have been an admirer of Robinson Crusoe.

Pierre Poivre, botanist, *Intendant* of Île de France, founder of the Pamplemousses Botanic Gardens there, wanted a nursery in the right latitudes for spices he had spirited out of the Dutch East Indies. Seychelles was in the same latitude as Amboina, and might be suitable. Since the late 1750s Poivre had been thinking of using the Île des Trois Frères – as Mahé was sometimes called, after its three-headed mountain – and in 1770 he sent cases of nutmeg, cinnamon, pepper and cloves on the seven-day passage to Mahé for planting along the broad bay henceforth called Anse Royale.[11] The nursery's guardian was the former French East India Company soldier Pierre Hangard, from Normandy, who founded the oldest landed family of Seychelles – a coloured family. In 1785 Hangard's daughter Marie-Jeanne, born in Seychelles and not quite

fourteen years old, was married to the twenty-five-year-old Breton
Jean-Marie Le Beuze. Marie-Jeanne's mother, Annette, was Malagassy,
and it was said that the groom was now condemned to perpetual
exile in Seychelles – certainly he could never go now to live in
Île de France, where he would have counted as a coloured person
by virtue of his marriage. The pair married on St Anne, inheritors
of the wreckage of the colony established there by the presumed
admirer of Crusoe.[12] The latter was a one-time promoter of lotteries
in Rouen, Brayer du Barré, who had come to Île de France
obsessed with the vision of a trading empire stretching from India
to Brazil; the empty Seychelles were an obvious if humble place
to begin. Barré, unlike his prototype Crusoe, did not need to
visit his desert island before establishing his colony on it; seated
in his study, he sent off his settlers – fifteen whites, a black woman,
five Indians and seven African slaves. They got nowhere with
their planting, and anyway Poivre's spice business encroached upon
that of the colony. Gillot – that unfortunate, unhappy hermit of
Seychelles, as he described himself – was doubly commissioned by
the man of science and the man of dreams, and Barré had cause
to complain that his people were diverted from making him rich
to making the spice garden grow.[13]

Barré was an indefatigable importuner, brilliantly inventive; and
if, as his eventual judges said, he did salt his new project with
stories of a silver mine only waiting to be precisely located on
St Anne, then in this he was the father of expectation in Seychelles:
tales of hidden treasure always abound there, and an individual's
success in business was likely to be ascribed to his having got
started by finding a crock of gold pieces under a fallen coconut
palm. Only a little maize, rice and manioc to feed the first settlers
came from St Anne, and they deserted it within a couple of years.
Appeals and projects still flooded from the embattled promoter
in Port Louis – for the loan of ships, a treaty with the King of
Portugal to guarantee regular supplies of slaves from the Portuguese
factories in Mozambique, soldiers, materials for a fort, means to
get the interloping Hangard off St Anne, and measures to stop
despoilers from Bourbon and Île de France from harvesting turtles
and timber without concern for the future. It was all in vain.
Ruined and disgraced, Barré died in Pondicherry.

From Poivre on the other hand came an indirect but lasting
a legacy. His garden at Anse Royale on Mahé, though a failure,

was nonetheless a great security risk for the next royal commandant of Seychelles, de Romainville, who arrived in 1778 with a file of soldiers to erect permanent buildings for the King and benevolently lead the few of his subjects then resident to live at peace with one another. In May 1780, when a nervous French ship bore up for Mahé flying English colours to deceive an expected British guarrison, this no less nervous commandant rooted out what was left of Poivre's garden.[14] It had served one purpose: the cinnamon had escaped, its seed carried by birds into the hills where, flourishing to 40 feet high, the cinnamon trees came to clothe the granite as man cut out the rain forest. The great *bois de fer* was cut from its habitat on the lower slopes of the mountains, and much of the *bois de natte* and the *capucin* too. Along with all this, Gillot as commandant in the mid-1780s had to deplore feuds already endemic among the *habitants*. '*Je suis malâde de chagrin de toutes ces sottises et de ce désordre,*'[15] he groaned in 1785 when physically sick too but uncomforted by the surgeon who was part of the King's colonial establishment. Among the despoilers were men now remembered in the place-names Port Glaud and Anse Boileau. Hangard had taken over not only St Anne but much of Mahé itself, making a fortune from the rape of the islands, selling tortoise and turtle to the slavers from Madagascar and Mozambique which had been making Seychelles a regular port of call since 1770 on passage to Bourbon, Île de France or, in the case of a few Americans, the Caribbean and the southern States. Without the fresh food of Seychelles, they would have been even more hard-pressed to get an economic proportion of their diseased human cargoes back to the purchasers in Port Louis and St Denis.

From these years the people of Seychelles derived an obsession with quarantine. In June 1784 came the slaver *Belirair*, firing a gun in token of distress, all her crew down with scurvy and most of the slaves too. Smallpox was more common, and communicable. Among other provisions she needed rice, which Gillot in Hangard's absence took from his too-plentiful store against the expostulations of Annette, paying her in slaves from the stricken cargo but not at her price, and Hangard, returning, claimed that he had been robbed.[16] Hangard commanded here, said Gillot bitterly. He ruled surgeon, soldiers, everybody, because he had money obtained by trading recklessly with Captains Boileau, Gilbert and Drancourt, who cleared for Seychelles ostensibly to load coconut oil but actually for turtles – meat or shell – which they sold in Bourbon for coffee, devastating Seychelles in the process regardless.[17] Hangard's friend Jean-Baptiste Quiénet fell out with Volamaefa, the free Malagassy woman for whom he had left the King's service because she was rich in slaves – richer than the King, half of whose slaves were always maroons in the mountains. If they could get hold of a pirogue, maroon slaves made off to other islands. The royal slave Dominique had got away to Silhouette. Gillot sent a detachment to shoot him and promised to stake the runaway's head in the pathway to encourage the other blacks to stay at home, all forty or fifty of them. He might have liked to perform a similar service for the half-dozen white *habitants* too – shiftless people, he found them, accustomed to changing their country as they might change their shirts.[18]

There were more settled men in prospect by 1785 like the sometime naval officer from Bourbon, François-Blaise Savy, accompanied by one son and a slave who died within a week.[19] Settled now since 1665, Bourbon had become over-populated or was seen to be so in those spacious times. Aristocratic families with capital travelled regularly between Bourbon and France, while *petits blancs* or poor whites led a peasant existence in the hills. There was every inducement for other members of the volatile Savy clan to follow, like François' brother Charles-Dorothé, a giant of a man who was to die in his fine granite-built house on St Anne in 1853 at the age of eighty-seven. His giant of a son was poisoned before he could harm the Lilliputians around him. François Blaise Savy had served with Gillot in India during the last war with the British. A gallant man, says Gillot, far removed from the rest of them here. Savy was poor for a time and worked his lands himself alongside his wife and four children, with not a single slave.[20]

Already on Mahé, building granite steps up to his Anse à la Mouche house, was Pierre-Fourmier-Louis d'Offay de Rieux, retired infantry captain from Strasbourg. He had served in India and France for twenty years.[21] After only two years on the island, his younger children were speaking the Créole patois of their eight slaves, or so Gillot said with condescension.[22] What they all wanted, said Gillot, was a fool of a commandant whom they could govern at will; what the Islands needed for conservation and rational development was a hard man who would take a stick to people there.[23]

Such a man came next year, in 1786, to shake his head over the shallow soil and note the granite boulders with a pessimistic eye. He was Jean-Baptiste-Philogène de Malavois. The British had seized the strategic atoll of Diego Garcia as a short-lived base, and he was sent to advise how Seychelles could be fortified against attack. He concluded that it could only be done very expensively. More practically, he encouraged Mahé settlers to turn from their pillaging ways into sober agriculture, though with limited success. They were to become proprietors. No bachelor was to receive a grant of land but only responsible *pères de familles* – a rule made to be broken, for soon there were more single than married men on the Island; a coastal reserve was to be kept for the King – it was soon encroached upon; and no proprietor was to sell his land without permission from the authorities in Île de France, who in future grants would give preference to Créoles of the Mascareignes and Seychelles, along with people skilled in seamanship. Oil was not to be made from coconuts on land so far unconceded, nor were either proprietors or visiting ships to kill turtles without authorisation, unless for their own consumption. And the dozen or so families that this more settled order of society was to tempt away over the next five years from the hurricanes and land shortage of Bourbon and Île de France to join the eight white households and four free black ones whom Malavois found – these new families were to be people who did not change their country with their shirt.[24]

On the whole, the newcomers conformed to this pattern. When in April 1790 the *Intendant* of Île de France sent over a new *Garde Magasin du Roi*, or Royal Storekeeper, and a surgeon for the royal establishment, together with their common brother-in-law, he could take credit for these new proprietors' solidity as citizens and settlers. André Nageon de l'Estang, keeper of the King's store, had been born some forty-five years earlier in Île de France, son of another André who left Brittany as a sea-officer of the Compagnie des Indes. The family was from the small Breton nobility, and the exiles dreamed of returning with a fortune from the Indies to restore the fame of their house. If a published letter is genuine – in which case the Nageon genealogy is defective at one point – a member of a collateral branch, Bernardin Nageon de l'Estang, sailed out of Port Louis in pursuit of that fortune in *corsaires* (privateers), and actually acquired maps to gold and doubloons buried by a successful privateersman in Île de France. However, the genealogy shows that this adventurer was the Seychellois André's son, Jean-Marie Juston, and seems to demolish the treasure story. Both story and genealogy have the Nageon in question dying aboard a corsair off Tamatave in 1798; and since this corsair was crewed by Seychellois the genealogy is probably accurate. The rest of the family were generally content to live more quietly ashore on the profit of their cotton; a barrel-vault fronted by a small chapel guards many of their dead on one of their former Mahé estates, at Anse aux Pins. The surgeon who accompanied them on their arrival, Jean-Joseph Conan, left only a place-name, Pointe Conan; but the third *père de famille* in the party, Jean-François-Marie Jorre de St Jorre, established a *grand blanc* family like the Nageons. The three households ran to eighteen white men, women and children, with thirty-six slaves between them to work the land that Malavois was parcelling out, according to number of children, in nuclear concessions of 108 arpents (acres). Each concession or *habitation* was a strip running to the mountains from a frontage on the sea.

The new influx of white women was welcome to old stagers. André Nageon's teenaged daughter Marguerite Pelagie Appoline was following the custom of the tropics when she married the middle-aged widower François-Blaise Savy. She gave him five more sons to enliven Seychelles, and after he had gone satisfied to his grave in October 1804, she rapidly found or was given another husband. And Charles-Dorothé Savy had many children by a St Jorre girl. So the households were formed: cattle and a few horses were ferried ashore from ships anchored in the serpentine channel through the coral inshore in Mahé's harbour; furniture, kitchen equipment, some silver, glass and much wine were un-packed. Slaves were put to work on soil which experience showed to be far shallower than the luxuriant vegetation promised. At first, all the same, it produced good cotton and maize, rice in the coastal swamps where streams were blocked, and manioc for slave-subsistence on the sides of ravines. And houses went up.

Later generations were to evolve a style of fine wooden houses on man-high stone foundations with granite steps up to verandahs and steep roofs of capucin shingles pierced by shuttered windows. The first generation, though, built in two styles: most commonly, a low thatched structure perhaps at the head of steps; more rarely, a regular mansion like Château Mamelles on Mahé and the Savy house on St Anne, their thick walls built of fire-broken stones, their two full floors crowned by an attic storey under the same steep roof. Mangoes and the potentially towering breadfruit were planted for terns to wheel among. Gardens were laid out on terraces, their broken remnants a wonder and a shame to later generations who let them fall into decay. Behind the houses were a *cour* formed by the separate kitchen, the cotton-house, the straw *cases* of the field-slaves and the *bloc* or lockup where they did solitary penance in darkness for offences against the masters' discipline on which the security of the Islands was reckoned to depend. In front, on the seashore, a creaking coconut-oil mill was turned by a bullock or a black man; throughout the Mascareignes, these two might be placed one below the other on the same auction list or bill. A great press was built for the first generation's major cash-crop, cotton, which served as a currency for the purchase of estates, schooners and slaves. There was a turtle pond, a park for the giant tortoises that made undemanding pets before adding to the diet; and four or six granite posts held a roof of latanier thatch over, say, a whaleboat and a couple of slender pirogues. From the first, the sea was the only easy means of communication, with the coasts indented and the *habitations* isolated from each other by spurs from the central spine of the Island. However, footpaths were cut and some luxurious spirits, especially women, would travel in a hammock or chair slung under an awning between slaves' shoulders.

Words also travelled, and even imperilled the hold which masters had over their slaves. These people had all known each other in the parent islands; they forgot nothing in the long nights now. One arrival from Île de France in 1789, Jean-Baptiste Morel Duboil, had not installed his family in their new home for more than three months before word came to his ears that his daughters were being insulted. Deterred by Malavois from having immediate recourse to his sword, the enraged *père de famille* was further provoked by hearing that droll stories were being told about his brother; and in retaliation, rashly daring, he described one of the narrators as the greatest 'Jean-François' or simpleton it had been his displeasure to meet in this new world. His story was that Jean-François-Marie Jorre de St Jorre had taken his stick to a certain seventy-two-year-old M. Maisonrouge in Île de France,

had been gaoled for it and had been with difficulty spirited away
by his alarmed family. St Jorre was widely connected among the
pères de familles in the community, they closed ranks, and Morel
was hauled before the Assembly of Seychelles – all seventeen members meeting in the commandant's leaky house at the *établissement*,
or township – and was forbidden the Islands. His judges were incompetent to try him, he complained. One of them – Jean-Marie
Le Beuze – was married to the daughter of a sometime slave,
which stripped him of his civil rights as a European. What dangerous
impression must be made on minds of blacks at large by such
treatment of a white?[26]

The Assembly of Seychelles had been newly summoned into
being in response to the heady news of Revolution in France. A
royalist admiral with an Irish name was to be butchered by a
mob in a shop in Port Louis, *cahiers de doléances* were being called
for from all quarters and colonies of France, and Seychelles were
as much part of France in revolution as the mother islands Île de
France and Île Bourbon. Proprietors on Mahé insisted on that.
When they reflected on all they suffered from Île de France over
turtles, lands, coconuts and much besides, they felt it was time
that they corresponded directly with the metropole.

On 19 June 1790 ten of the twelve heads of families then
established in Seychelles, armed with the absentees' proxies, con-
stituted themselves an assembly. Elected president, Nageon read
a letter from the general assembly of Île de France inviting Seychelles
to join as one colony. After that Nageon resigned, having been
too short a time on the Island to form an opinion. Quiénet was
elected, the fact of his Malagassy lady not then appearing as an
impediment to anybody. And the legislators, with their slaves
squatting outside ready to row them home through sea kicked
up by the south-easterly, accepted the advice Malavois gave to
decline the proffered embrace from Île de France. They all knew,
he said, that people there had only vague, contradictory and er-
roneous ideas about Seychelles. Next week there issued the first
statement of independence Seychelles ever heard. The *pères de
familles* would accept no sovereign power other than that of the
National Assembly in Paris, they said; and they wanted most of
the restrictions on them removed. Praslin, Frigate, Silhouette and
North Islands should be reserved to existing proprietors of Mahé.
No newcomers should be granted concessions anywhere without

majority consent. They asked for new plants and a *curé* for their souls. They required that the concessions granted to the free Indian, Ramalinga, from Bourbon should be transferred to some European since Ramalinga had not yet occupied it, and they demanded that no more land should be conceded to free blacks at all.[27]

They therefore wanted a fairly ample autonomy – freedom for proprietors from rules made in Île de France, and absolute separation in law and practice for whites from all black persons, whether slave or free. All that year they went on insisting that they were responsible only to the metropole. Eleven islands around the Seychelles Bank over 300 leagues from Île de France should be part of Seychelles whose Assembly alone should authorise occupation. Only this Assembly should draw up an interim constitution for the new colony. During January 1791, when by chance it was learned that Île de France had advised Paris against their claims, d'Offay de Rieux wrote in stern and fluent rebuke to put the supposed mother island in its place. Four of the seventeen white heads of households now in Seychelles were Créoles of Bourbon, he said; only one was a Créole of Île de France. Six more had indeed been *colons* there, but almost all of them swore they had left because their Île de France existence was so disagreeable. Mostly they had paid their own passage to Seychelles, so they owed the state nothing. And if the metropole only knew and responded to their needs, d'Offay continued, they would make Seychelles a valuable place indeed. Their coconuts, indigo and grain promised better than those of Île de France; their timber sold well in India; their harbour was a unique port of refreshment for ships bound from Africa to the Mascareignes and even the Americas; and as a depot for slaves it would be as useful to commerce as to the conservation of that unhappy portion of the human race who were the object of this particular trade. Sooner or later the port – Labourdonnais, the proprietors wanted to call it – would become important for shipbuilding and repair. It could be a major rallying-point for mercantile and fighting expeditions. '*Voilà ce qui doit être mis sous les yeux de l'Assemblée Nationale et qui, Messieurs, est vraiment digne d'exciter en faveur de nos Îles le Patriotisme de Messieurs nos Deputés*'.[28]

Patriotism at least ensured that Seychelles should not miss out on flying visits from commissioners charged with explaining the Revolution to the Frenchmen in the Indian Ocean. The first pair

came from Île de France *en route* to India, having been instructed
to spend as little time as possible in petty Seychelles but to inquire
into the Morel Duboil affair among other things. They were at
Mahé near the end of July 1791. On 1 August the new national
flag was hoisted in the town. The Tricolor floated above sixty-five
white men, women and children, twenty of whom were active
citizens, and above twenty free people of colour and – much of
the provisions sold to slave-ships having been paid for in the fruit
of Africa – more than 487 slaves.[29]

'*Vive la Nation, la Loi et le Roi*': and, ceremony having thus
been observed, the Seychellois pointed out that they wanted more
from the nation than mere pageantry. They wanted proper port
facilities for one thing, terrified as they were of smallpox. In this
they had good reason: the slaver *Thérèse* had just come in from
one of the main Mozambique entrepôts, Kilwa, where smallpox
was raging, and there were four more ships behind her. When
Commissioner Lescallier arrived from Paris next year *en route* for
Pondicherry, he found the frigate *Minèrve* quarantined at La Digue
with yet another commissioner as well as the governor of Bourbon
himself cooped up on board.[30] Thus it was by shouted words
from the ship's rail to nervous boats lying off at a wary distance
that Lescallier told the proprietors that the National Assembly in
Paris earnestly desired to extend the benefits of the constitution
it had lately devised to all Frenchmen, even those in such distant
parts of France as Seychelles. In proof of the solicitude of the
nation's revolutionary representatives, here was an interim constitution for the Islands – making them an administrative dependency
of Île de France, but with a colonial assembly directly answerable
to Paris. Membership of the assembly was open to any French
citizen over the age of twenty-five; blacks and people of colour,
that is of mixed parentage, were eligible if they were the legitimate
children of free parents – in most cases that question was shelved
for at least another generation. Widows and unmarried women
of property were excluded, however white they might be, but
they could vote for the election of a genuine *père de famille*. Military
matters remained under the direction of the commandant, and
civil administration was to be conducted by elected representatives.
With the object of simplifying matters in so tiny a place, civil
powers were also granted to the new commandant Esnouf, who
was permitted to land when the quarantine period expired.[31]

Esnouf is remembered in legend as the man whose lot it was to apply the metropole's decree against slavery to the slave-owners of Seychelles. They are held to have boycotted him in consequence and, of course, to have ignored the decree. If indeed he had attempted the rash stroke of emancipation which Danton and his confederates later directed, doubtless Esnouf would have been boycotted at the very least. The decree of 16 Pluviose An II of the French Republic, One and Indivisible, came near to causing counter-revolution in Île de France itself.

As one of the metropole's shaken emissaries to that island explained, the horse, cow, ass and African or Malagassy were all seen as animals provided by Nature for the European's use. He associated them together accordingly, in work as at auction where human beings were sold off like beasts. And yet the local-born European, the Créole, was a good fellow, brave and generous, who loved the name of Frenchman and would do all in his power to uphold it – so said the man from Paris. A Créole would have his black flogged with *sang froid*, persuaded that such an action was natural and indispensable.[32] There was no inconvenient agent in Seychelles to press unfathomable views upon the proprietors and wickedly excite the slaves. Danton's decree was passed not in Esnouf's time but on 4 February 1794, after he had left Seychelles, by which time the Islands were on the verge of claiming independence not only of Ile de France but even in a measure from the *Mère Patrie*. And they were about to be provided, notionally, with the Union Jack, colours of a country which happily had not yet acknowledged all the rights of man, although parliament under pressure from mass petitions was beginning the process that ended in the abolition of the British slave trade in 1807 and caused great insult and injury in the end to slave-owning proprietors in Seychelles while releasing ex-slaves into the world to earn their living as best they could.[33]

News of the Franco-British revolutionary war had reached Seychelles by July 1793. The French made it *guerre de course* in the Indian Ocean – privateer warfare, against Britain's rich India trade. Privateering was to make Île de France and Bourbon-Réunion rich for ten years, before a concentrated British blockade brought them near to ruin. French maritime heroes were made in the boarding of Indiamen. Readily to mind come the brothers Surcouf, of St Malo and Île de France; a little less readily, the brothers Hodoul, of La Ciotat in Provence and of Seychelles, slavers now moving temporarily into more profitable waters. Corsairs were at sea within days of the news of war reaching Port Louis in June. By August twelve or thirteen more were fitting out there. Two big privateers passed through Seychelles before the end of the year – *Le Volcan des Mascarins* and the *Vengeur*. By February 1794 the British ruefully reckoned that they could identify sixteen, mounting from *Le Léger's* sixteen guns to *La Ville de Bourdeaux's* forty.[34] Neither list noticed the brig *Olivette*, Captain Jean-François Hodoul: not yet a corsair, the young Provençal mariner was content to carry slaves to Seychelles. He had bought the *habitation* Ma Constance at Anse l'Etoile, and planned to marry the fifteen-year-old Marie-Corentine-Olivette Jorre de St Jorre. This at least the Royal Navy did not prevent,[35] although it carried off the *Olivette*. In February 1794 Commodore Henry Newcome had sailed from Table Bay to cruise for privateers off Île de France in the 32-gun frigate *Orpheus* with the fifty-gun two-decker *Centurion* and the 44-gun *Resistance* in company. On 6 May after close action the *Orpheus* took the 32-gun corsair *Duguay Trouin*, which had been the Indiaman *Princess Royal* until the privateers carried her by boarding.[36] That gave Newcome two prizes, the other being a Danish vessel carrying war stores for Île de France. He had some wounded men and spars too, along with numerous prisoners. He consulted his charts, hauled to the north and on 16 May 1794 dropped anchor under French colours in Mahé harbour. What the French had feared from the first had now occurred. Newcome's journal entry was:

> AM at 8 the Marines of the Squadron under Lieut Matthews landed when the Island capitulated. Squally with rain. Engd Watering & preparing to heave the Bowsprit out.[37]

The British commodore might be taciturn, but the French commandant needed more words to explain away his surrender. Esnouf, in Île de France, was much in demand from the Seychellois as their agent against oppression from that quarter. His successor wrote a long and ingenious letter to explain his capitulation, saying that he had at first refused to supply provisions as demanded by the British when they dropped their disguise – the ruse had not deceived him at all – after seizing the *Olivette*, which the parsimonious

Hodoul had not run ashore according to his promise. The commandant described how he had yielded to pleas from the proprietors when the British offered to exercise their combined broadside of eighty-four great guns upon his paltry four-pounder battery and the muskets of the anxious *pères de familles*; many years later a long-lived slave told newcomers stories of their visible alarm. The commandant emphasised the honourable term of his surrender; and mentioned his regretted inability to save the slaver *Deux Andrés* from capture when she appeared inopportunely round St Anne.[38] She later got away by overpowering the prize-crew – no thanks to the Seychellois, she may have thought.[39]

What Seychellois and the commandant had in mind was more than the usual island capitulation. This meant a volley for the honour of the flag which then came down but might reappear when the interloping squadron was safely over the horizon. The commandant was a subtler man – Jean-Baptiste Quéau de Quincy, civil commandant of Seychelles since August 1793 and in that or another office in the Islands for the next thirty years. Born in Paris in 1748, attached in youth to the household of the future Louis XVIII, de Quincy had come to the Indies around 1770 as an officer in the regiment of Pondicherry. He claimed all the virtues of a solider and wore none of them lightly. He was a man of honour, he would say, frank, impartial, utterly truthful, the very mirror of propriety, scorning prevarication or deceit.[40] Up till his death in 1827 he said so in a manner to invite suspicion. At the least, what he said of his enemy Malavois could as well have been said of him: '*Son age serait bien celui de la retraite, mais son caractère ne lui permet guère la paisibilité*'.[41]

De Quincy had yielded up Seychelles on terms, principally involving the Islands' neutrality for the future, which the departure of Commodore Newcome's squadron would, in the normal course of events, have rendered transitory in the extreme; but for Seychelles' own sake de Quincy had every intention of leaving the formal sovereignty in the hands of the British until after the war was over. Given the reputation of the Royal Navy and its likely reappearance at will, the advantages to Seychelles were obvious. The colonial assembly of Seychelles agreed to remain without a flag until Île de France sent guns and men, so enabling the Seychellois to defend themselves with dignity – in other words, for ever. The Seychellois confirmed de Quincy in his post. Their awareness of the need for this confirmation indicated their recognition that a minor revolution had occurred. As for France, they would serve her by providing her ships with a neutral port. They called on Esnouf to defend them against patriotic resentment in Île de France.[42] This was powerful pleading. Esnouf spoiled it a couple of months later by soliciting a cargo of wine, flour and cotton print. Seychelles was absolutely bare of stores from Europe and India.[43] But such deprivation was unusual. It would take the Seychellois twelve days to sail to Mozambique in the favourable weather between April and September, ten days to Zanzibar, twelve to Bombay, fifteen to Moka, and it was an easy journey on to Muscat. The blue flag they devised with *Séchelles, Capitulation* upon it was seen in British ports on the Coromandel coast; the Seychellois were allowed to trade their turtles for prints.[44]

And until the Peace of Amiens put a brief end to war in 1802, Île de France learned to accept that Seychelles were only tenuously French. Only apologetically, because he knew that in the eyes of Seychellois the capitulation formally extinguished France's legal authority in Seychelles, would the Governor-General grant permission to sell a concession of land. In 1801 when he heard that the First Consul had lighted upon Seychelles as the appropriately inconsiderable place to exile Jacobins whom it was convenient to blame for an attempt to assassinate him with a bomb, the governor-general even brought himself to hint that Bonaparte did not understand the delicate status of these Islands. In strict law, the exiles might have had to be released as soon as they set foot on this British soil.[45] When the first batch of them arrived aboard the frigate *Chiffone*, her captain found himself very unwelcome with the cargo for other than the obvious objections to bloody revolutionaries. Some wandering British frigate captain, anxious to exercise his gun-crews, might see their landing as a breaking of the capitulation – that precious piece of paper under whose protection the white population had increased to eighty or eighty-five families, as the Seychellois told him with a little pardonable exaggeration, and 1,800 or 2,000 slaves.[46]

Seychellois made great play with their capitulation when it suited them. They had it renewed in September 1798 when the *Centurion* came back with a new captain searching for a Danish ship reportedly at sea with a cargo of French bullion. The Seychellois sold the *Centurion* six bullocks, and she seized a slaver with blacks aboard and others hidden ashore.[47] De Quincy was embarrassed when the slaver's crew recaptured her between Ceylon and the Cape. The virtuous man had sold some of her concealed slaves for his own profit when he was supposed to guard them for that of her captain.[48] With a growing family to support, married as he was to a lady whose civil divorce he had arranged soon after his arrival in Seychelles, the commandant knew what was due to a man in his situation. De Quincy built a big house he called Bellevue – one of the stone two-storied houses, with nine rooms. When inventory was taken at his wife's death in 1809 he possessed seventy-four slaves from Madagascar and Mozambique, and one from India, with names like Aglae, Hercule, Cézar and Latulippe.[49] His drawing-room with its twelve chairs, four framed etchings and pendulum clock, his library with its volumes of works by the *Philosophes*, gave his life some elegance. He was at the social apex of the Island, a *grand blanc* like Nageon, St Jorre and Charles Savy de St Anne, as opposed to a *petit blanc*, or a *blanc brûlé*, sunburnt from stumping the mountain tracks instead of being carried in a chair.

Next year, 1799, Seychellois of all degrees were put to greater pains to preserve their charter. In August that year they found themselves hosts to the French corvette *Surprise*. She had fitted out at Île de France to take ambassadors to the Directory in Paris from France's ally in India, Tippoo Sahib. They were a certain General Dubucq and a couple of Indian gentlemen, and had been carried from Mangalore to Port Louis by an officer from the corsair *Apollon*, well-known at Mahé because her captain was Jean-François Hodoul. The *Surprise* was still there in September when Captain Alexander inconsiderately came in with HMS *Braave*, with 40 guns, before whose weight of metal the smaller Frenchman had no choice but to surrender.[50] Off from shore came de Quincy, swearing on his honour that the Tricolor had not flown here since 1794. The *Surprise* had clearly been flying it, and strictly he had no right to allow her to be repaired in the Islands, which the capitulation declared to be actually surrendered, and not merely neutral. He asserted that he wanted to give every possible assistance to British vessels – and was told that this meant handing over the ambassadors who were now hiding ashore, an armed group of seventeen. Alexander sent de Quincy an ultimatum, which de Quincy passed on to the proprietors with his own order to hand over the fugitives, only to receive a withering lecture on patriotism from one of the latest arrivals in Seychelles.[51] This was the advocate Jean-Nicolas Lebouq, deportee from Bourbon – or Île de la Réunion, as it was called now that the Bourbons were no more (it became Île Bonaparte when the First Consul elevated himself to their empty throne, and Bourbon again during the Restoration period after Waterloo). Lebouq was among a group deported from Réunion in 1798 for an insurrection in defence of pure revolutionary principles: this was how they saw it, claiming an inclination in the Réunion authorities to declare the island independent of the indivisible Republic, and even to hand it over to the reactionary British. Packed off for the Indies in the brig *Laurette*, they had got its master to land them instead in Seychelles – to the dismay of François Blaise Savy, whom the proprietors had appointed municipal agent in the temporary absence of de Quincy on board a slaver bound for Port Louis.[52]

Several of these deportees stayed, settling especially on La Digue, hitherto unoccupied. One was Maximilien Morel, from the rebellious district of St Pierre. Marie-Célérine Payet, his wife, petitioned to be allowed to join him on his corner of La Digue, down on the plateau between the massif and the sea, with their five children and four slaves. She went, and they prospered. Twenty-five slaves were owned by the family in 1815 when the estate was valued after both parents had died; the successors inherited 108 acres of land and 4,551 pounds of cotton worth, in the coin employed in Seychelles, 132.72 piastres or pieces of eight; it all added up to an estate worth 3,639.72 piastres, the slaves as always making the greatest part of the estate's value.[53] Seychelles did more for this generation of proprietors than Réunion ever could; and others in the year of Mme Morel's application – 1799 – foresaw a similar outcome in their own case. A spate of applications came from St Pierre, launched over names well-known in Seychelles today – Gontier, Hoareau, Payet. All felt that their inconveniently large families would be better off away from the restricted soil of Réunion. As Pierre Gontier put it, even though his expectations might be based on illusion, he still found them impossible to resist;[54] his family settled on Mahé at Beau Vallon. However, Mahé was no place for the ardent Lebouq, despite the chances of adding to his capital by trading in tortoises from Aldabra or, with half as large an investment again, slaves from Mozambique. He thought the slow pace of life would send him mad, with people so bored that social relations tended to be expressed in quarrels over minutiae far removed from matters of principle such as a revolutionary might entertain.[55] The *Surprise* affair involved a principle, although de Quincy would not see it. Lebouq would not surrender Tipu Sultan's ambassadors if they came to his house, even to maintain the capitulation, as he told de Quincy when the warning reached him. Quite rightly, he did not believe Captain Alexander's threats.[56] And Mlle Lebouq who was besieged by the *Braave*'s officers proved more constant than Tipu's chief ambassador General Dubucq – who, having sworn never to surrender, did so with his party before the *Braave* sailed. He had disposed of his despatches, though, and Alexander let him go. The British had no particular interest in the persons of Tipu Sultan's ambassadors, having just killed Tipu himself at Seringapatam.[57]

If HMS *Braave* had come a few days earlier, she would still have seen how Seychellois interpreted the capitulation when no British man-o'-war was present, and would have made a more valuable prize. This was the corsair *Général Malartic* – at least as effective a weapon of war as the courtly and, to the Revolution, complaisant old governor-general of Île de France had ever been in the flesh. She was back again in Mahé roads the next year, reprovisioning for the cruise that ended in her capture.[58] Seychelles saw most of the corsairs at one time or another. The *Hirondelle* was lost on Île aux Vaches on 4 September 1809, her crew stunned by Mahé's hospitality – which Robert Surcouf himself enjoyed only a little less disastrously on two occasions. Most successful of the French privateersmen, and one of the few never captured, Surcouf arrived in 1795 on the first privateering cruise he ever made, and had to run for safety when two large English vessels hove in sight; back in 1800, he lost three men to the great white sharks for which Mahé waters were noted.[59] And Captain Malraux of the *Iphigénie* revictualled at Mahé before sailing to his spectacular death in the Gulf of Arabia. He had captured a rich prize but was engaged by the British corvette *Trinkomely* which, outgunned and undermanned from the start, and with all her officers killed, fought on until she blew up, taking the corsair down with her.[60]

The Hodoul brothers came through Seychelles in privateers

they sailed in after the *Olivette's* capture. Jean-François Hodoul repaid himself from East Indiamen. In 1796 he was prize-master in a vessel cut out in the roads of Viringapatnam. The profits from this put him into the twelve-gun *Apollon*, 197 tons, as co-captain with other Seychellois in his crew.[61] André Nageon's son Jean-Marie died on board this vessel off Tamatave in May 1798, if the family genealogy is accurate. By then Hodoul had prospered so much that he commanded the unusually powerful *Uni*, a miniature frigate with her thirty guns. He was captured by HMS *Arrogant* in August 1800 after a long chase in which he threw most of the guns overboard to lighten the ship – an uncommonly slow ship, if she could be outstripped by a seventy-four-gun two-decked line-of-battle ship like *Arrogant*.[62] When Hodoul retired to Seychelles after two years in Fort William prison, Calcutta, he was not poor: among his least valuable prizes was the *Harriet*, a foolhardy British eight-gun privateer which, believing in the Britishness or at least neutrality of Seychelles, allowed herself to be captured by the *Uni* off St Anne in 1800.[63]

Neutrality always meant what Seychellois wanted it to mean. Only the year before, another British privateer, the *Collector*, had been captured by Malraux off Mahé.[64] Although they did not actually fit out any corsairs in their own Islands, the Seychellois sailed blithely to prey on their supposed captors. *Le Chasseur* in 1796 got more men from Praslin than she lost through sailors jumping ship there.[65] When *La Gloire* was captured by the *Albatross* sloop-of-war in 1801, Matthieu d'Antoine of Mahé lost his personal papers. This was an inconvenience to him nine years later when he married Barthélémy Hodoul's widow, Françoise Jorre de St Jorre;[66] Barthélémy had died at sea, perhaps killed in another similar engagement. Most were more fortunate. Jean-Joseph Jouan joined the corvette *Gobemouche* at Mahé in 1808, and when she was captured by the frigate *Nereide*, he convinced the obliging British that he was a passenger and got himself put ashore.[67] Apart from the islands being a source of fresh provisions and crew, corsairs were drawn to Seychelles because of their strategic position between India, Africa and Île de France.

Seychelles became a haven for prizes. The captures lay there quietly until hurricanes and scurvy drove away the British squadrons blockading Île de France; then the corsairs came back, ideally with more prizes, and carried them across to be stripped or sold in Port Louis. Although the British had some inkling of this, they were slow to act, but in 1801, finally, they sent two ships independently to look into Mahé expressly for privateers. The first was the *Sybille* (thirty-eighy guns) which had captured *La Forte* despite the French frigate being more heavily armed – and despite the gallantry of Lebouq's son who was on board. The *Sybille* came under orders from Admiral Rainier, commander-in-chief on the East Indies Station, who took the most cynical view possible of the capitulation and could not understand why his own nephew had renewed it as captain of the *Centurion* in 1798.[68] The *Sybille* renewed it too – even while having every reason to doubt the Island's neutrality from everything she saw on entering Mahé harbour on 19 August 1801. Lying there in the *barrachois*, the protected inner harbour, was a frigate under French colours with her foremast unshipped for repairs – the *Chiffone* (thirty-six guns), bringing the first batch of Jacobin exiles.[69] The *Sybille* moved in close to pistol-shot range under French colours, then hauled them down as she fired her first broadside. It was all over in little over a quarter of an hour. The *Chiffone* had put four of her twelve-pounders ashore just below de Quincy's Bellevue house, with a furnace to heat the shot red-hot, which should have helped to even the odds against her heavier opponent;[70] but she let the British get to the point-blank range they favoured. Her cable cut by a shot, she swung end-on to their raking fire. The *Sybille's* eighteen-pounders did frightful execution among the *Chiffone's* crew, killing thirty-five and wounding fifty. Little damage had been done to *Chiffone* herself when her flag came down, and the British immediately sent her to sea under their own colours.

That was a bad day for shipping at Mahé. A prize sent in by the corsair *Nymphe* was sunk during the action. The slaver *Sophie* lost four of her black sailors to stray roundshot from the frigates, and had to sell seven slaves for 538 piastres to pay for her repairs.[72] And the wooded heights had not yet heard the last echoes of heavy guns. More work was in store for surgeons in that benign Mahé air where even amputations could be relied on to heal sweetly. The spirited twenty-two-gun corvette *La Flèche* was off Seychelles with the rest of the Jacobins. After an exchange of five with a stranger on 2 September 1801 she continued on into harbour at Mahé where she could count on being found.[73] The stranger was the twenty-gun sloop-of-war *Victor* (Commander G.R. Collier).

Sent from the Red Sea to search Seychelles for privateers, Collier had watered at Diego Garcia and was coming to investigate Mahé when he brought *La Flèche* to this brief chance action. The Frenchman, firing high in accordance with the philosophy of his service, so cut up the *Victor*'s rigging that, ship-rigged though she was, and the Frenchman in theory less weatherly, the *Victor* could not hold him. 'Night fast approaching' – confides an uncharacteristically garrulous Collier to his admiral – 'added to the chagrin I felt on observing the Corvette sail better than the *Victor* on a Wind.'[74] He worked his way on to windward all the same and caught the corvette in the *barrachois* four days later. *La Flèche* was flying red flags of defiance, and met the *Victor* with a raking fire as she warped up the winding channel to that pistol-shot range again. Then, as Collier described it,

> Having two springs on the Cable our Broadside was soon brought to bear, and at 3/4 past 11 a.m. a well directed fire was opened, which was kept up incessantly from both Vessels till twenty minutes past two, when I plainly perceived the enemy was going down, in a few minutes her Cable was cut, she cast round, and her Bow grounded on a Coral reef.[75]

La Flèche went down in shallow water soon after British boarders had put out fires the retreating French had lighted. She had been a fine new ship, like the *Chiffone*, and lost heavily in men, while the *Victor* had not a single casualty, having presumably overwhelmed the French eight-pounders with her short-range but heavy carronade guns. Even after all this, the capitulation held. Captain Charles Adam of the *Sybille* had preceded Collier in putting his signature to the impudent, so much evaded capitulation document which was a triumph for de Quincy's diplomacy. Adam sailed with just a couple of captured Île de France ships in tow, leaving five local vessels to ply peacefully under their neutral flag with its white letters spelling out 'Séchelles capitulation' on a blue field.

The *Courier des Seychelles* was one of these, the *Amazone* and the *Favorite* were two of the others. The partners Michel Blin and Constant Dupont ran a couple. In mid-1802, with the Peace of Amiens agreed, Blin in the *Rosalie* acted on de Quincy's order to hoist the Tricolor formally over the Amirantes, in case the wreck of the despatch-boat *Spitfire* there the previous year should give the British ideas about claiming them.[76] Jean Sausse – a friend of de Quincy, whom he eventually got into trouble – had the *Amazone*. An old seaman from Fréjus who had sailed the Antilles in his time,[77] Sausse lived partly on Praslin and partly on Île Bonaparte between his regular voyages to Mozambique for slaves.

Turtles, tortoises, oil, timber, cotton, maize, slaves – these were what the local ships of Seychelles dealt in. They themselves were never privateers; neither impudence nor ingenuity could have been stretched that far. Jean Planeau from Bordeaux was building more of these handy brig-schooners, brigantines and schooners from 1801 at his shipyard on the *barrachois*. In May 1808 he and his sixteen slave craftsmen had a 50-tonner ready for launching. Jean Albert built *La Marie* that year. The *Favorite* was captained by Denis Adrien Calais from Normandy – a bold man in his day for, himself illegitimate, he was among the first to cross the colour line by marrying into the Ramalinga family of Bourbon which had defied the white community's objections to free black land-owners and had come to Seychelles from Bourbon after all. Calais was very much part of the coloured community of the Islands. The *Favorite*'s owner was Hélène Naz, an Indian *émancipée* whose lover, the Portuguese seaman Emmanuel Naz, vanished at sea after marrying her in 1806 and legitimising their three children. The widow sold the ship to Hodoul in 1808, indemnifying Calais for the voyage he had been engaged to make in her to Aldabra for tortoises and to Africa for slaves. At a mere 45 feet long on the keel and not much above 50 feet on deck, she was expected to carry a disproportionate number of both, packed very tight. Planeau's new *Aimable Marianne* was about the same size. When Captain Sausse bought her from the builder he planned to force eighty slaves into her,[78] all specified in the bill of sale after the manner of cattle and with the same eye to acquiring breeding stock: '*Quatre Vingts têtes d'Esclaves don Trente Noires pièces d'Inde, Quinze Cupons, Quinze Négresses et Vingt Negrillons ....*'[79]

So the slave population grew, much faster than the white. There were 215 whites of all ages in 1803; 86 free black, freed or coloured; and there were 1,820 slaves. In 1810 the whites totalled 317, the free blacks and coloureds 135, the slaves 3,015. And while the pessimistic old Malavois, now back in Île de France, doubted whether an increase of the free population was sound policy when so much of Seychelles was too rocky to cultivate,

no-one objected to the build-up of slaves. Le Beuze, J.-P. Langlois
and Charles-Dorothé Savy all increased their slave numbers – Savy
almost doubling his, from 56 to 100; while from 1803 to 1810
Hodoul, Sausse and sailors like Louis-Marie Tirant took at least
twenty-two cargoes on to Île de France also, and others to
Bonaparte.[80] Hodoul's own slaves increased from forty-seven to
eighty-nine, on his 50 acres of cotton and 50–100 acres of cane
from which he made sugar and arrack.[81] When he sailed in company
with the corvette *Gobemouche* in 1808, himself bound for Africa
for slaves in the *Favorite*, four other Seychelles slavers were at sea
ahead of him. Seychelles were ideally placed for the slave-trade.
It was a soldier's wind, meaning the wind was on the beam with
no need to tack between Seychelles, Mozambique and back again.
With nothing quite certain at sea, Captain Planet the year before
had spent sixty-four days bringing a cargo from Mozambique; the
slaves were sick with scurvy by the time he got them ashore.[82]
They might not have been too bad a loss in their emaciated state
even so, for the slavers of Seychelles had favourite places along
the African coast which not everybody knew about. Captain Constant Dupont knew a bay 4 leagues north of Cape d'Algardo
where he could fill up with no fees to pay and at very low
prices.[83] For proprietors, slaves represented the biggest investment
they would ever make, as inventories of deceased estates clearly
show. Here slaves are given values and listed under names reflecting
sometimes their own characteristics but more frequently the humour
of their owners: Lundi Chapeau, Figaro, Dominique Révolution,
Mousqueton Fusil. The owners often gave themselves jocular nick-
names too. New slaves were branded with the slaver's mark –
Hodoul's was H on the left breast – and bore the marks of their
country, in body and facial scars, which they tried to get rid of
as they discovered the superiority asserted by Créole slaves over
those born in Mozambique or Madagascar, who had not lived in
slavery from birth.

Backed by the masters' discipline, the influence of the Créoles
was far-reaching. They taught new slaves to give up their own
languages for Seychelles' version of the widely-disseminated French
Créole *patois*. This was a speech which over the ensuing generations
was to become highly political, since it was regarded as fit only
for black people. Its origins may be as much regional and archaic
French as African or Malgache. A particularly convincing view is

that Seychelles Créole derived from a root developed in Bourbon between 1665 and about 1725, when French settlers with their many Malagassy women and their African slaves – who were not then preponderant in number over whites – had evolved a *patois* owing most to northern and western France of the seventeenth century but much also to the Antilles. The French Antilles lent the Indian Ocean colonies many words, including '*Créole*' as a term for the blacks alone, while the sea and India added a few more.[84] Once broken into this tongue – with its terms of deference, '*Mon Blanc*', '*Mon Bourgeois*' – the Malagassy, the Mozambican, the occasional Malay and highly valued Indian found that he – or, in much smaller numbers, she – entered a world in which integration was paid for with the loss of much of what they brought in the forms of folklore and art.

The day for the slaves was regulated by the bell calling them to work before dawn, and their movement was restricted by the firing of the cannon ordering them all out of the tiny town at dusk. Their personal lives revolved around the straw hut, garden plot and bamboo *casier* or fishtrap. Their world was likely to be a matriarchy – children went with the mother, who ruled the household even when it included a man or men. Neither partner might set much store by a permanent relationship, although men often paid for their freedom with loneliness in old age, while a woman could usually count on having at least one child left to care for her. Slavery itself, of course, encouraged impermanence in unions and, on the Seychelles evidence, may have been responsible for promiscuity from an early age. Certainly family life was not encouraged when the slave-household could be divided because the newly-wed master's son was going over from Mahé to develop an *habitation* on Praslin or Silhouette. Nor did responsible sexual attitudes readily emerge in the man whose role was strictly limited by the daily agricultural and domestic requirements of the owner of his woman and children. And the slave world was almost directly geared towards producing an evasive, self-defensive quality in slave personality and behaviour such as was found through the West Indies too. At the same time slave society in Seychelles was enriched by its stories about Soungoula, folk-hero of Seychelles. A 'rabbit' in Swahili, the Soungoula of Mahé and its sister Islands is more of a monkey. Unlike his Jamaican counterpart Anansy (Ananse of the Gold Coast), Soungoula is not a bitter character but

mischievous, good-humoured, a wiseacre as well as a trickster —
which may indicate that, as has often been claimed, slavery was
gentler in Seychelles than in the West Indies. A slave of de Quincy's,
given him by a Portuguese envoy to Île de France from the major
source of slaves in the Mascareignes, Mozambique, was actually
named Soungoula. Their imaginative life at least partly satisfied
by this gentle rascal, the slaves related to the physical world with
the help of *gris-gris* — magical rites, white and black, by which a
lover could be won, sterility relieved, an enemy disposed of, and the
arbitrary will of the universe momentarily brought under control.

Slaves had some direct physical protection in law, and in theory,
under the *Code Noire*. Although mutilation was prescribed for
running away and death for striking the master or a member of
his family, slaves were not to be tortured at will. But to find out
what relation even this much protection in law had with reality,
recourse must be had to the attitudes expressed in word and
action by slave-owners. Not much, evidently, on the estates at
Cascade of Louis-Jerome Dumont who, when he died in 1823,
owned fifty-four slaves worth 6,420 piastres. Dumont was from
Réunion, perhaps a deportee but rich, a notary, and a friend of
de Quincy, and he had firm views on the place of the slave. If
he wanted to insult a white enemy, he would compare him to
a slave and promise him the punishments it was proper to mete
out to such a creature. In Dumont's system of plantation economy
slaves could be dragged to the *bloc*, thrashed or shot.[85] According
to local edicts, they were to be flogged or put to work in irons
if found in town at any time on a feast-day or a Sunday, and on
any other day after 7 p.m. without a chit from their masters.
They were accurately seen as a potentially subversive, actually and
persistently thieving and hard-drinking society. Masters themselves
were open to punishment if they did not keep slaves on the estate
at almost all times, and they had to be inhibited from profiting
by their slaves pilfering from other proprietors.

Slaves ran away, forming as a rule transitory communities of
maroons. They could be shot if *en marronage* they resisted capture,
and their owners were compensated from public funds. *A commune*
was established in 1806, and most of its functions were concerned
with the recapture of slaves.[86] Mahé is small, but even so quantities
of slaves could hide on its remote beaches and among its still
remoter hills. When two proprietors, one perhaps a widow not

yet decided on whether to accept a new husband, contracted to pool land and slaves, the document would deal with loss of slave property by *marronage* as it dealt with gain by natural increase. And when a slave woman was found murdered, maroons were suspected. She had been stripped, and one thing the Island would not provide was good cotton print. The captured maroon who was charged with the murder and the slave he accused of it were both found dead in gaol.[87]

With the Jacobins' arrival in 1801, proprietors' insecurity greatly increased. If this brief influx of seventy-odd supposed revolutionaries is of more picturesque than practical significance to the Islands, that is because the proprietors took care to get rid of them. Malavois actually fled at the sight of them, and so even did Lebouq, while Hodoul talked of sailing in a *corsaire* again.[88] These Jacobin exiles recognised that they had oppression in common with the slaves. They were an excellent new market for blacks to steal for; even more, they laid plans to free everyone who experienced oppression as they did – but they talked about it in their cups at Volamaefa's hospitable house. This lack of discretion was speedily punished by the removal of half their number to Anjouan in the Comoros, where either the Sultan did not allow them to linger before he poisoned them or an epidemic killed them off. The rest mostly got away from Mahé by various means over the years, leaving voluminous memoranda of complaint as the principal memorials to their presence there. There was more theft on Mahé while any of them remained, and more reason to worry about maroons. Accordingly the Island was divided into four districts, so that they could be hunted down systematically. If any came in of their own accord, as maroons often did when starving or sick, they were handed back to their masters after punishment.

An obedient and hard-working slave might be freed. Enfranchisement was expensive and officially discouraged, but it seems to have happened more often in Seychelles than in Île de France and certainly more than in Bourbon. Two of de Quincy's blacks might perhaps have been thought to merit freedom for their services aboard the *Chiffone* in her fight with the *Sybille* if they had not been killed in the action. As it was, their owner obtained compensation from among the slaves belonging to the Republic. The chief man of these, Pèdre, might once again have found his freedom, but he died of a heart-attack on Curieuse caused by fear of a crocodile.[89] A good many of Hangard's slaves, on the other hand, actually were freed. He seems to have made this a policy, perhaps influenced by his Malagassy woman, Annette; and two of his *affranchis*, Port Louis and Joseph Banane, married their women, which then and afterwards remained unusual except in the landed families. 'Good service' was the reason normally given for enfranchisement, and the notary may have smiled as he made out the deed when women were in question. Certainly much good service was done for the bachelor sea-captain and notary Jean Loizeau from Guitres in the Gironde district of France, by his young Indian *affranchie* Babet; he had a stream of children from her.[90] When Matthieu Guet freed the sisters Charlotte Zoé and Laurencia Flippenta and endowed them with slaves and land which they passed to the nineteen-year-old Laurencia's son Charles Marie Saint-Ange, sex was obviously in it too, although the St Ange family does not see Guet himself as their white progenitor. Another Guet *affranchie*, Fanchon Joubert, was obliged to buy her son Henry from Gilles Houareau, but she had slaves of her own to give for the boy – Argent Vidole and Daris Régent.[91]

In Seychelles Don Juans of the slave-huts were plentiful. There was, for a start, a high proportion of unmarried white men, and so coloured families came into existence, at first with a separate register to record their rites of passage, the children often legally recognised by their fathers whose name they invariably took, recognised or not; they were not always freely given it by *grands blancs*. Jean Loizeau left Babet's children his considerable fortune when he died in 1825 but it is possible that he never recognised them. And none of Babet's ostracised sons cherished affection for the French rulers of Seychelles – not even for de Quincy, in his nine-roomed *château*, surrounded by volumes of the slavery-detesting Rousseau and Voltaire. Appropriately, the works of the *Philosophes* were falling prey to the rigours of the tropics.[92]

Maybe the *Philosophes* did nonetheless help de Quincy in that life of service to which, as he claimed, selfless devotion to the public alone impelled him. He would rather have reclined at ease in the bosom of his family, he said.[93] He never showed the faintest inclination not to govern, though; and still less to seek martial glory on the battlefields of Europe. In this he could not compare with Malartic's successor as governor-general of Île de France, who was bombarding the First Consul with expressions of his desire to serve;[94] when the guns fell silent briefly for the Peace of Amiens in 1802-3 this admirer was replaced by a younger though no less lyrical one. He was General Decaen, a staff officer who had been bred to the law in his dour home town in Normandy. Disapproving of capitulations, he now combined the theoretical martinet with the pettifogging bureaucrat in unfriendly fashion so far as de Quincy and Seychelles were concerned. The Tricolor floated once more over Seychelles after the peace, de Quincy reported; all was restored to order.[95] It was only a pity that shortly before the peace a couple of Englishmen had come in and burnt the refloated *Flèche*. La *Flèche* was a potential privateer, they said; let the Portuguese merchant from Mozambique who had purchased her go to the devil, *père de famille* though he might be.

For his own part, de Quincy wished his superiors to understand that his zeal had been indefatigable. Without means or assistance, he had faced all difficulties and brought off every feat he had attempted, hoping always for that happy day which had now dawned, when Seychelles were French once more.[95] He had placated the English, and kept down the more bellicose Seychellois. Not only Lebouq had flaunted an officious patriotism. In June 1799 Malavois's son-in-law M. Bellevue had won seventeen supporters at a public meeting which he called to contest the capitulation,[96] but he was lost at sea soon afterwards. What tribute de Quincy had levied from interests in Seychelles not closely associated with his own was less clear. Not everyone there was prepared to stand up and cheer him – not the widow St Jorre, certainly. In difficulty with ungrateful offspring over division of the estate, as families were so frequently to be, she did not scruple to say that Seychelles had always been in the hands of a clique. She saw no help for it but to contemplate marriage with one of the Jacobins. The clique monopolised offices and the fruits of its own brand of justice, she said, oppressing virtuous people like herself.[97] No satisfaction came from Decaen. He sent legal instruments to make Seychelles a more settled community, associating a civil commissioner with de Quincy, but de Quincy remained the power as president of the new *tribunal de paix* and of the *commune de Seychelles*; from these additional eminences he freely assured Decaen of his own probity, frankness and sense of fair play. De Quincy had a

harder row to hoe when war came again, all the same. The Peace
of Amiens was made to be broken, but Decaen could not bring
the Greek Kalends any closer, having no more ability to protect
Seychelles than his predecessors. Frigates of both the warring nations
came in again. And there was still no rational recourse other than
capitulation in face of the Royal Navy. On 24 September 1804
de Quincy wasted no time in sending off a flag of truce to HMS
Concord which had been piloted over from Praslin by Sausse after
gorging her crew on turtles there for five days. She hoisted British
colours over the *Établissement* and seized a brig and a schooner
before sailing on 27 September, well-found in livestock, leaving
her captain's signature on a renewal of the capitulation. A couple
of two-pounders were allowed to remain, as before, as signal guns
in case of a slave revolt, while Sausse and the retired privateersman
J.-F. Hodoul were each allowed to sail a 30-tonner under the
blue flag.[98] Of course, Hodoul might well have been hanged, if
the frigate-captains had felt him worth the paperwork, for
preying on British shipping while a resident of a country under
capitulation; as it was, they were content to make use of his
sailing directions.[99]

All this sober recognition of reality by Seychellois aroused fury
in Decaen. He ached to attack India, but cooped up in Île de
France instead had not much humour to spare for Seychelles.
Was it not ridiculous that de Quincy should have handed over
the Islands without waiting for the British to demand surrender?
Had not Sausse deserved to be put on trial for treason? No capitulation would be recognised unless the enemy left behind a force
sufficient to sustain it.[100] He was unmoved by appeals from the
Seychellois who looked forward to benefitting again from their
own brand of neutrality – '*ce que ne Peut attenuer Leur Sentimente
de bon Français, dont ils ont toujours & Sincèrement fait & feront Profession*'
– so they promised.[101] When Decaen's colleague at sea, Contre-
Amiral Linois, brought his powerful squadron to Mahé in 1805,
he found no flag flying at all. The Tricolor went up at his invitation,
but Linois – another gentleman of the *ancien régime*, who detested
new men like Decaen – agreed with de Quincy that there was
no other way to deal with the British. Seychelles had only about
sixty white families scattered around nineteen or twenty leagues
of coastline. Naturally it would be dangerous to arm the slaves.[102]
The Islands were safe only when Linois' *Marengo* (seventy-four

guns) was there, preferably in company with the frigates *Belle Poule* and *Sémillante* – that *Sémillante* in which one of the Hodoul brothers sailed, and from whose deck he charted Aldabra.[103]

None of these formidable French men-o'-war was there to protect Seychelles in November 1805 when the British frigate *Duncan* came, or twelve months later when the *Pitt* and the *Terpsichore* looked in on their way from the regular blockade being attempted on Île de France. British captains were all cynical about Seychelles' neutrality now, even though they did not discover till 1808 that, when signal-stations on Île de France were flying a red signal flag with a bearing pendant, the returning corsair took his prizes off to de Quincy's kingdom.[104] Between August and October 1807 alone the Île de France corsairs not only took thirty-three ships in the Bay of Bengal but got most of them home too.[105] The blockade of Île de France was not much more than a joke, with the few ships available to maintain it, and some of the British frigates were out of patience. The *Pitt* and the *Terpsichore* tricked de Quincy into committing himself, by coming in under French colours themselves. When he hoisted them too, they showed their teeth, putting troops ashore and holding him prisoner on board until they sailed next day.[106] As for the *Duncan*, she had given him no chance at all to go through his paces. A repeated visitor, *Duncan* came in cleared for action but never found either a corsair or the level of discipline that would discourage her own people from deserting. She then had to chase them all over Mahé – men, in all probability, who had never set foot in Britain and might speak any mother-tongue but English. Even so they occasionally served as means of long-term escape for runaway slaves. In 1805 she seized Dupont's slaver *Courier des Seychelles* at anchor off Île Thérèse. Dupont's 170 new Mozambique blacks were safe ashore after being packed into the small vessel's stinking hold like sardines in a can, three or four to the ton. The *Duncan*'s captain suspected he had been cheated. He landed fifty men to pillage and burn on pretence of hunting up the valuable slaves and his own deserters. He sent his boats to capture the *Sirius* brig, also newly arrived from Mozambique, which balked him by throwing herself ashore in Anse Boileau in an unusual display of patriotism. He burnt the *Rosalie* at Anse à la Mouche, then sailed on without hoisting his flag ashore or bothering in the least about assuming possession of Seychelles.[107] De Quincy was mollified in June 1808 when, returning in company with a vastly superior officer aboard the *Russell*, the *Duncan* behaved in a more seemly fashion and renewed the *Concord*'s capitulation. This time, according to a prisoner aboard her from the captured corsair *Île de France*, the *Duncan* lost thirteen deserters.[108] In August the *Albion*, the *Pitt* and the *Drake* once again allowed Hodoul and Sausse to keep their ships – although Sausse nonetheless entered a clause in his contract with Planeau protecting him in case his new slaver, the *Aimable Marianne*, were captured, as she might have been after 1808 when the British began to attack Île de France's slave-trade. And for de Quincy to be held prisoner by the *Terpsichore* and the *Pitt* so considerately in November 1806 had put that upright man in the seventh heaven of delight. Not in the least impressed, Decaen went on pressing Seychelles for risky services to the cause. As Decaen had it: even in those glorious battle-camps where victory assured to the Emperor the happiness of bringing peace to the whole world, despite obstacles thrown in the path of his vast and generous plans by a *puissance perfide*[109] – even despite these more than global preoccupations, the great Napoleon had not forgotten that Seychelles were there to revictual and refit his small ships in the Indian Ocean. His big ones had been captured on their way home, although it took the 98-gun three-decker *London* to subdue the *Marengo*. The corvette *Venus* was accordingly refitted at Mahé in 1808. So too was the twelve-gun *Gobemouche*, which sailed in company with Hodoul in the *Favorite* but then, running into the frigate *Nereide*, had no blue flag under which to shelter.

A prize of the *Gobemouche*, the *Ceres* privateer, had no better luck. Her recapture at least added spice to the life of Polidore Denis, a slave accompanying his master, M. Uzice, from Seychelles to Île de France. Polidore took the opportunity to ship as a seaman in a British frigate; it was a grim life – the *Nereide* for one had lately been in a state of mutiny – but he could have known worse. He had seen India before – back in Île de France, perhaps returning to Seychelles – he was reclaimed as runaway property by the Uzice family.[110]

Property of any sort, human, cultural or inanimate, was not intended to be affected in Seychelles or anywhere else in the Mascareignes when Île de France with its Dependencies fell to the British in

December 1810. As Île Bonaparte or Île de la Réunion, Bourbon had gone five months before – falling almost with relief, although at the first British attack in 1809 the general commanding the troops had felt obliged to kill himself before, as he said, a revolutionary clique could send him to the scaffold as a traitor for failing to defend the island. Decaen himself fought for Île de France but surrendered to superior force almost as handsomely as de Quincy. All attributes of nationality in land, laws and religion were guaranteed. '*Vive la loi*', if not '*la Nation*', not that Seychellois themselves wanted to be included in this new capitulation at all. They had been more than ever attached to their own ideal since March 1810 when British frigates burned a Mahé schooner because Decaen had replaced her capitulation papers with a regular French *congé de commerce*.[111] And they were not wrong to be apprehensive. The new conquerors promised to be more demanding than Newcome. When Captain Beaver arrived in April 1811 with the frigate *Nisus*, bringing formal news that Napoleon no longer possessed an empire in these tropic seas, he actually claimed the islands forming the harbour's seaward side as prize of war. The bile resulting from his failure to make the claim stick may have hastened his premature death from inflammatory constipation at the Cape next year.[112] Seychelles were not of much value, though in Beaver's view Britain would get little advantage from possessing them – 'other than of keeping the Enemy out of them', as he followed so many wise French officers in saying.[113] The Governor of Mauritius – the old name to which Île de France now reverted – felt differently at first. A lyrical view could be taken of Seychelles' strategic importance, thought Governor R.T. Farquhar, himself a servant of the East India Company before this and Governor of Penang for the Company in his youth. As a great naval, military and commercial base, ideally placed for expeditions to Ceylon, Goa, Bombay, Persia, the Red Sea and Madagascar, Seychelles could be used to overawe all the states between Egypt and India, relieving Britain of the need to continue squandering money and reputation in subsidies to the faithless and impotent Persian court so that it would no longer be at the mercy of unsteady powers on the borders of India.[114]

Meanwhile here were Seychelles with a population running to 3,486 souls – if the 3,015 slaves did possess souls, a doubt which the British parliament had not settled in 1807 by declaring an end to the slave trade that Bonaparte had renewed for France in 1802 and France was not to declare illegal again till 1817. Here were 2,720 acres in cotton, 2,432 in foodcrops, 220 in sugar, some in coffee and a great deal under poorly-yielding cloves. Here were 1,450 head of cattle, sheep, pigs, goats; turtles struggling to survive under the thin protection of laws passed by a despairing de Quincy who foresaw extinction if the breeding season were not respected; crocodiles, fast being killed off; and hillsides showing ever greater scars as the timber was cut out and the soil washed down to the sea.

There were conflicting human allegiances too. Scarcely a month after the *Nisus* left, in came the French frigate *Clorinde* as a fugitive from an engagement with British frigates off Madagascar when her two consorts had fought until they could fight no more, while she hung back from the action, at one point even striking her colours – for which the Emperor wanted to hang her captain.[115] De Quincy threw up a battery to protect the *Clorinde* and got her back to sea repaired and reprovisioned in six days,[116] relying apparently on the simplicity of the British since he had a hostile witness – Lieutenant Bartholemew Sullivan of the Royal Marines. Sullivan had been landed from the *Nisus* to recover from wounds received when a squadron of British frigates was annihilated at Grand-Port, Île de France, before the island fell. During these difficult six days he was kept under gentlemanly restraint in Hodoul's house, according to tradition – no hardship, since Hodoul's table was comparable to the best in Paris. The situation lacked dignity, all the same, and Sullivan would have been less than human if it had not rankled when he became civil commandant a few months later. Here was the beginning of another revolution for Seychelles, which lasted through all the years of colonial rule till independence in 1976, yet always retaining the chief element with which it opened – namely, for slaves especially, semi-tragic farce.

2

THE DEPOT OF SMUGGLED BLACKS

1811-1840

As first British Civil Agent in Seychelles, Sullivan encapsulated in his years there the British experience as colonial overlords for the next 165 years. Like a lion he came in, and left with his tail dangling. Sullivan was an active soldier, not an elderly uniform with a preference for politics. Although he had to get around on crutches, he was too lively for some Seychellois – particularly de Quincy and his cronies. To his amazed young eyes they revealed themselves as more than a little corrupt. His despatches reveal a baffled feeling that the local society was altogether too much for even an Irishman like himself to get the weather-gauge on. Immediately he dismissed de Quincy from the *tribunal de paix* and was then amazed to find the old fox offering himself for re-election. De Quincy's claim to any position was inadmissible, Sullivan insisted, until he had given up his French commission and received Farquhar's permission to live in Seychelles as a private citizen. De Quincy had actually been talking about returning to France, but that might be a daunting move after more than forty years in the East; instead, he waited on Farquhar to argue his absolute indispensability in Seychelles,[1] leaving evasive and uncandid sets of financial accounts there. Making spoil of state property before it fell into the hands of the interloping British had been an agreeable pastime for de Quincy and his associates Dumont the notary and François Le Roy the civil commissioner. Money in the treasury had been divided among them, with deeds to land disposed of to friends after the final capitulation ante-dated to make them legal. Sale of government slaves had been discussed. If Sullivan had known morality in other islands, like those of the West Indies, he might have found all this less a Gallic trait than in the nature of small societies, where the élite are apt to engross limited resources. As it was, he struck stiff Anglo-Saxon attitudes:

39

From the little opportunity I have had of judging of these persons, I am confident that no sense of honour, shame, or honesty will deter them from endeavouring to practise upon Englishmen every species of deception, as indeed they consider us a people easily duped.[2]

A clean sweep was indicated. Le Roy was set down as 'one of those wretches to whom the Revolution has given birth' and returned under arrest to Mauritius.[3] As for Dumont, former *sansculotte enragé* as Sullivan discovered him to be, he said at the top of his voice that the Englishman was planning to assassinate him. First Dumont was insulted at being brought a summons to attend Sullivan's office by a mere slave, but no doubt he had other compelling reasons to stay away. He had encouraged some impassioned sea-captain to abduct a coloured woman he fancied, which the sailor was not content to do, complained Sullivan, without 'saying he did not care a Straw for the Authorities of the Island, crying hoora'. When he did come, Dumont made so free with threatening passes of his parasol that the crippled soldier threw him out. Dumont fell to the ground shouting that he was assassinated, adding as admiring friends led him away: 'You treat the French like Slaves, it is in that manner you Assassinate people in England.'[4] Then he wrote appealingly to Farquhar with a little of the pathos at his command: '*C'est un fonctionnaire Public, C'est un Père de famille, c'est un Vieillard à Cheveux Blancs de près de soixante années, qui depuis quelque temps est en But à Monsieur Sullivan ....*'[5]

The magnificent periods rang out, precursors of so many across the next five generations of furious French-Seychellois, forcing the British to back down, easily convertible into a rhetorical anti-colonialism that often safely assumed acquiescence in the slave and post-slave population. Cold Anglo-Saxons, for their comparatively ineffectual part, never ceased to marvel that extreme fertility coupled with old age free from criminal convictions should be thought charters entitling a man to any licence he felt his circumstances required regardless of consequences to his neighbour. The uproar was too much for Farquhar. He anyway understood there were certain outer islands in the Amirantes still unconceded which some of his own friends might like. He reappointed de Quincy *juge de paix*, whereupon de Quincy took the oath of allegiance before Sullivan – but a far from appearing as a private individual, he presented himself in the court uniform of the *ancien régime*, with side-arms.[6] His signature was indecipherable and he was later made to sign again. Sullivan had resigned in exasperation before that and been replaced by Lieutenant Bibye Lesage of the 22nd Regiment of Foot, who had useful grants in the Amirantes to add point to hints (and guarded requests) that he received to keep Seychelles quiet. However, before Sullivan left he stirred the Islands up much more over the now illegal slave trade. He was told by a free black informant one night that a cargo from Agbe had just been run by Captain F.C. Romarf into Praslin where Sullivan 'immediately on landing found in Huts close to the Shore, the Thirty-seven Slaves newly introduced, or rather their Skeletons, as they appeared to have been nearly starved during the Voyage'. He accepted an invitation to dinner on Praslin, recaptured some slaves who were spirited away during the meal, and was then prosecuted in the *tribunal de paix*; it had no right to hear a criminal case, but did so and convicted the civil commandant. Seychellois were particularly appalled that Sullivan should have led government slaves armed with muskets and pistols into a white *habitant*'s dwelling.[7]

That judgement was one last cut at the British interloper, but it matched the reputation that Seychelles had from now on as the depot for men and some women, all mostly young, being smuggled from Mozambique and Madagascar into Mauritius and Réunion as illegal slaves. Planters were utterly dependent on a non–self-sustaining unfree labour force. Around Réunion prowled Lieutenant-Colonel H.S. Keating, future Réunion planter himself, and Lieutenant-Governor until Farquhar removed his civil powers in 1814 because Keating could not have pursued slavers more earnestly if he had been the emancipating Wilberforce's own brother. Far too active for *habitants* and Farquhar too, the hyperactive Irish soldier was faced with 'an extensive and opulent conspiracy of Slave Dealers', as he finally assured the Prince Regent in a petition against Farquhar's relaxed approach.[8] The Scotsman, by contrast, thought the white Réunionnais a gentle people who did not deserve to be dragged out of their beds at night by Keating's soldiery in their searches for illegal slaves.[9] The Governor believed in slavery, thought the slave trade statutes did not or should not apply to the captured French islands, and remained of that private opinion when the Secretary of State for War and Colonies assured him he was quite mistaken; outside *grand blanc* circles his own greatest friend in Mauritius was his subordinate Charles Telfair, the naval surgeon from Ulster who owned land in Seychelles and for years ran big plantations in Mauritius, one of which he owned jointly with Bibye Lesage, where their slaves' devotion contrasted agreeably with the insolence of the lower orders which Telfair had known in Europe. Telfair told the world about this in a pamphlet after Parliament in London pilloried him as a slaver.[10]

There was an active market for slaves in Seychelles themselves, and, with demand so lively in Mauritius and Réunion as it continued to be into the 1820s, were Seychellois to deny themselves profit in order to satisfy a scruple that went against all history and was an official British scruple at that? At the long-established French slaving port of Nantes, to which Liverpool and Bristol had formerly been comparable, pious shipowners of the early 1820s prayed to God that not too many blacks of the cargoes being carried to the Mascareignes in their slave-brig *Le Succès* would die, so that the voyage would be profitable. Her supercargo saved the face of the Bourbonnais – as they became again for fifteen years after the restoration – and himself from the letter of French law by dropping manacles and other incriminating gear overboard at a buoyed spot in the roads at St Paul before being caught in the Amirantes on her next slave passage from Zanzibar.[11] Seychelles were far-flung, the vast area of sea surrounding them being largely at the command of any fast ship that could keep her identity ambiguous or her course unclear, and the new British civil agent, Lesage, with land of his own to develop, seemed less hot against slavers than Sullivan. Lesage claimed to know of four cargoes run into Seychelles in his time[12] – perhaps for owners there, perhaps to be seasoned for the Mascareignes, perhaps again to replace old slaves from Seychelles who had already been smuggled over to Bourbon or Mauritius. One Seychellois slaver, Captain Jouan, had broadly suggested that Lesage was a slaver himself, and challenged him to fight the Emperor, at that point still riding high. This attack was unwelcome to the *juge de paix* too, for he found Lesage congenial, perhaps for the reason Jouan proposed or perhaps simply because Lesage was an intimate of Farquhar's with shares in the Belombre plantation in Mauritius which was owned by the Governor's inner circle. At any rate, Captain Jouan was hustled off to Mauritius by de Quincy himself to stand trial for seditious words. Lesage was wounded in the attempt to arrest the fourth slaver he admitted to knowing about, the *Revenant*.[13] This was in 1814, a bad year for some slavers: the *Revenant* herself was wrecked on Bourbon, the *Diligent* was captured there with slaves from Seychelles, and the tiny 10-ton *Passe-Partout* lost half her cargo of sixty-nine Mozambique children when they died from smallpox on her protracted forty-five-day passage to Seychelles.[14] When Lesage left for Madagascar that year, he was being sent to organise an anti-slave-trade treaty with King Radama I. Farquhar, who sent him, may have had a sense of humour; certainly he used the young Radama as the power centre through which British influence could operate against the French in Madagascar, and equally certainly he preferred to attack the slave trade far from his own coasts, courts and colonial constituents when, under increasing pressure from Parliament and the Colonial Office, he eventually found that he had to attack it after all. Lesage sold his estates in Seychelles, and one of the purchasers, appropriately enough, was the new civil agent Captain E.H. Madge. Madge was in Seychelles for twelve years, and might have spent his life there had cries not been raised in Parliament during the early-to-mid-1820s about a supposed slave-trade in Mauritius through, and of course to, Seychelles.

It had probably been over for a couple of years, such was the slowness of reaction in Parliament, but the backwash was strong enough to remove Madge from the Islands in 1826, then from the King's service altogether in 1828. He was unfairly judged – not quite a scapegoat but someone whom, in a barrel of half-rotten apples like Mauritius in these years, it was convenient to see ejected. The courts and police there were effectively in the hands of pre-conquest Mascareignean Créole functionaries like the Procureur General Jean-Marie-Martin Virieux and his younger brother the policeman Jean-Marie-Denis, while the Governor was concerned above all to conciliate white Créoles. The new Chief Judge George Smith was unwilling to enforce the 1811 Felony Act against slavers themselves and content merely to convict slave-ships in the Vice-Admiralty Court; no fines that he might impose were ever exacted. Thus Mauritius was not a dangerous place for people smuggling in slaves – except in 1817 when the garrison's hands were freed during Farquhar's absence on leave. The parliamentary commissioners whose enquiries led to Madge's fall rather felt he had been harshly treated in comparison with de Quincy who, at a great age, had passed beyond their reach.[15] He had always contrived to keep beyond the reach of Captain Madge.

As he saw his own life until he arrived in Seychelles, Madge had been more accustomed to the frowns of fortune than its smiles. However, he had money from accumulated pay to buy Poivre and Desroches – islands in the Amirantes fit for cotton. It was easy to become a proprietor. Land was to be had on credit. Living was cheap because it was not luxurious, and the simple necessities of life were grown by the labour of slaves, whose cost could also be paid off over three or four years from the proceeds of cotton. Maize and turtle could be harvested too from an island like Poivre. And as the managing partner there, Madge could even have the lost Dauphin of France, the rightful Louis XVII himself:[16] this was the exalted personage that Madge's manager Louis-Pierre Poiret revealed himself to be on his death-bed in 1856. He had been smuggled out of the Temple prison after Maman had followed Papa to the guillotine, he recalled. Hidden for some years with a cobbler whose name he took, he had, by one account, been smuggled to the Indian Ocean aboard the *Marengo* in 1803 and after 1807 lived on Mahé, acquiring slaves, land at Cap Ternay, and two successive coloured ladies, before working Poivre for a few years and then returning to Cap Ternay. There is no doubt that he believed himself to be the Dauphin; he wrote, or at least drafted, one or more letters to Europe in that guise, and left none of his children – formally illegitimate, but legally recognised before he died – without a 'Louis' or a 'Marie' among their names. No doubt many of the several dozen similar claimants in other parts of the world believed their own revelations too.[17] They were perhaps strange friends, or at any rate very bold ones, to smuggle the Dauphin out of France in Linois' flagship the *Marengo* with General Decaen himself on board; even stranger, certainly, to leave him there in Seychelles without either bringing him home to his throne or poisoning him. De Quincy did not marry him to one of his deserving stepdaughters, as he did an undoubted aristocratic refugee, the Vicomte de Brachet, who had swum ashore from *La Flèche*.[18] Poiret must remain more positively identified as an 'astucious' proprietor – 'more knave than fool', said the Slave Protector after deep thought – who once tried to pass off certain slaves as Seychelles Créoles when in reality they were probably new arrivals introduced in defiance of the anti-slaving statutes.[19]

The slave population went up by more than natural leaps after the slave trade was abolished there by the new British statutes introduced formally in 1811. Of 3,015 slaves counted in 1810 only one-third were women, and their fertility could hardly have produced the increase to 6,950 by 1815.[20] Hodoul, Tirant, de Quincy and his old friend Sausse all knew what had produced the slave-influx which was essential for them to seize advantage from the coming peace, as was demonstrated in 1816 when Madge captured the famous old Bourbon-based slaver Captain Sausse and his brig, the *Marie Louise*. New slaves she had just landed on the Praslin plantation of her joint-owner, d'Albarède, had spread smallpox there as well as on Mahé when they were smuggled over there for sale. Word reached Madge, and he commandeered the brig in the face of de Quincy as president of the *tribunal de paix*, his son-in-law André-Joseph Lablache who was its first *suppléant*, and its *greffier* Rémy-Jean d'Argent, an established slaver himself.[21] Madge, however, had no pistols to put into the hands of any slave-guard. By dawn, left in charge of her mates Kevern and Grandcourt, the *Marie Louise* was heading out of harbour for Bourbon where she took a new name but even so was eventually to be seized as a slaver again after making at least one more passage to Seychelles. Madge did prevent her from picking up the rest of her slaves from Praslin. Sausse, detained, escaped with fifty-four of the slaves from Mahé and with de Quincy's evident though hotly denied collaboration.[22] He could not deny Sausse as an old friend, and the documentary record is clear: with an outstanding debt of seventy-five bales of cotton for twenty-five new slaves sold illegally to de Quincy by Sausse in 1812, Sausse only extended the period for payment when de Quincy had committed himself to aiding his escape.[23]

After that, too many Seychellois who did not love de Quincy observed his own slaves provisioning the Sausse-owned schooner *Hirondelle*, the *juge de paix*'s well-known boats taking her out to sea into the wind,[24] for anyone to accept de Quincy's denials except within the Gallic circle of protection in the office of the Procureur-General in Mauritius. De Quincy therefore proposed to go there, and so Madge arrested him and went along to make the charges stick. Greatly embarrassed in his age and his dignity, de Quincy stormed away from the Islands which he by now absolutely identified as his own possessions amid fierce recrimination. Its members were so treacherous, he said, that they were even supporting Madge. What baseness, he said, for the ungrateful brutes to be found in cabal with their benefactor's own son-in-law Lablache. What absence of the generosity due to a septuagenarian with five interesting children to launch into the world advantageously; he had even raised his late wife's two daughters, whose actual father was in a British war prison. He, whom the world had always recognised as a man of honour, was beset in his old age by this one-time revolutionary Lablache, deportee, fugitive, maybe a bigamist, to whom in his charity he had even given one of his dead wife's daughters – although, had she been alive, she never would have permitted it.[25] There was, behind it all, a quarrel between de Quincy and Lablache over inheritable property – at any one time there was usually a crop of such quarrels ripening in Seychelles. The plundering of minors' estates by relations appointed as family trustees under provisions of the Civil Code was a pastime, as it was throughout the Mascareignes.

Other longlasting social and psychological stances also emerged from de Quincy's outbursts. Madge was an outsider deceived by Lablache; the word of blacks, given against him, could never be accepted by anyone alive to Seychelles and the slave world because it was commonly assumed that money or arrack would buy the testimony of any slave. Taking slave evidence against a white was illegal, anyway, and Madge's appeals for more evidence to people at large, slaves included, endangered the solidarity of the white ruling group. De Quincy's other solid argument – that the *juge de paix* should know the Islands but not be connected, like every other proprietor, with each family in the place[26] – would have ruled him out too. De Quincy was not universally well-regarded in Mauritius either. Chief Judge Smith took him to be 'literally a lump of Passion, Prejudice, and Partiality'.[27] However, Procureur-General Virieux stood firm, taking care not to see evidence that would have obliged most men to convict de Quincy as party to a felony. Back he went to Seychelles, still *juge de paix*, appealing to the Prince Regent for leave to prosecute Captain Madge, while Virieux sat on papers that Madge needed for his reply.[28]

The upshot was more than one petition from proprietors against the partiality of de Quincy's administration of justice. In one succession case he gave judgement to protect a fraudulent guardian who was a client of one of his sons-in-law, a notary, so that the man could make off to Mauritius with the spoils and fight the appeals with it.[29] He was the least qualified of any man to be *juge de paix*, thought Smith, who was himself one of the most partial of judges alive. De Quincy would let no-one appear before him as public prosecutor, on the grounds that there was no provision for such an official in Decaen's original law – although in the past he had appointed public prosecutors enough and to spare, until one of them entered on the court record some facts inconvenient to the *juge de paix*. There de Quincy was, however, and there he must remain. To the very end of his long life, he could still put up a brilliant performance in front of those who, mostly *étrangers*, took him at his own estimation. In 1824 he convinced an obliging emissary from the new Governor that he possessed a character replete with every honourable sentiment although it was unhappily true – so the emissary continued – that in a few cases his age and ignorance of the law had enabled others to use him.[30] That same year, one of the ingenuous British naval captains in whom de Quincy particularly delighted put up to him precisely the image that he liked to project himself:

> At a party at his house, I paid him a handsome compliment upon the benefits which he had conferred upon his country, when the old man was so overcome by the unexpected and gratifying allusion to a subject, on which he with good reason prided himself, that he burst into tears, and was for some time quite overcome by his feeling.[31]

Among his own countrymen he had had cause more for tears of mortification. When the *commune* was reconfirmed in 1817, the members selected were reluctant to sit with him and one of them absolutely refused; and when it petered out in the 1820s, at great cost to civic-mindedness in Seychelles, de Quincy's senile domination might have been as much responsible as Sir Robert Farquhar's determination to allow the Islands no institutions that were not possessed by any district of Mauritius.[32] However, De Quincy's self-image won even the Seychellois in the end. He was buried in the apparent place of honour, on a knoll where the flagstaff and battery stood, to one side of Government House – although it was always open to his enemies to say that they did not want him lying among their own dead in Bel Air cemetery. And he always beat Madge, who was sent back to Seychelles in 1817 with a flea in his ear for arresting de Quincy over the *Marie Louise* affair.[33]

Nor could the British civil commandant get his hands on Sausse in 1819, when the slaver arrived from Bourbon in a French corvette on business connected with France's colonial designs upon Madagascar but prudently stayed aboard.[34] Madge did capture *Le Lutteur*, the unlucky Captain Romarf's new schooner which ran a cargo into Anse à la Mouche after Romarf was drowned off Madagascar. Charmed by this windfall, proprietors spirited the blacks into the hills. Madge recaptured some of them but drew the line when Mauritius pressed him to arrest the Seychellois involved. They included some of the Island's most eminent *grands blancs*, a Nageon de l'Estang among them. He would not do it, Madge said – he could not, bereft as he was of assistance.[35] He had only slaves as boatmen, and his deputy the easy-going Ensign George Harrison. Ensign Harrison was more at home in Seychelles than most other Anglo-Saxons; his wife, born in Geneva, had been educated in France; some said he was Sir Robert Farquhar's natural son. Harrison outstayed his friend and plantation-partner Madge, taking over for several years after he was withdrawn in 1826. Madge was constantly being required to attempt the impossible, but at the same time was rebuked for exceeding his powers; no-one seemed able to define what those powers were, but everyone was sure they were very limited.[36]

Seychelles, depot of smuggled blacks – that was what the Islands had been to Colonel Keating's men.[37] Madge probably did not connive at this, but it should not have been surprising that his zeal vanished. No slave-trader, he was a big slave-owner. With nineteen in 1815, he spent some $1,200 more during the next four years on another ninety-five, one of whom was the slave whose purchase cost him his job. This was Moustique Le Fleut, from the *Marie Louise*. Aged about twenty in 1827, he remembered how he had been kidnapped as a small boy called Golom at Makoa in Mozambique, sold on by the Portuguese, and landed from a two-masted vessel at Praslin. Part of d'Albarède's share of the cargo, he was purchased by Madge when these slaves were sold off; in law they should have been set free, having been illegally introduced, but the court in Mauritius had actually ordered their sale.[38]

Post-1815 figures leave no doubt that up till the early 1820s many more like Moustique Le Fleut were smuggled into and through Seychelles. By 1827 the slave population was down by 430 on the 1815 figure but 2,267 were recorded as having been transferred to estates in Mauritius, where slaves fetched a higher price than in Seychelles. The narrow coastal plateaux of Mahé, Praslin and La Digue and even the ampler flats of some Outer Islands were not comparable to the sugar plains of Mauritius; it made sense here to pay high prices with the intention of getting the most out of the slaves before their emancipation, which after all might never come – as in the end it did come in the 1830s. The Admiralty court records of Mauritius itself show how the seas were full of small ships running in black contraband, and the Outer Islands of Seychelles were suspected of being used as depots where they could be acclimatised and disguised. The Amirantes saw enough activity to lend colour to the suspicion. The captured *Favourite* was wrecked on Daros in 1821 by her crew after they had recovered her from prize-masters put aboard by the Royal Navy; they made off in a vessel belonging to the Island's proprietor, the Dutch-born sea captain Robert Rolph Young. He was rescued by the Langlois family's brig *Courier des Seychelles* – a new vessel under an old name, perhaps, though not necessarily sailing on a new errand; she was bound for Aldabra for tortoises, she said, but not everybody believed her.[39] That year HMS *Menai* captured the fast new Nantes slaver *Le Succès* with letters from the owners imploring the blessing of Almighty God on the enterprise. It had taken him forty-one hours of chasing her round the Amirantes, said the naval captain grimly, with too many reefs too close beneath his keel to make it a pleasant race.[40] And the gun-brig *Delight* took recaptured illegal slaves to the bottom with her in a hurricane off Mauritius.[41]

Moustique Le Fleut, happy in comparison, was freed from his illegal slavery in 1827. Other slaves can be identified by name too – as, for instance, some of those owned by the Langlois, a rising family consisting of Madame *Veuve* Langlois and her three sons. Thirty-one-year-old Pierre-Marie-Adolphe Langlois, master of the *Courier des Seychelles*, married the deceased François Blaise Savy's fifteen-year-old daughter Rose Virginie in September 1818 during a break in his alleged voyages to Aldabra.[42] His *Courier des Seychelles* surely often carried more smuggled slaves than tortoises into Seychelles. On about 23 May 1823 she brought three men who later told their story – Augustin Ribaud, Roquelaure Louis and Robert Sans Chagrin. She had sailed openly from Mahé under the baffled eyes of the new Protector of Slaves, Knowles; and she probably carried with her descriptions of imaginary slaves whom the proprietors had already entered in the obligatory registers so that the new blacks could be passed off as old. Louis recalled coming from Mozambique in a cargo of selected young blacks and being put ashore secretly on Silhouette where the Langlois, Savy, Tirant, Hodoul families all had land. Madge had land there too and by now plainly he was sometimes willing to placate proprietors. Next day Louis was landed on Mahé at the Widow Langlois' house, lodged for a while in her store-room, and then taken to her estate at Anse Marie Louise. This was how Robert Sans Chagrin and Augustin remembered it too. Augustin came with Louis and a great many others, and was lodged at Tirant's place on Silhouette where he stayed longer than Louis, because he danced during the festivities commonly held on plantations to mark the New Year and could speak Créole, before they shipped him over to Hodoul's house on Mahé where the *commandeur* took him immediately into concealment in the woods. After a few days lying low he was taken to his new master – the *juge de paix*, de Quincy.[43]

Then there were mainly anonymous slaves smuggled into Romarf's former depot on Praslin by the Port Louis sea-captain Nicholas Dodero: 150 landed in 1822 were credited to him, and another 157 the following year.[44] Among them were children from Madagascar who received the slave-names Isidore and Bourbon when they were bought by Jean-François Jorre de St Jorre; their story was not told till 1835, when St Jorre's former slaves, now 'apprentices' for four years until full emancipation, could being themselves to complain about his ill-treatment of them.

The prospect of freedom had its effect on the slaves, and perhaps made the masters more heavy-handed in expressing their resentment. Already by 1821 the slaves had, as Madge put it, imbibed 'certain Ideas of Liberty, which materially indisposed them to those established Measures of Discipline necessary for holding so numerous a Body in perfect subjection'.[45] Mr Slave Protector

Knowles might have got across to Silhouette too late to free Augustin, Robert and Louis; but his appearance on estates where hitherto the word of the master was law meant that the whip, the strap, the stick, manacles and the *bloc* or plantation prison were not so readily submitted to by slaves as the system required.[46]

Slaves gathered together at night in defiance of good order. Those of the actual slaver-captains, newly-introduced and not born into slavery in the Islands, were particularly unreconciled. One party stole Hodoul's small sloop; another got away with a boat of Tirant's, first surrounding the big house during supper with hatchets, ready to deliver a lethal blow to any member of the family who came out too soon.[47] Proprietors restored tranquillity by curtailing the sale of arrack and marching in night patrols; they promised Knowles every insult they could imagine, regretting the good old days when Seychelles, '*heureuse dans sa médiocrité*', found that its assurance of internal peace, '*bien plus que dans l'accord des habitans, était dans la disposition des esclaves, qui, satisfait d'un traitement humain, montraient du zèle, du dévouement, et une simplicité de moeurs qui les preparait à une docilité constante*'.[48] The prospect of freedom warmed even the coldest imagination, said the masters. For that matter, slaves had sought liberty often enough in the past by running away, but the incidence of *marronage* increased as the idea of emancipation took hold.

There were certainly plenty of maroons from now on. Four of Madge's own slaves made off in a pirogue, along with two he had captured from the *Lutteur*, and while chasing them with the soldiers stationed in the Islands from 1817 onwards a couple of de Quincy's blacks were drowned in a capsize.[49] When La Tulippe and La Fleur, slaves of Charles Savy, were wanted to give evidence against a slaver, Savy could claim that they were fugitives in the mountains.[50] For about four years in the late 1820s whites and their more obedient slaves identified a leader among the maroons, Macondé. He was in his early thirties, knew how to handle timber-working tools and, after three or four years in the woods, delivered himself up to his master; he then become useful in tracking down his former companions.[51] The concept of liberty being close at hand might lead a man to run for it – so might a simple attraction to life on Mahé. Outer Islands were places of exile. On Poivre in 1830, forty-seven of M. Hugon's slaves complained of enforced separation from their families on Mahé, as well as of 'being made to labour with the pioche under the lash of a Driver, which is repugnant to their feelings, having been domestics or accustomed to work less fatiguing and degrading... .' On Desroches a gang of Hodoul's absolutely refused to work, even though they seemed to be well treated. In the old days they might not have ventured on their revolt, if there is more than symbolic truth in the legend that he had once shot and buried a cargo of slaves in order to evade capture by a British man-o'-war. Now he simply brought these mutineers to court.[52]

In the runaway Cupidon Mozambique's case, even to accompany Charles Savy *neveu* as far as Silhouette was to be cast into a howling wilderness. He preferred to take to the woods behind Grande Anse. He was about twenty-five, became a maroon around the *saison des tortues*, as he said – i.e. between April and November – but got more bananas than turtle flesh on an old Nageon plantation where he had hidden with four others. That diet palled one fatal day in 1833 and the hungry band essayed a descent upon the house of Madame *Veuve* Landrous at Anse Majeur. This resulted in cries for vengeance from the widow and six years in irons for the maroons.[53] The names of their former masters show what other members of this band were escaping from. Théodore's owner was an epileptic who later killed a woman slave while supposedly under the influence of his affliction and, escaping Mahé's lightly guarded gaol one night, got away in his brother-in-law's brig. Baptiste had fled from Babet Loizeau, *affranchie* of Jean Loizeau who had left her and their children most of his property; her dealings with their domestic slaves, who were actually much more at risk from the tensions in the great house itself than the *piocheurs* or fieldhands were, in the end saw her sent to gaol.[54] White proprietors did not often suffer to that extent. Slave children were given as playmates to white ones, who were themselves brought up and sometimes suckled by *nénènes*, slave nurses. The relationship might be affectionate or exploitative on either side, or a mixture of both, and was commonly the latter. Something of these relationships was revealed in the Loizeau household during 1833. In a drunken quarrel at table, two of Babet's teenaged sons were unacceptably reminded by a slave woman, perhaps their old nurse, of the damage their forks might do. One son dragged her to the lock-up, but relented so far as merely to beat her about the face when she reminded him that it was his interests she was guarding.[55]

The slave protectors thought that much of the activity in these great houses could justly be described as domestic brutality; the masters would have called it domestic discipline. François Hodoul kept his slave Victorine in irons for two months as punishment for running away, as well as for theft and debauchery. She was distinctly a *mauvais sujet*, he complained, when the British fined him £40; and by way of proving it he got her sent to gaol for stealing a comb.[56] But that was a small triumph indeed, and absolutely no recompense for the life which British philanthropy was threatening to take away from him in return for a few pounds sterling per head of his slaves.

On the eve of emancipation the Islands were losing people fast; perhaps half the white and coloured population left for richer pastures in Mauritius. De Quincy's heirs went after his death, as did the Langlois and the Monvoisin family with their fourteen domestic slaves. Removal of so many house slaves had to be looked at twice for British authority to be sure that the family was not secretly breaking the prohibition on the transfer of field labour,[57] imposed in 1828 after Charles-Dorothé Savy and his son Ferdinand sold slaves whom they had obtained permission merely to transfer to their Mauritius estates. The transfer of slaves to Mauritius from Seychelles, except two domestics per master, was thenceforth forbidden.[58] Later the Treasury paid less compensation for slaves whom the British had forced to be kept in Seychelles, on the grounds that their labour was of lower value among the granite boulders of Seychelles than in Mauritius.[59]

Proprietors were already suffering from Farquhar's determination, in an airy dismissal of 1,000 miles of sea, to treat Seychelles as a district of Mauritius – which for fifty years subsequent Governors followed loyally. In 1817 Farquhar had decreed that Seychelles trade must pass through Mauritius. This put 20 per cent on cotton exported, and 40 per cent on the calicos and wine it went to buy – a heavy price for the subsidy which the administration of Seychelles received from Mauritius. The Seychellois were comfortable on their cotton so long as the price stood high, not bothering with money but conducting business by bills-of-sale on their crops, and living well off the country; but life had become almost insupportable for the energetic after 1822 when cotton fell on world markets.

Up till that time, Seychelles had exported 16-18,000 bales of cotton each year, but by 1825 this was down to half and sold for half the former price.[60] Yet some Seychelles proprietors found a magnetic attraction in their rocks, and for others Mauritius was too humid, too barren and perhaps too big.

Seychellois often had a satisfying life in their own Islands; and so in the 1830s, in a minor key, did many Créoles. So little money could be made by working the fieldhands in the last years before freedom that they were barely worked at all; hence they were strong and healthy, and raised pigs and bees, and tobacco for the market – in contrast to their often hard-driven counterparts on the sugar estates of Mauritius and Bourbon.[61] The physical back-drop of Seychelles always favoured a relaxed life, and the climate was good. It was true that St Antony's fire, dropsy of the scrotum and elephantiasis were recognised local afflictions along with dysentery and some leprosy, particularly among the blacks, but the number of those who reached extreme old age was high. Time could be passed pleasantly. Cards and billiards were the major acknowledged diversions for Seychellois men – with sexual diversions acknowledged almost if not quite as freely. French was becoming slurred on the lips even of the *grands blancs* and they had often lost the fire that was thought to characterise their metropolitan cousins. For the most part they had little need of it. They could walk freely, unarmed, around their Islands, or be carried in their hammocks. Maroons notwithstanding, Seychelles made a peaceful homeland. There might be much theft among the blacks, many high words among the whites and much chicanery at large when the opportunity offered to advance individual or family interests, but there was little actual violence. Seychellois valued hospitality and politeness; the women loved dancing and took full advantage of the open house provided by Charles-Dorothé Savy on St Anne when the corvette *Favorite* brought a French circumnavigating expedition commanded by Captain Laplace in 1830.[62] Simplicity in the usual timber-and-latanier-thatch houses was what commonly struck Laplace in Seychelles, somewhat in contrast to the ceremonious reception of the visitor by the mistress sitting under a rattan canopy with her slave girls; but his engraver shows one *château* at any rate as built for ceremony. Two elegant storeys of stone rose to a couple of attic windows set in the steep roof of capucin shingles. The Savy house was full of girls while the ship lay nearby, not

all pretty as Laplace admitted, but all agreeable; and on the night
of a ball torches helped guests from the landing-place, last year's
Paris fashions appeared, and light danced off the granite, until he
wondered what he was seeing – and, still more, hearing when
violin and tambourine got to work for a *contredanse* too violent
and intricate for metropolitan abilities.

The landed class of the Islands led a private, family-oriented
life. One's duty was to love, honour and respect the family, and
ensure that others respected it.[63] In some families slaves too were
to be respected by outsiders. The community was nothing. Every
man for himself and God for us all – this was the motto outside
the nexus of related families. They were also sometimes inter-related
to an unusual degree: one of the Tirant sons married his father's
sister, with a licence from obliging Mr Harrison. There were no
gentlemen in black to talk about prohibited degrees of affinity or
to officiate at any marriage, baptism or funeral. The *curé* requested
in 1790 had never come, and de Quincy appropriated the land
set aside for him. All rites of passage were conducted within the
austere embrace of the Civil Code.

It was too austere for 453 people who were baptised in June
1830 when a Church of England clergyman dropped in en route
to India. *Grand blanc* names like Savy and *blanc coco* names like
Calais crowd the register alongside Créole Figaros, Esparons and
Laflutes. So ripe for harvest did the field seem to the Reverend
William Morton that he came back for twelve months in 1832-3,
with a government stipend as Civil Chaplain plus a grant from
the Society for the Propagation of the Gospel in Foreign Parts.
However, his particular gospel could only be propagated in English;
and he was followed by not a few others of his Anglican creed
who made a mess of things. The sexual luxuriance of Seychelles
was often too much for what store of tact the established church
had to dispose of. The Islands offended the next parson, the Reverend
Mr Banks, who arrived in 1840. He was not surprised to find a
more flagrant licentiousness among proprietors than blacks – *grands
blancs* insisted on being French, while the former slaves were civil
and quiet and had actually celebrated 200 marriages among themselves in the previous two years, and flatteringly insisted that they
liked the freedom-giving British better than the local élite who
would never cease repining for their lost slave labour. As Mr
Banks put it, 'The lower classes do not appear as sensually debased

generally as the others & Mahé with its surrounding Islands afford a very strong proof, that unsanctified knowledge only fits a man to be Satan's more effective servant.'[64] Not much formal knowledge was imparted at all, sanctified or otherwise, except navigation. Seventy or eighty pupils had been taught under the philanthropic Mico Trust since 1839, the impoverished Misses d'Offay gamely ran a dame school, and the Scotsman J.M. Collie took twenty 'better class' pupils whose parents had some ambition for them but could not afford to send them to school in Mauritius.

Few could. Proprietors had never given much attention to the soil, having been careless even in the early days. By 1830 Mahé could not feed its population but had to rely on maize from Silhouette, Marianne and the Amirantes. With the cotton price down, the Seychellois were surviving by getting permission to ship occasional cargoes of sugar and arrack direct to India from the three mills built on Mahé in the 1820s. Some money was to be made from the whalers, which started to call in November 1823; by 1837 there had been eighty-two.[65] There was profit in them for shipwrights too. J.-F. Hodoul went into business with his son in 1830 near the islet that bears his name,[66] but the main shipbuilders were Hélène Naz's son, with his partner and brother-in-law the London-born Thomas Crook, who had bought out Captain Planeau. They launched vessels ranging from 20-ton luggers to a 300-ton barque for the Port Louis merchant Thomas Blythe. In partnership with one of the Hodoul family, Crook and Naz built the wryly-named schooner *Emancipation*.

Emancipation put short-term money into proprietors' pockets. Louis Poiret for instance got £371 4s 5d for his twenty slaves; many years later he decided he ought to have had more, although he did not say he was the King of France when he petitioned for it.[67] Nor apparently did he defiantly spend his capital on extravagance in Mauritius and Bourbon, as the Savy of Ste Anne had done when Laplace came back on a new circumnavigation in 1837.[68] He found the girls more finely dressed than before, more expert dancers, less timid; and yet he had liked them better before their exposure to the more mannered society of their cousins in the two big islands. Seychelles themselves were sad with overgrown plantations; houses were deserted and some already falling down; the huts of the freed slaves were spreading across the neglected estates. Laplace was sure that Seychelles would soon be left to the black people, and sailed away cursing all philanthropists. Even in Bourbon, where slavery still persisted, he foresaw trouble as a result of the weakening white hegemony.[69] *Grands blancs* joined the malediction but not the prediction that Créoles would take over Seychelles. The Savy did not sail for India, as Charles-Dorothé told Laplace he was thinking of doing, although their beautiful St Anne house did fall into ruin, like de Quincy's abandoned Bellevue. And basic standards continued to be maintained – the standards governed by colour which for generations ruled society in Seychelles. The *grands blancs* there were never quite so successfully exclusive as their Antillean counterparts, the *Békés* of Martinique, but they had done pretty well at this stage and were not about to give up. The family was the central institution, however freely men, and sometimes women too, roamed sexually outside it. And by its marriages, with their reassertion of values and re-enforcement of property, Seychellois society revealed itself most clearly of all. *Grand blanc* families were jealous about whom they admitted to their legal beds. Charles-Marie St Ange married a woman of mixed parentage like himself, daughter of a British policeman by a freed slave. Jean-Marie Le Beuze's daughters were rich but had to take Dutch and American sea-captains, strangers to the Islands, and when widowed acquired new husbands from only minor white families; while the Loizeau children, among the richest people in Seychelles, found wives among the Ramalinga and similar families. Their cousins, not wealthy at all but completely white, married into *grand blanc* houses.[70] This was all symptomatic of caste, and privileges followed. By mid-century it had made men like Adolphe Loizeau resentful enough to brood upon the ancient example of coloured people's role in the great revolt in Haiti and talk openly about using the dagger in Seychelles.

3

THE AIR OF SEYCHELLES
1840-1920

Revolution was an intermittent threat or promise in Seychelles. One day in December 1852 Adolphe Loizeau, coloured sometime slave-beater, son of the Indian freed slave Babet by a rich white landowner, harangued a crowd from the front of his store in Port Victoria about the lessons of the revolt in Haiti in the 1790s. So the metropolis of Seychelles, which should have been called Labourdonnais,[1] had been christened in 1840 at the motion of Ensign Harrison's successor as Civil Agent, the former Mauritius Registrar of Slaves C.A. Mylius, who had been reluctant to seek consent from, as he said, the distinctly un-British white Seychellois. Although they did consent, they resented the name almost as much as the foreign government's established intention, in principle anyway, to overturn the natural ordained order of society by not merely enfranchising slaves but contemplating the extension of social equality to coloured people like the Loizeau family.[2] Beside Adolphe Loizeau stood his brother Théodore, one of the two notaries authorised to practise in Seychelles; their fees had just been questioned by this same Mylius[3] who spoke for generations yet unborn in reckoning that notaries' charges would have made Barabbas feel less of a thief. In the harbour the 94-ton *Josephine Loizeau* discharged turtles, maize and coconut-oil on to the wharf built by Mylius at one end of the Long Pier.[4]

People of colour like the Loizeau family had cause to regret the retirement of the splenetic old Civil Agent in 1850. As Registrar of Slaves in Mauritius, Mylius had formed an opinion of *grands blancs*, as well as of the feeble local implementation of British metropolitan policy, which his eleven years in Seychelles only served to confirm. He was delighted with Emancipation Day there, 11 February 1839, when black Créoles celebrated with 'peaceable demonstrations of joy and gratitude'.[5] As for the Islands themselves, though, a more neglected corner of the globe he never wanted to see. No church, no schools to speak of, no market, no hospital – it was impossible, surely, that civilised existence could be conducted without these. The very graves of the *grand blanc* families at Bel Air on the hill above the town had been rooted up by pigs: 'In our present degraded state', as he put it with heavy irony, 'we are hardly worthy of being owned by so great and liberal a nation.'[6] Liberality was altogether lacking in Mauritius – which met the deficit on basic administration costs for the sake of Seychelles' strategic importance but would venture little for development, having no belief in the Islands' agricultural future. And the heart of the nation itself was liberal only with high-flown speech. That very soul of the mid-nineteenth-century Colonial Office, James Stephens, gladly used Seychelles as the peg on which to hang a small treatise on the needs, expectations and resources of small dependencies *vis-à-vis* the obligations of the Empire at large. The Island situation of so many British colonies was a fertile source of trouble and misgovernment, he said; a few thousand people separated from any large population required political and ecclesiastical institutions out of all proportion to their comparative importance and their ability to pay,

> ....and the multitude of these miniature States must from the very nature of the case exhibit so many strange anomalies. They must either live without a due participation of the advantages of people inhabiting larger and more populous countries; or they must purchase these advantages at the expense of a ruinous taxation, or they must become costly incumbrances to the state to which they belong.

Those who lived – and perhaps more especially those who ruled – in places like Seychelles tended to see all the defects of the Island environment as through a magnifying glass. The Colonial Office looked at them as through the wrong end of a telescope. And so the great object was

> ....to correct each of these delusions, and looking all round at the resources of the Empire, and the demands upon them, to determine how much can be spared without injustice to greater interests, for those of such a place as the Seychelles.[7]

Very little indeed could be spared. The Commissioners of Eastern

Enquiry in the 1820s, their brief not limited solely to investigating
the extent of the illegal slave trade into Mauritius and Seychelles
after 1810, had recommended something like a full colonial establishment for Seychelles, but London left the final decision to
the discretion of Mauritius, and its officials were pleased to tell
Mylius that he was a mere clerk and that the Islands he wanted
to regard as a colony were no more than a minor dependency
of Mauritius.[8] The commissioners had recognised that Seychelles
needed their own port of entry, with independent customs, but
the Collector of Customs in Mauritius overruled this. The Islands'
trade would best continue to be regarded as a coasting trade organised
from Port Louis. Seychelles could never in his view become the
seat of an extensive legal commerce; illegally, the Mascareignean
historian M. Le Duc among others was trading between some of
the Outer Islands and Madagascar without benefit of clearance or
port dues.[9] Mylius was left to peer liverishly down his microscope.
When he trained it upon local society he saw that the Loizeau,
St Ange, Dupuy and other coloured families had every reason for
their complaint that discrimination was used against them. Up till
his arrival, as they said, 'some persons of the white population,
of French origin, employed in this Colony the vilest means to
oppress and vilify the coloured population, who were then in the
minority.'[10]

It was done through the courts as much as any other way. As
judge, de Quincy was succeeded by Guillaume Antoine Anne
Fressanges from Mauritius who was aged, half blind and half deaf
and of little use on the bench, except to lose unwelcome depositions
on the manslaughter of former slaves. Fressanges gave judgements
which made Mylius feel that things had been better in the pre-
Emancipation days when the slave protectors could intervene.[11]
'It has occurred in our celebrated Court', said Mylius, 'that witnesses
have deposed in one way, and their testimony consigned in a
diametrical opposite one on the records, from, no doubt, the
extreme deafness of our learned and talented Judge.'[12] Necessarily,
he had a wider jurisdiction than the District Magistrates in Mauritius.
Appeal to the higher courts there was impossible for anyone except
proprietors; having access to credit if not cash, they could keep
an appeal going for so long that it became pointless to sue in the
first place. It was also scarcely worth while to try anyone for
serious crime; although in the 1840s the court was given jurisdiction

in all offences under the Penal Code up to those punishable by death, it could only inflict a year's imprisonment. Where the court felt a longer term in gaol to be appropriate, it had to report to Mauritius, then send the case there – where, without fail, the accused would be found not guilty. It became easier to confine the obnoxious to gaol indefinitely by simple fiat, and this was done when Créoles were involved – like a certain unfortunate Hector whom Fressanges imprisoned, even though Hector was the *plaintiff* in a case of 'criminal connection' (adultery).[13]

The defendant was the Reverend G.F. Delafontaine, Civil Chaplain since 1843 and till 1851 the only clergyman in Seychelles. He followed the two brief incumbencies of his Anglican predecessors in reckoning that to bring even a few people into his makeshift church was a glorious victory.[14] Mr Delafontaine at least had the police clumping obediently into church behind Mylius, until Mylius began to sense that the service he was hearing from this Swiss clergyman was not what he expected in *his* Anglican church – he meant the possessive literally, but so did the clergyman, who declared that he would not even allow *la reine Victoria* herself to interfere with his services. He proposed to launch a manuscript news-sheet carrying the pointed motto 'Render unto Caesar the things that are Caesar's, and unto God the things that are God's'.[15] People had the impression that he would take the lion's share of God's things. There were lively times in Seychelles during the 1840s. The Stipendiary Magistrate Clement, Fressanges's colleague, was in trouble with Charles-Dorothé Savy. The giant found it difficult to get house-servants in the new emancipated age – in this he was not alone since it was a universal Mascareignean problem, with the ex-slaves abandoning plantation houses as well as plantations – and was driven to acquire the guardianship of three young Africans, whom he used around his house with such necessary discipline as dragging them by the hair into the cellar. Rescuing the children from this, Clement brought on his own head all the foreseeable recriminations about violation of the sacred hearth.[16]

Prudently, Clement went on leave the next year and, as Mylius complained, stayed away an unconscionable time. In that time the Civil Agent's favourite servant was murdered and the murderer, freed on very minor bail by Fressanges, was then urged by Captain Payet to try his hand on Mylius himself. The only reason the proposed victim could hazard was 'the extreme indulgence shown him here whilst in command of the *Trio*...on the occasion of his violating the law of Nations, and the Quarantine regulations'. Payet's idea of indulgence evidently differed from Mylius's. Such a threat was not new; in 1844 the Civil Agent had a price of 1,000 dollars put on his head because he insisted on billiard rooms being closed during divine service.[17] Mylius left telling evocations of Seychelles and their people: André Lablache's son Charles, chief of police, who was 'a friend of the negro and the poor, qualities rarely to be met with in a Slave Colony';[18] the building of the *Marie Laure* from fastenings pillaged from the Liverpool vessel *Tiger*, lost on Astove in 1836 with cargo worth £80,000 – only £3,000 was ever recovered by people with any right to it, and the chief mate, Thomas Spurs, prudently settled in the Islands with money in his pocket;[19] the Reverend Mr Delafontaine, at bay in court on Hector's embarrassing charge, abusing the government medical officer in the midst of his evidence 'to the great merriment and sarcasm of an anti-English audience';[20] and the land situation, which shocked Mylius's puritan soul. Two-thirds of the concessions were legally due for resumption, so little had the original conditions been complied with; and as to principles ruling the first parcelling out, the maxim *'cherchez la femme'* most shockingly applied: 'Petticoat influence, and gallantry, have procured the enjoyment of whole Islands, and hundreds of acres of land – free! Those were the chivalrous days of Sechelles.'[21]

Ladies still continued to make themselves available for enjoyment, and men had not become so unchivalrous as to refuse them a commercial reward. New days were coming, even so. When Fressanges was retired from his tottering bench, Mauritius showed some sense of humour by replacing him with a coloured lawyer, an ally for Loizeau. Charles Molloy Campbell, who arrived as District Magistrate in June 1852, was the son of Lieutenant 'Black' Campbell, who had been aide-de-camp to the slaver-hunting General Gage John Hall in Mauritius in 1817. C.M. Campbell left no doubt in Seychelles that he belonged to the coloured party there, for all his education among white Seychellois in Mauritius; at his birth, his father had set all white Mauritius by the ears by demanding his enrolment on the whites' register. A subscription ball was to be given by the coloured families of Seychelles, perhaps in C.M.

Campbell's honour. Over tiffin among a circle of officials, it was suggested that of course white families would not attend. If they were not willing to send their children to Mr Delafontaine's attempts at schools to rub shoulders with black and coloured children, why would they dance with the parents (unless horizontally with the wives in private)? Campbell swore that he would put a red cross against names of any *grands blancs* who dared to stay away.[22] Proud, unstable, socially marginal in the profession to which he had attained, he was in a sense betrayed by the Acting Civil Agent, D.W. Ricketts, who hailed from Mauritius too and was apparently a connection of Campbell's on the white side of the blanket.

But when his remarkable appointment to Seychelles was first announced, Campbell found his services much in demand from Seychellois then living in Mauritius. He understood that he was to be their advocate and judge combined. He was supposed to give judgement for M. Maigrot against Charles Lablache who, Maigrot alleged, was plotting against his (Maigrot's) half-brother Corgat. Maigrot required of Mr Magistrate Campbell all the partiality that Campbell would surely receive from him if the position were reversed; he begged Campbell to be more than firm with people in Seychelles, given over as they were in his experience to intrigue and ill-natured gossip (*cancan* in the patois). He promised to stand by Campbell as his friend in Mauritius in case of need, and was much mortified when Campbell gave a judgement not to his proprietorial friend's liking. A share in a succession was at stake, and Maigrot needed either justice or vengeance; his nephew, who was directly involved, must get what he wanted or blood would certainly flow. Let Campbell follow the uncle's directions minutely, making all the court orders Maigrot specified, or Maigrot himself would come over to Seychelles and confront the judge to discover whether his promises before leaving Mauritius had been empty words. Plainly they had been: Charles Molloy Campbell felt that as judge in Seychelles he was independent and did not need to do the bidding of such people.[23]

Another of his correspondents thought so – and since this was Charles-Dorothé Savy's son, Campbell might have taken warning. Charles-Joseph-Napoléon Savy, born on St Anne in 1808, was now a lawyer in Mauritius. He claimed to represent the Seychellois – not all his cousins thought he did so[24] – and sought to live up to his splendid Christian name. Napoléon Savy might have been the martyr of St Helena reincarnated, so bitter was his hatred of the British *canaille*, those bloodsuckers upon the pioneer French – some of the bloodsuckers, in his view, would have been hard put to it to name their own fathers. Mere trumpery-ware, he held them, who wasted their time trying to apply unsound theories of philanthropy to idle former slaves.[25] Napoléon Savy's family had a particular problem, house-servants apart; he told Campbell, as whose devoted colleague he at first signed himself, that it would be the work of a good judge, good Christian and good *père de famille* to get Napoléon's brother Ferdinand out of a problem centred on disputed rights to the old shipyard that Ferdinand had tried to buy. Lawsuits were burgeoning over it since networks of families had an interest under the Civil Code's subdivision of succession rights; Ferdinand was actually indebted to Adolphe Loizeau for some of the capital invested. Napoléon's friend Charles would see everything clear, but Charles Campbell saw the matter more plainly: 'He would have me favour his friends to the detriment of other people. Do his will, I am another Daniel. Be opposed to his unreasonable wishes, I am a Jefferies or something worse.'[26]

Campbell identified himself with what he saw as the emancipating British as opposed to the slave-owning French – not till the 1848 revolution did France abolish slavery itself – which meant that he would have passed a doubly uncomfortable youth in his native Mauritius too. He held that English should be the principal language used in his court instead of French. Mauritius – meaning the British governing minority – had actually ordered that English should be the official language of Seychelles.[27] This was unreasonable enough, and Campbell timed his edict badly since an aged Seychellois court clerk with no English at all had been appointed at the same time as himself. Moreover the *grands blancs* were fighting back. There was much reassertion of identity, both French and Catholic, among them in the early 1850s. This was heightened by the arrival of the ardent Capuchin Father Léon des Avanchers from Aden in March 1851, en route to joyous martyrdom in Abyssinia nearly thirty years later. As Père Léon said, the white families of Seychelles flocked to his masses, and clearly his magic had greater appeal for the population at large than the paler Anglican rites. He performed many baptisms before being driven off to Mauritius by the then Civil Agent, R.W. Keate, who chanced to be from an Anglican family, son of the legendary flogging headmaster of

Eton, and actually built a chapel on Praslin. Here, he said, was an open field for the Anglican Church, because some of the Seychellois were nominally Catholic, but all were actually as heathen as any missionary could wish. This unreasonable view ignored the fact that the choice of a church always had a political dimension. As one of the Savy summed up the feeling of the old white families to Père Léon, France had indeed been beaten in 1815, but even conquerors could hardly insist that French Catholics should take communion only from an Anglican parson. '*Ce serait porter trop loin les mots térribles de "malheur aux vaincus"!*' [28]

Seychelles at this moment was no place for a coloured judge like Charles Molloy Campbell to preach equality to the despised class to which he announced he proudly belonged, to discriminate against the French language, and to denounce the whole French tribe. Ranks closed when Campbell dismissed his court clerk, J.E. de St Perne, holding over the man his daughter's attempt to get her old *nénène* or nurse to do away with the daughter's newly-arrived love-child. [29] Nonetheless, this was still the moment when Adolphe Loizeau chose to make speeches about the need for coloured people in Seychelles to follow the example of Haitian slaves so many years before, and unsheath daggers. [30]

It was open war between coloured people and *grands blancs*, Loizeau declared, but he was doing little more than expressing his personal pain and sense of deprivation. [31] Although one resident of Mahé claimed descent from a victim of the massacres in Haiti, the Haitian freedom songs were never heard among slaves in Seychelles, nor apparently did they find local echoes. Loizeau was gaoled and Campbell was disposed of by a special commissioner from Mauritius, whose report revealed the magistrate dancing drunkenly on the beach in his shirt, profiting from a succession, and covering up a case of manslaughter aboard a schooner part-owned by one of his associates. 'In the name of outraged Justice and of that of the gown I wear, I now solemnly protest against every act of Rapine and Embezzlement Mr Campbell has committed in this District,' concluded this pious commissioner, C.R. Telfair. [32] Nephew of a leading light of Sir Robert Farquhar's old slave- and plantation-owning circle of self-aggrandising British officials and, until his bankruptcy in the 1830s, principal partner in Belombre plantation in Mauritius, he became District Magistrate in Campbell's place, and soon discovered other matters to protest against. Seychelles, he wrote to the Governor of Mauritius, certainly had 'a set of French White-men, old Slave holders, who would if they could, grind the Mulattos to powder'.[33]

Coloured families then watched with malicious satisfaction as Telfair and the new Civil Agent G.T. Wade fell foul of *grands blancs* in their turn. Great exception was taken to flogging Seychellois for breaching gaol discipline – although Créoles were birched for lesser offences; and some of the Seychellois families involved in the disputes over ownership of the shipyard were aggrieved when Wade formed a joint-stock company to buy it, with the idea of running a regular schooner round the archipelago and a small clipper on to Mauritius. This company was an idea of Governor Higginson of Mauritius – who actually visited Seychelles, so anxious was he about the possibility of bloodshed – and was planned as an evangelistic enterprise. Catholic and Protestant, coloured and white man, Frenchman and Englishman – all were to be involved together for the first time in the history of human settlement in Seychelles, said the promoters.[34] But instead it immediately became a platform for the coloured families, who alone would cooperate with the British. They became its directors while the élite – meaning, according to Telfair, 'a few worn-out French families, sunk in sloth and poverty'[35] – held aloof and reckoned that Robespierre was come again.

With a nice sense of the symbolic, Loizeau and his friends proposed to take possession of the Islands' history in the same moment as they rejected the white élite's church. They wanted to re-erect the neglected stone of possession on a handsome new plinth at their shipyard; every year they proposed to deliver a Masonic oration before it, with a collection afterwards for the poor.[36] Duly provoked as the *grands blancs* were, their counter-attack took the form of personal abuse – collected by Napoléon Savy and sent to the Colonial Office.[37] Telfair tried to compose one of the interminable quarrels over property, and found himself charged with intimidation by the man who had sought his help in the first place.[38] 'Honor, Honesty, Industry, Conjugal fidelity are as empty names among the men', Telfair concluded, 'as Chastity and Thrift are among the women.'[39] Here was Ferdinand Savy *fils* accusing Telfair of adultery with Savy's own wife. Gaoled for this slander, as it was judged to be even if it was not actually one, Savy really might as well be released, as Telfair savagely reflected, because after all 'defamation of Character, lying, and libels, are the daily pass-times ..., and are to a certain extent hereditary ....'[40] His friend petitioned to be set free on the grounds that he was a *père de famille*, rejecting an offer of release which would have involved retracting his story; this, he said, would be displeasing to his God.[41] Savy's gaol companion Charles Jouanis, imprisoned for saying that Wade was a 'damned drunkard', likewise swore in the sincerity of his soul, as a man of honour, that he would never accept any lessening of his term as an act of grace rather than of justice. It would be said in the distant Colonial Office that they were all wicked people, Jouanis wrote to Napoléon Savy, but really they were simply embittered and with good reason; as for Telfair, Jouanis supposed he must be mad.[42] Revolution was talked about, *grands blancs* proposing to rise in arms against British bureaucrats, but the air of Seychelles after all encouraged only talk. Telfair fled the fatal islands for fear that his wife might come to believe Savy's stories.

Loizeau died suddenly before the age of forty. His brother Arnold's attempts to despoil the estate gave ammunition to be used against the coloured party to the new District Magistrate, Hollier Griffiths, an Englishman given to strong language who detested any tincture of colour and had nightmares about Haiti. Falling foul of Mr Civil Agent Wade, whom he reckoned to be Loizeau's patron, Griffiths initiated the Seychelles tradition of judges who believed they were the only people of consequence in the place.[43] Not that Griffiths lacked ammunition. Arnold Loizeau's (well-insured) schooner *Voyager* went up in flames with only the brother of one of his mistresses on board. A duel threatened between Loizeau and a rival over the disputed possession of another lady whose favours were for sale, but by that time Griffiths had been found in bed dead of apoplexy and the coloured Seychellois Etienne Dupuy had taken his place. However, there would not yet be any shortage of diversion: this magistrate fell out with the Acting Civil Agent, a cousin of Telfair, who was demanding more active legal protection for a daughter of Charles-Dorothé Savy, who was much beaten by her husband, than Dupuy felt able to give. Telfair summed it all up: 'Really there must be something in the air of Seychelles that evaporates the poor remains of brains that people bring into it.'[44]

This was connected with the sense of loss and cultural deprivation suffered by *grands blancs* in being cut off from France – something which the first Apostolic Delegate to Seychelles, the Neapolitan Father Jérémie de Paglieto who arrived in 1853 with a fellow Capuchin from Savoy, tried to help them overcome. They were all descended from Frenchmen, he would announce on social occasions like funerals, and they should not forget that His Majesty Napoleon III, Emperor of all the French, was particularly anxious for them to attend (say) the forthcoming Feast of the Assumption.[45] A fine church went up in Victoria under Père Jérémie's direction. Far too big for the population, it was built by private subscription until government help had reluctantly to be solicited in the 1860s.[46] Only in 1868 did priests receive salaries, although government had maintained the Civil Chaplain from the first, even while admitting that Anglican clerics had achieved little. Delafontaine's successor in this post, the Reverend Dr A. Fallet, had to content himself with 106 communicants on Mahé on Christmas Day 1857 and eighty-nine on Praslin a few days later. The Catholic Church had the rest, as spectacular processions on feast-days bore witness. From the 1860s it had schools worthy of the name too, teaching in French since that was the language of religion. The Sisters of St Joseph de Cluny founded a girls' school in 1861, and the Frères des Ecoles Chrétiennes one for boys six years later. But the main reason for the brooding air around the crumbling big houses was simple poverty.

At the end of the 1840s not a single property was under regular cultivation. The Islands' estimated 100,000 coconut palms yielded only 7,000 *veltes* (1 *velte* = 7.5 litres) of oil, 4,000 of them consumed locally. Cocoa, coffee, cloves, rice and tobacco were grown, but only in patches. Sugar grew more widely. Rum alone was made from it now, in the mills run by Albert at Anse Ballein and Dargent at Frigate. Fine, fertile Frigate, a home of the indigenous magpie robin, was an island principality of its own, protected by breakers whipped up by the south-east monsoon. Napoleon I presided from the *salon* wall over the plantation house under the banyans after the island had passed into the hands of the Savy family, and duty was not paid on all the spirit distilled on Frigate until the police raided it one night during the calm north-west monsoon.[47] For most people coconuts seemed the best crop – along with turtles for which luggers went to the Outer Islands, the crews at risk because owners could not afford to renew the rotting sails.[48] They left meat to waste out of all proportion to the value of inferior shell that could be got from the green turtle. In 1863, 1,800 green turtle were slaughtered for £90 worth of shell exported, though some were brought back alive to Mahé for food, kept in the pond at the wharf and offered for sale, in the market that was built in about 1852, alongside straw hats, charcoal, piles of fish and coconuts.[49] Coconuts needed less capital and labour than most other crops and there was no capital to buy labour; when at last, in 1861, the authorities in Mauritius obtained India's consent for Indian labourers to be indentured in Seychelles, there was no money in the Islands to meet the cost of recruitment and transport.[50]

By then the Islands were on the brink of a very fortuitous deliverance in the manner most acceptable to landowners who, like their own forebears as well as their contemporary counterparts in the Mascareignes and West Indies, were ill-adjusted to managing anything but slave-labour. They had spent the generation after Emancipation vainly trying to reintroduce slavery by demanding a poll-tax to drive the Créoles to work and had struggled on, in practice, with the *moitié* system by which squatters worked three days for the proprietor and three for themselves. Deliverance came as a new form of slavery. On 14 May 1861 the steam sloop-of-war *Lyra* landed a couple of hundred Africans rescued from Arab slaving dhows in the Mozambique Channel; there were eighty-eight women, mostly aged between ten and twenty-five, and 114 men aged between ten and twenty.[51] Thus Seychelles came by its new working population. Although in law the new arrivals were obviously free people, no one offered any other idea than to hire them out as labourers, on wages, in return for a premium from employers to meet the government's small cost. A cargo taken to Mauritius the previous year had been put to work there, but the need in Seychelles was far greater. And the Islands were so convenient to the Arab slave routes that it became the rule to land on Mahé any slaves freed at sea south of the Equator; those captured to the north of it went to Aden. Some British blood was shed, and not a few slaves drowned when they leaped overboard in panic, as naval boarders came whooping aboard the crowded dhows. Doubts were expressed by one commander over whether the Africans, particularly the women, would not have been much better off in the Koran-ruled households of the Muslim world than on plantations where profit governed.[52]

Nonetheless the *Lyra*'s people, first of the 2,532 souls who were to be landed in Seychelles up till 1872, obligingly assured the Civil Agent, Captain Wade, that they would certainly be killed or sold again if they were returned to Africa.[53] Freed slaves seem to have retained a tradition of gratitude. On 30 June 1897, the sixtieth anniversary of Queen Victoria's accession, 2,000 Liberated Africans, grouped according to their various Mozambique towns of origin, and each with a flag, gathered in Victoria to present a loyal address; as translated from the Créole, it reflected that they were 'a living memorial of the Queen's glorious reign, for during that period, we have all been freed from slavery'.[54] They had always been devoted to the English, said an Ulsterman writing two generations after the arrival of the first shipload – they were good workmen, and they retained many of the dances they had brought with them but found their Seychelles-born children aspiring to be absorbed into the old Créole community which now counted itself the aristocracy of the black population.[55] Liberated African parents had found their own row hard enough to hoe at the beginning, and the Civil Agent whose private hints to the Royal Navy may well have brought the pioneers in the first place did not see them far along it, since he died of dysentery before the end of 1861. His successor, Swinburne Ward, took a dimmer view of their prospects. Once assigned to masters they were beyond his protection, because labour legislation was lacking although nowhere needed it more. Ward loved the islands and seas of Seychelles, for he was a great fisherman; he wrote to the Royal Botanic Gardens at Kew: 'the scenery is nearly perfect, and they are quite unique in their way. I never was in any part of the world at all like them.' He loved Frigate's excellent rum too, and drank at least his share of the 10,000 gallons of the liquor consumed annually by a population of 7,200 men, women and children; he appreciated the emotion with which a seasoned toper told him that it took at least two days to recover from a bout of drinking the deadly local pineapple brew.[56] Of the Seychellois as employers, however, he wrote: 'They are cruel, cowardly, very exacting, and expect the maximum of labor for the minimum of food and general care.'[57]

Liberated Africans were frequently brought by their private employers before the District Court to be punished for negligence at work. This obviously sprang from discontent, but nobody inquired into the reasons – it was nobody's business to do so. They even preferred to work for government, building roads or extending the pier. If in old age they should come to be treated like the Créole aged, their future would be gloomy. Old people were turned out of their huts when they were no longer able to work; the aged and the sick could not be sure of receiving care even in the little Créole colonies of the hillsides and ravines.[58] There was thus a need for a public refuge for the sick and destitute, a poor law under which proprietors would contribute to the maintenance of their worn-out employees, and a Protector of Liberated Africans in recognition of their rather special claims. For the moment, Mauritius decided that it would suffice to see whether the District Magistrate could do the protecting. Events proved that he could not, and rum soon got such a hold on Swinburne Ward that the wages paid to government on behalf of African minors disappeared in his hands.[59] Nobody except African minors felt any compelling interest in the defalcation until proprietors began to find themselves in court when a Protector had finally been appointed. This was in 1873, nine years after a less alcoholic Ward had recommended it.

Particularly harassed by the Protector, though not much touched, were the two biggest proprietors now in Seychelles, Camille Lemarchand of Baie Lazare and Val d'Andorre, and Edouard Sauzier of Forêt Noire – new arrivals of the late 1860s from Marseilles and Réunion respectively. The regular visits of Her Majesty's ships for ten years brought not merely labour but capital in the form of money spent by pursers on food and by seamen on drink and women; but the old families were not quick off the mark in buying big areas of land when they became available. And these new proprietors, with money invested by themselves and not by their grandfathers, took a keen interest in getting it back through their Liberated Africans' labour on the coconuts and coffee up at Forêt Noire and the vanilla at Val d'Andorre. The proprietors seem hardly to have worked their Liberated Africans lightly. They had been bought from the government for five years, and the investment had to be made to pay. *Ramasseurs* were sent out with their gunny-sacks to pick up the fallen nuts at 5 a.m. when the sun rose, and were kept at it for ten or eleven hours. Economies practised at their expense by the two big landowners especially were on a grandiose scale in the wages and rations withheld. Not for nothing was Sauzier the brother-in-law of the District Judge, M. Esnouf.[60] It was all a shock to the first Protector Dr William MacGregor, an earnest, self-taught Aberdeenshire ploughboy who ended as a colonial governor almost as distinguished as he was rich through speculation on his own account. He was shocked by the nakedness of Lemarchand's labourers, and by the reaction of Seychellois ladies whom he, like others, gravely asked whether their benevolence did not tempt them to teach the Africans to read; the idea of a literate African was laughable indeed.[61] The Africans' situation had appeared still more shocking the year before to Missionary Bishop W.G. Tozer, from the Universities Mission to Central Africa; on holiday during 1872 he was moved to offer a personal gift of £10 a year for five years to the Church Missionary Society if it would only undertake to redeem the neglected souls of unfortunates who did not seem to have benefitted at all from having been landed in Seychelles.[62] Accordingly, the Reverend W.B. Chancellor arrived in 1875 and came rapidly to the usual conclusions of the Anglican parson about Seychelles: his predecessor had reduced his congregation by falling out with everybody, and Satan was very strong here, with concubinage, polygamy and women crowding the wharf whenever a warship approached.[63] Chancellor was more robust than most of his cloth. He held that the best way to handle government in Seychelles was by taking the initiative – and to maintain his own health amid tropical Mahé's 'civilised immorality', he believed in the efficacy of claret and cigars. He gave a powerful description of the Liberated Africans' condition, and intervened on their behalf in and out of season. One of the proprietors called an African labourer 'Chancellor' in derision. There were myriad complaints against the Africans, said the authentic Chancellor, but 'What with curtailed wages, stinted rations, insufficient clothing, bad houses, an excess of work, and maltreatment, the African has been compelled to lie, to steal, to attempt murder and to run away from his hard task master.'[64]

The African was painted as an inferior being, whom it would be fruitless to educate. This racially induced conviction was, illogically, bolstered by political convenience. Seychellois 'say that if the Mozambiques are educated &c in time they will become the masters of the place.' The proprietors, said Chancellor, 'know too well that they will not be able to bully and cheat enlightened people'.[65] Enlightenment was sought by many adult Africans through baptism, some hoping to be healed by its miraculous powers, others – as Chancellor recognised – expecting that it would improve their status. So great was their ignorance of the true meaning of the rite that he usually had to refuse – a scruple which gave advantage to his Roman Catholic competitors who expected understanding to follow the sprinkling. Chancellor pinned his own hopes to the boarding-school he established on the mountain behind Victoria, 7 miles from the wicked town – a place to which sailors and other loose characters would find the journey too arduous. Known as Venn's Town to its patrons, after a C.M.S. saint, this was 'the University' to satirical Lemarchand, object of Chancellor's nightmares with little Africans waiting almost naked at his table. At Venn's Town the first 'crocodile' of thirty-two children toiled up in March 1876 at 4 o'clock in the morning, to avoid the blazing sun; they were to be clothed in prints and piety. The next year Chancellor was promised fifty young girls whom the government proposed to take away from estates, and he candidly did not expect one to be a virgin.

At the end of twelve years, 138 girls and 101 boys had been admitted to Venn's Town, and forty-one were still there. Some gained marriage-partners, but not one learned even the rudiments of a trade. Psalm-singing was their chief study, whether the teacher was Chancellor, his subordinate the West Indian Pickwood, or Chancellor's successor, the Somerset blacksmith Warry – who had fancied that he had a call but was cured of it in Seychelles by falling into the usual sin of sexual incontinence. Psalm-singing, and Bible-reading – though they had precious few Bibles to practise on; economy, even above the love of Christ, was the school's watchword. Not all the children found the lessons they heard on the fall of man and the first promise of the Saviour overwhelmingly compelling; 'how true it is', sighed the passionate blacksmith, 'that all our teaching can make no effect on the heart unless the Holy Spirit comes with his quickening power to show what sin is and how hateful it is to God.' Many of his recalcitrant little Africans, having no sense of sin whatever, escaped from him at the first opportunity, or were taken away by their parents until he came to wish that all were orphans.[66] Life in Venn's Town was dull at best; a pious life, to be kicked over during forays into the lower world of Victoria where hospitable ladies of the town carried their willing naval quarry off to rickety houses of pleasure in darkest Hangard Street. The little Venn's Town saints had a famous reputation down there as thieves. Of course, that lower world was well-known for its spirited untruths; so a visitor to the minor city of God reflected while she sat painting up there in 1883. This was the globe-trotting primitivist Marianne North, whose paintings reflect a malevolent innocence in Seychelles, all glossy with forbidden fruit. Even so, that city of the world, Port Victoria, sometimes had the measure of Venn's Town. Some of the big boys from Venn's Town were caught stealing salt-fish from the Civil Chaplain's own kitchen, and were punished with a diet of dry rice. 'Oh that they may be awakened to come to the Saviour while there is yet room.'[67] Across the valley from Mr Warry's prayers the drums sometimes beat all day in time to the *moutia* dancing. It was there in the hillside hamlets and on the estates that the Liberated Africans became socialised into Seychelles, not at Venn's Town before it closed down, a failure, in 1892.

They were fine estates now as seen through the eyes of the only governor ever to spend any time in Seychelles while Mauritius ruled. Sir Arthur Gordon, a Scots aristocrat and one of perhaps half-a-dozen British colonial governors worth remembering in the Empire's history, was only the second Governor of Mauritius and its dependencies who set foot there – his precursor had spent just a couple of weeks in 1853. Gordon stayed in Seychelles a number of times during 1871-4 to escape the fury of planters in what, to him, was the hateful island of Mauritius, whom he required to treat their Indian indentured labourers more nearly like humans.[68] Fine groves of coconuts stood along the coasts of Mahé. At Port Glaud M. Le Fléchier's estate had the appearance of a park, the palms planted a regular 36 feet apart with a carpet of short grass beneath them; the house was a striking one, raised on stilts, the reception-room rather gorgeously furnished, the bedroom above it made noisy by the clock let into the parapet. More fine palms stood at the Michaud property Port Launay, with a pen for Aldabra tortoises; cashews grew in the hills, finer than anything to be seen in the West Indies; and Pierre Poivre's legacy, the cinnamon, magnificently climbed the mountains.

Without cinnamon to hold the soil, there would have been more avalanches like the disastrous one of 12 October 1862. Following two days of heavy rain, a landslip beginning high up on the Trois Frères buried the upper part of Victoria under mud and boulders. Here and around Mahé, in a population of 7,560, seventy-five lives were lost, many of them in the house of the Sisters of Charity. People crowded there for safety but Père Jérémie alone was dug out alive. It was only surprising that such major slips had not happened before, widening the coastal plateau at other parts of the Island besides Victoria. Here it was possible to lay out a recreation field where the slip had filled the sea, years later to be named Gordon Square after the hero of Khartoum in recognition of his inspired identification of Seychelles as the true Garden of Eden.

In the early 1870s, with memories of the avalanche fading, the risk of further ones was increasing as Sauzier cut out more timber on the heights to make way for his coffee. Sir Arthur Gordon could nonetheless walk through magnificent scenery along the gravelled paths that were Mr Civil Commissioner Franklyn's pride (this former merchant captain was too fat to use them himself unless he rode on men's shoulders like the *grands blancs*). A good path ran south from Victoria to Cascade where the boulder-strewn mouth of the stream stopped it; another, northward, rose and fell along the coast past the ruins of de Quincy's house; and another, crossing a shoulder of the Trois Frères, went through a coconut grove owned by one of the new arrivals, the retired French naval officer Bonnetard, before descending into Baie Nord-Ouest past the ruins of a sugar-mill. Hammock or pirogue apart, hard walking was still the necessary means of travelling – perhaps more so than ever, for the horses of the first settlers had not thrived in Seychelles.

Half a mile by pirogue took the traveller from Cascade to Pointe la Rue with its fine view – mountains of Mahé to one side, islets sheltering the harbour to the other; there might be another pirogue to seaward, making for its wicker fish traps under a sail of woven matting – though, if Lemarchand had had his way, no one but proprietors would have been allowed to fish at all, and they would have been able to buy the rights to whole bays

in the interests of cheap food for their labourers. At Anse aux
Pins there was a Catholic church and an Anglican school, at Anse
Royale a bigger Catholic church before the track swung sharply
over the mountain to descend into Anse à la Mouche; then on
to Lemarchand at Baie Lazare and Père Valentin at Anse Boileau.
The Capuchin drank citronelle in a tiny two-roomed presbytery
built into the front of his church; Père Valentin was an ideal
monk, simple and kind, but he had a great many complaints
against M. Lemarchand.

The planter – squint-eyed, well-read, amusing, and ever ready
to tell of his neighbours' depravity in allowing Créoles or time-
expired Africans to squat on their lands *moitié-moitié* – had a long,
low single-storeyed house with a verandah supported on tree-trunks,
crotons upon it in tubs, caged birds hanging. His palm-leaf bath-
house, floored with sand, trapped a mountain stream through
branching white coral into a pool, then let it out into the sea;
his cigars were lighted by little black La Tulippe, who wore an
exiguous fig-leaf tied round with string; and he quoted Molière
while his son read the Marquis de Parny's poems. The Réunion-
born Parny had written verse during the Revolutionary war against
the British as well as under the Directorate, describing the Trinity
on a visit to Olympus where the Virgin engages in a love-affair
with Apollo. In the *cour* at night the Africans who were going
to leave Lemarchand the moment their time was up performed
an elephant dance for the appreciative British Governor. It was
an opera more than a dance,

> ....for the whole hunt was sung and acted as well as danced. A fire
> was lighted in the middle of a shed: three naked little black boys
> crouched and squatted near the blaze beating biscuit tins for
> tom-toms, with short sticks; the women stood on one side, the
> men on the other. They sang incessantly, dancing slightly. Then
> another goes out alone, and comes back frightened; then two go
> out together, one alone again, and finally two twos who return,
> having slain the elephant, and there is much jubilation. When the
> two go out on their quest, one has a bow and arrow, the other
> an assegaye, and they boast what they will do.[69]

Away at Val d'Andorre the vanilla put out its leathery pods and
from all round the coasts came the creaking of the oil-mills with
a bullock turning the shaft and an African lad sitting on top to

hold it down. On Praslin and La Digue, where Gordon was the first British governor ever to appear, that sad creaking sound had particular prominence; coconut oil was almost all that the 3-4,000 people there had to live on. The 600 Diguois nonetheless seemed more lively than the people of either Praslin or Mahé itself, the revolutionary pulse from La Réunion still beating strongly. This was a quieter life than Mahé's, all the same. Much vermouth was drunk behind closed shutters. '*Quelle chaleur épouvantable*' was the refrain uttered in polite conversation when callers came, and probably about the only words spoken when the caller happened to be one of those outwardly severe Anglo-Saxon ladies whom the French tend to find lacking in sympathy. The greatest display of animation Marianne North ever saw was when the creaking stopped – silence would send Seychellois out to shout at bullocks and blacks until the mill started again.[70] On such a Praslin estate Gordon was shocked to be told that one tiny white tot's greatest pleasure was to beat the little blacks – not that the blacks seemed to feel or mind this, but it did not strike the Governor as a very healthy preparation for adult life. He did not beat his own lower orders, although he had strict ideas about who in Britain was a gentleman and who was not.

Seychellois surprised him, as they surprised Miss North, with their occasional marriages across the colour-line. If the generation since Adolphe Loizeau had failed to break into white society, money had blanched a number of the coloured families and even one or two Créoles – but similar tolerance did not extend to their cousins who had no money. Back in Victoria at Government House near the flagstaff where de Quincy's tomb stood, Gordon, looking out from beneath his verandah, could enjoy the young coco-de-mer reflecting moonlight from its huge leaves, and the outline of Ste Anne at sea; but when the dog-packs had been through later at night, gnawed human bones might be found on the lawn; they came from the cemetery on the hill behind the house, where the first of the Hodouls, Savys, St Jorres and d'Offays lay, endangering the health of the town.

That was one face of two generations' neglect. Another in the same charnel-house motif was the leper-asylum on Curieuse. This had been established in 1829 with about 100 lepers, mostly banished from Mauritius. There they had been left to dwindle, with no doctor for some years after one drowned on the passage through the reef at La Digue. Living as they did with death, the lepers' chief concern seems to have been that they should not be buried in the friable blankets which were all that an unfeeling government provided; they acquired solid coffins instead from the proceeds of their pigs and chickens, and kept them prominently in their houses to shock the tender visitor. Neglect was to be found in the schools too. Anglicans alone had been subsidised so far, a little of their pittance finding its way into the Civil Chaplain's pocket rather than the teachers'; it took an actual visit to make the Bishop of Mauritius admit that the Reverend Mr Vaudin's schools barely existed. Only the Convent with its 300 girls was outstanding, although the boys' College was a real school too; its pupils showed an astonishing self-possession at their annual prize-giving as they competed for sham laurel crowns. These schools, which had been good in their day but within ten years seemed old-fashioned, were an integral part of the Roman Catholic hegemony. Catholic ritual had won the day, with the help of the French language's affinity with Créole.

At the Feast of the Immaculate Conception 1,200 people could be expected to go in procession around Mahé – with white veils, white jackets, the sisters in blue and black habits, russet monks, images and a brass band, all steaming under the sun, all in honour of a conception which most of those present would have found, in their own lives, a little pointless. It charmed Sir Arthur, committed Anglican though he was, to think that His Lordship, Bishop Royston of Mauritius and Dependencies, invincible bigot, would be on Mahé in time to be scandalised by what he would perceive at the idolatries of Corpus Christi. As the first Roman Catholic Bishop of Seychelles put it, his people loved religion – particularly processions and other ceremonies, which were the only diversion in their monotonous island life.[71] He underestimated the interest not merely of sex – he expressed horror at the prevailing concubinage – but also of politics, whose *accoucheur* was Sir Arthur Gordon.

Seychellois had indicated very plainly that they were eager to be free of Mauritius at the end of 1869 when they petitioned the Governor for permission to call a general assembly of all proprietors to consider the failings of government. Officials were to be prepared to explain themselves.[72] Mauritius refused, protesting that this was tantamount to setting aside all lawful authority; but Gordon considered the domination by Mauritius an absurdity and the neglect criminal, and soon after arriving on his first visit to Seychelles in August 1871 he was ready with his own petition to the Colonial Office for proprietors to sign. His drafting proved acceptable to 6–700 Seychellois who gathered at the Court House on 21 September. Reintroduction of Liberated Africans, temporarily suspended, was called for, and greater legislative and administrative independence. The Colonial Office finally accepted the proposals, strongly influenced as it was by the recollection that it had recommended similar measures twenty years before, and a local legislature, the Board of Civil Commissioners, was set up, which first sat on 26 November 1872. The Civil Commissioner, now styled Chief Civil Commissioner, presided over a board composed of the newly-created Treasurer, the District Judge (as the District Magistrate was restyled, to match his wider powers) and the Government Medical Officer on one side as official members, with Lemarchand, François Hodoul *fils* and Charles Dupuys on the other as nominated unofficial representatives of the Seychellois.[73]

So Seychelles had a constitution. Customs and finance too were made more separate from those of Mauritius, and the bulk of imports no longer had to pass through Port Louis. A Board of Education was empowered to divide increased government grants more rationally to all schools, regardless of religious affiliation, according to quality and results (this horrified Royston). The Board of Civil Commissioners passed regulations exacting a land-tax at one shilling per acre, provided for the management of the public hospital which the interest of the Chief Medical Officer, Dr J.H. Brooks, in private patients had long helped to keep uncompleted, and decreed a new cemetery, a house of refuge for paupers, and a £5,000 loan to put a light for shipping on Ste Anne along with a lighthouse on dangerous Île aux Vaches – which in the event remained dangerous and unlighted till 1883. As Lemarchand said, there really should have been decent roads on Mahé too: every time he came into town to perform his functions as a Civil Commissioner it was at the risk of a broken leg. And surely, in his opinion, it was not too much to ask that the Board should legislate effectively to get the benighted Créoles and Liberated Africans out of their ravines, off the half-worked estates of small proprietors

into productive labour on the lands of active men like himself.
Larceny by servants worried him too.

With the subdivision of estates at successions, there were now
many small proprietors who did not trouble to look closely at
the origin of the produce brought them by their *moitié* tenants;
often, anyway, they passed most of their time quaffing rum and
bacca (fermented cane juice, the national drink of Seychelles).
Worse, there were small shopkeepers known to Lemarchand who
had no land of their own, not even for a single coconut palm,
but still somehow made 3,000 veltes of oil a year without visibly
buying a nut. He would wager that 990 nuts in every thousand
sold to the oil-makers were stolen.[74]

Seychelles began legislating, then, to meet the perceived needs
of tropical agriculture in islands restricted in size and geological
configuration, with a comparatively small propertied stratum and
many landless people with every incentive and matchless opportunity to steal. Property in coconuts was reaffirmed by a prohibition
on moving them from an estate without a licence – which was
like defying a force of nature. There was now money to be made
in coconuts, and new traders – some Indian and some Persian
–were coming in to get their share. A coir factory opened but
did not flourish. The Marseilles firm of Roux de Freycinet appeared
and fell foul of *El Medico*, otherwise Dr Brooks, who with his
partner Aristide Dupuys had hitherto been the main importer and
storekeeper, with a particular corner in coals for navy vessels and
the occasional mail-steamer.[75]

New factions developed in politics. Established retailers, supplied
from firms in Mauritius, found their prices undercut by direct
importers from Europe, and petitioned for a return to something
like the old customs system in order to push back competition.
Proprietors wanted their oil to continue going to Mauritius duty-
free. It was gradual independence Seychelles wanted, said François
Hodoul, not sudden radical severance.[76] Even so, the trend continued to be towards independence, not merely from Mauritius
but also from the colonial administration as represented by the
Chief Civil Commissioner. That was helped by the appointment
of two additional unofficials to the Board – the current André
Nageon de l'Estang with the lawyer Eugène Serret – and then by
personalities who split the administration after C.S. Salmon's arrival
as Chief Civil Commissioner in 1875. Dr Brooks was disaffected,

a hungry professional man deprived of his chance to make his fortune. Barrow, the Treasurer, was embittered because news had got about that as a young man he had been transported to Australia for forgery. Salmon fell foul of both and, according to one faction among Seychellois, wanted to spend £100 on another brass band when the wharves were falling to pieces.[77]

The factions formed around issues like Nageon's natural if illicit desire to expand his house-site on to Crown land next door, and Serret and Hodoul drawing fees from government as, respectively, Crown Counsel and schools inspector. Out of 740 pages of writing sent off to Mauritius in March on the supposed public affairs of Seychelles, all but a dozen were devoted to the squabbling of leading residents and officials.[78] Everybody's grievances were fanned by Mr Attorney R.M. Brown, a future Judge of Seychelles in the mould of an earlier District Magistrate, Hollier Griffiths. If anyone on the Island was to trip over a heap of stones on the Chaussée at night before falling into the St Louis river through the hole in the Customs House bridge which the stones were supposed to mend, it had to be the fulminating and infallible Maître Brown. He was running his own case for libel against Lemarchand and, by showing Louis Deltel from Mauritius a letter in which Lemarchand defamed Deltel, caused Lemarchand to be challenged to a duel.[79] These were vintage small community heroics, with sticks more in employment than swords, but big employers like Lemarchand and Sauzier did take sticks to Africans, and would have dearly loved to take them to the authorities also.

One of Sauzier's labourers let it be known that he was making off to the Outer Islands, and had put his violent-tempered employer to the trouble of threatening legal action against the chief of police for not sending a boat after him, before the labourer was picked up strolling peaceably around Mahé. Lemarchand's people drove him to distraction with their requirements in the matter of hospital care. Here was Lemarchand's own inappropriately named syphilitic servant Napoléon sent to be cured at the employer's expense! If the Secretary of State really knew Seychelles, Lemarchand supposed, he would not be content just to throw out Salmon and Barrow – he would take a bludgeon to every official who persisted in showing dangerous sensibility towards Africans and talking humanitarian claptrap. As for himself, Lemarchand was a practical man; he had won prizes for his vanilla, coffee, cloves and coconuts at the Paris Exhibition.[80]

Petitions flowed from Seychelles. In 1880 a new Governor of Mauritius, Bowen, fuming that this colony of small islands gave more trouble than one of the Australian colonies would have done, wanted to clip the new legislative wings.[81] Seychelles on the contrary demanded longer feathers. Serret, Hodoul and Lemarchand petitioned alongside the officials for power to legislate for the suppression of vagrancy, to reorganise the customs tariff, and to regulate distilleries; there should be a mortgage office, power to try capital cases in Seychelles instead of in Mauritius, extension of the court's legal powers in other matters, and an end to the Mauritius Council of Government's power to legislate for Seychelles in any matter at all; an end also to the anomaly that Alphonse, Providence, Farquhar and Cosmoledo Islands had been removed from the boundaries of Seychelles but were still under the court's jurisdiction. All this, they said, would enable Seychelles to progress still more morally, intellectually and materially than they had ever done under the 1872 constitution.[82]

It was truer, in the view of some people, to say that the Islands had progressed materially, with new merchants setting up business, on the oil from the coconuts planted since the 1850s. However, the Colonial Office was sympathetic to home rule, and over-rode Bowen in favour of views put up by the then Chief Civil Commissioner, Captain A.E. Havelock. A sometime protégé of Gordon, Havelock had filled the gap after Franklyn's death in 1874 and was doing so again in 1879-80 after Salmon's removal. From now on, the Chief Civil Commissioner was to have considerable independence, and would stand to Mauritius as the President of St Lucia, say, stood to the Governor of the Windward Islands – subject to general oversight but with independent initiative and responsibility. The Board's legislative authority was increased, and a judge was supposed to come regularly from Mauritius to hear murder cases with a Seychelles jury rather than accused and witnesses continuing to be sent to Port Louis.[83] The judges there put a stop to that idea, unhappy at the prospect of moving from their comfortable seats and carefully moderated amount of work; thus did the Secretary of State diagnose the essence of their objections.[84] A fully competent District Judge would have to do, London decided – if one could be got for the money, which was doubtful. In the end, Maître Brown took the post and stayed for years with undiminished vigour amid wonderful unpopularity, marvelling at the protracted, internecine nature of cases over land boundaries and libel, not to mention the dubious professional standards of notaries. Bankruptcy, divorce and misconduct of legal practitioners were transferred to his court's jurisdiction, and some notaries ended up in gaol or decamped. But the transfer of murder trials was delayed, since murder was very rare in Seychelles. Trial by jury on the spot should be adopted as an anglicising and civilising influence much in need here, said the British; but although the Seychellois took a gloomy view of the standards of their community, they did not want to be anglicised. This was one of the most passionate, most dangerous places in the world, said Maître Serret when the point was put to the Board again in 1890. Whether guilty or not, a man might have no single witness either for or against him, depending on the support he commanded.[85]

That was pessimistic enough, though realistic, and the same could be said of the petition advanced by 413 people in 1882 who actually wanted a return to the pre-1872 state of dependence on Mauritius. This was all the more curious to Mauritius and London because only the year before Chief Civil Commissioner H. Cockburn Stewart had been pressing for Seychelles to be made a separate colony in their own right.[86]

No country was more favoured by nature, he supposed, and the Islands were only as undeveloped as they were, with a mere £13,000 of revenue, because no money was invested. Britain had never heard of the place. Seychellois at large were apathetic. If he could borrow £12,000 he could open up Mahé with a decent road-system in place of its mountain paths; the increased flow of coffee to market would repay the loan, along with the cloves, pepper and cinnamon that still went to waste, and the ginger, saffron and arrowroot that nobody cared about, so long as they could make Rs 250 an acre clear profit from a *vanillerie* of five acres worked by twelve labourers.[87]

Again, nothing less than total autonomy would do for the site of the Garden of Eden, as General 'Chinese' Gordon had just discovered Praslin to be. Plainly the coco-de-mer was the tree of knowledge, as the breadfruit must be the tree of life; and the

Indian Ocean was made up of the waters of the Flood. Nothing could be clearer to a slightly unbalanced artillery officer, in the less than lucid moments he allowed himself from his brief on how to fortify the unfortifiable Seychelles. Also nothing was clearer to him in 1881 than that they were a rising colony while Mauritius was declining. But nothing much about Seychelles seemed to be rising to the 413 dispirited patriots petitioning in the following year. Eden had many small products but Adam still relied heavily on coconut oil; the prolific Adam family of Praslin could swear to that. The market had dropped, there was beetle in the trees, and small proprietors in particular remembered that constitutional sophistication meant loans, indeed debt, and greater expenditure on those government establishments which already ate up a disproportionate amount of revenue. James Stephens had known what he was talking about, nearly forty years before. Led now by Rosemond Gontier, Denys Calais of Cerf and shopkeeper Jean Hereau, the 400-odd patriots put up a powerful case for going quietly, even returning to the apron-strings, in their horror at the prospect of higher taxes and being left alone unsupported on their granite chips.[88] Minority that they were among nearly 4,000 ratepayers, they were easily routed by the new Chief Civil Commissioner Arthur Barkly, son of a former Governor of Mauritius. While his wife made notes for her rather anodyne sketch of Seychelles – Bishop Mouard toddling up to his north-west monsoon retreat at cool La Misère; the Créole's taste for brightly coloured, over-ribboned versions of high fashion – Arthur Barkly talked of increased and even doubled revenue. He reported nine schools with 903 pupils, where there had been four with 421 in 1872, and 394 licensed traders instead of only 150 in that milestone year; 'and most important of all, that great lesson in self-dependence, foresight, prudence and responsibility which a share in the management of their own affairs can alone successfully teach a people'.[89]

Not enough responsibility was in fact allowed by third-rate colonial officials to the well-developed Seychellois feeling for stringent quarantine. A new Government Medical Officer failed to diagnose a case of small-pox landed from a British warship, and deaths mounted while he talked about chicken-pox. Dr Lepper could play no cricket henceforth because embittered unsporting Seychellois stole his ball; and revenue fell when the eventual stringent quarantine threw trade out of gear. Cruel sums were done:

a special committee of the Board discovered that establishments cost Seychelles Rs 81,909 even though the import-export figures scarcely totalled Rs 600,000.[90] Eden had autonomy enough, certainly as much as it could afford. The pace slackened. In December 1888, the Board of Civil Commissioners was created a Legislative Council and the Chief Civil Commissioner was gazetted Administrator; in 1890 eight varieties of Seychelles postage stamps appeared. Only in 1903 did the Islands wholly separate from Mauritius, and then it was as much as anything at the behest of an Administrator who yearned to be styled His Excellency the Governor. In the last fifteen years of the nineteenth century the Seychellois mostly let their constitution alone and worried instead about their increasingly valuable vanilla. The two sometimes coalesced, as in 1892 when Judge Brown, the Acting Administrator, was applying legislation against vanilla theft with an iron hand. Sixty-one people, who felt their interests endangered as well by this as by direct controls on notaries, petitioned for an elected majority on Legislative Council with no seat at all for the Judge. As Judge Brown put it, with perhaps a little partiality, 'there appears to be a strong tendency...to advocate freedom of fraud among professional men, and impunity to vanilla thieves and receivers.'[91]

Markets were good and the *moitié* system enabled everybody to benefit. Very few of the landless, Créole or African, would work in agriculture for wages in the 1890s. A landowner would provide the vanilla vines and allow a labourer three or four acres, sharing the rewards. Vanilla was used as a local currency, like cotton in earlier times. The police were kept busy not catching their cousins the thieves.

Agriculture in the tropics flourishes, if at all, in cycles; its success depends on afflictions like hurricanes in other tropical countries and on the fickle tastes of Europe. Even so, vanilla had a good run. As an adjunct to copra it kept Seychelles more than going for twenty years till 1902 when Germany came up with a synthetic. Fortunes were made in the 1890s as the price doubled to Rs 32 a kilo – small fortunes, of course, commensurate with the limited size of the Islands and their population of 9,000. If every square foot had borne a vanilla-vine climbing its capucin sapling, one fair-sized steamer a year could still have carried off the entire crop. As a result no steamer-line with heavy costs of its own was in love with Seychelles – not the British India Steam Navigation Company, Union Castle, Deutsche Ost-Afrika Linie or even the Paris-subsidised Messageries Maritimes,[92] whose travelling inspector A.A. Fauvel acquired such a personal affection for the Islands that he collected transcripts of all documents relating to their history that he could find in French archives for Governor W.E. Davidson to publish; but it was the strategic position of Seychelles, not their past or their produce, which attracted Messageries Maritimes in 1888 when it made Mahé the coaling-station and port of junction for its Europe-Australia line and its Mauritius-Réunion-Madagascar steamer.

In return for a small subsidy from Seychelles, vanilla went quickly by Messageries Maritimes to Marseilles where it arrived in good condition and in time to take market advantage of the two months' advance that Seychelles' harvest had over Mauritius and Réunion. When obsessive quarantine forced the French line away to Colombo in 1896,[93] Seychellois were driven into the reluctant embrace of British India Steam Navigation. BISN had been carrying a little Seychelles copra to India, and returning with the quantities of rice that kept the Créoles alive and the importing merchants wealthy. Now monthly steamers were laid on from London to Mahé but they were often delayed at the bars of East African ports; old and slow, they were particularly distasteful to Seychellois passengers because they charged extra for wine. Messageries Maritimes were doubly welcome when they came back to Mahé in 1901 but, as before, they were at the same time a source of alarm to proprietors with their demands for dockyard labour. British India steamers apart, two big ships of Messageries Maritimes would appear every four weeks – dwarfing the dhows from Aden or Bombay and making the local schooners insignificant; and the labour opportunities they offered did the same for the labour market on the estates. One of a handful of new Anglo-Saxon immigrants who came to Seychelles in the 1880s had been Harold Baty, a parson's son from England, a hearty fellow on good terms with the Créoles. He formed Baty, Bergne & Co. to handle the lighterage requirements of the port, and the high wages he had to pay to be sure of 200 men's concentrated labour for three or four days in thirty upset the proprietors immeasurably. Dying young, Baty left some good stories for his partner Bergne to tell about him. Governor W.E. Davidson recorded one in his diary:

> Mr Robartes, a slight delicate man of refinement, was staying with Baty who was physically the opposite. At dinner, Baty caught in his hand a large moth – *Buffes bananes*, we call the kind – it was just before his face and as he opened his fist the frightened moth made a dash into his open mouth and he had perforce to swallow it. Having done so, he made the best of it: and Robartes, who hastily assumed that it was Baty's habit to seize and eat such food, hastily left the table. The next night at Dinner, Baty was negligently following with his hand a half tame little Gecko on the table cloth, when Robartes turned pale and rose saying 'Pray consider me! I have been unable to eat since breakfast yesterday'.[94]

Other English arrivals were perpetually upset. *A Home for our Boys, the Seychelles* was the title of a misleading pamphlet published from Mahé by a wandering British misfit in 1883. The 'boys' it helped attract to estates on Mahé were unappreciated locally and few lasted out the century. All, however, stayed longer than the Oriental Bank. This opened its doors in 1888 in a fine new building only to close them four years later, leaving the field to local money-lenders. Chief among these was the Persian Abdool Rassool. Blind, astute, with a complex family web that made for famous disputes over his succession, he had come from Mauritius to trade in Seychelles as Said & Co. He acquired property on Mahé, a big coconut plantation on La Digue, along with Poivre, Desroches, Daros, half of Île aux Vaches and Providence. His schooner, the *Zipporah*, Captain Charles Ferrari, brought in copra and shell from the Outer Islands and took back labourers who, once out of Victoria harbour, were obliged to commit themselves to his managers, with no access to a magistrate and at liberty only to swim for it if they felt aggrieved. As one Island manager equably put it, 'The men coming back from the Islands always have grievances when they land here...but these grievances vanish when they are sober again and then they draw their money and no more difficulties are experienced.'[95]

Competitors of Rassool in money-lending and business were the Parsee merchant S.J. Olia and Jivan Jetha, a Jain. The Dauban family ran model Islands and estates from their base on Silhouette but were not involved in wholesaling or finance. Chinese immigrants, mainly from a single village near Canton, were mostly shopkeepers. Persian and Indian entrepreneurs by contrast ran minor empires, and their ties with Bombay drained Seychelles of specie, exported by the chest-full to pay for India's rice and cotton-print; produce went to Europe and Mauritius, some to Réunion and Madagascar, little now to Bombay. An issue of local banknotes to stop the drain had to wait till 1914.

Coconut products and vanilla might dominate the export trade, with valuable additions of guano after the turn of the century; but cane bulked large on the local market and in politics. For cane made bacca, and bacca meant release for the poor, as well as money for the proprietors, along with work done on their estates at *festins* – occasions when a working-party could be got together with the promise of present pleasure and subsequent oblivion. Almost every Créole man, woman and child drank bacca in handsome quantities, according to Edouard Lanier, a Seychelles-born entrepreneur with a French father and Mauritian mother who died in his sixties in 1936. With his double chin, white moustache and aquiline nose, this man of enterprise and humour had a profile fit for a medal. Lanier knew the bacca market, his distillery producing 80 per cent of that consumed on Mahé in 1910; about four litres were needed to get drunk, it was reckoned. A thousand acres were in cane, and there were 200 crushing mills of various sizes on Mahé alone. Consumption varied in proportion to police surveillance, according to one producer; for the law had something to say on the bacca question.[96]

Bacca had been designated a 'question' by government long before the 1880s when it began to legislate in the name of those twin gods of administration: public order and public revenue. It was in difficulties because bacca was extremely easy to produce, and it was an innocent brew one hour and alcoholic the next, which was bound to confuse the law. In the early 1880s legislation announced penalties for anyone found in possession of 'strong', otherwise fermented, bacca who was not a licensed distiller paying a sizeable fee. Judge Brown outlawed it altogether; but then only strong bacca over 3 per cent proof was banned, while the unfermented was made legal. Thus not only did fallen man in latter-day Eden possess a God-given drink which, unfermented at 1 p.m., could be strong at 2, but he also possessed a cousin of practical as well as playful wit in the person of Edouard Lanier. Lanier devised a boiling process which held up fermentation by fully two days, and sold the innocent liquid at 6 sous a litre with the promise that it would be worth the money in forty-eight hours.[97]

Commercial manufacturers wanted just enough restrictive legislation to make it impossible for a labourer to ferment his own bacca from a couple of rows of canes. Both as distillers and as big planters, they wanted this for the sake of the *festins*; though smaller proprietors, unwilling to pay the licence fee but still needing the labour, had different interests. Having had all the issues except the labourers' enjoyment discussed exhaustively between 1910 and 1912, the law in 1916 accepted the legality of strong bacca if sold at certain mills, with a duty to make up for what the revenue would lose in customs on Mauritius rum (Frigate's far better product was no longer being made). This was a blow to the proprietors –how much so, appeared in 1925 when Lanier himself put up a member of Legislative Council to propose that bacca should only be sold off the premises in demijohns holding thirty bottles, but this was one of the few occasions before the 1940s when proprietors lost in this Crown Colony.[98]

Seychelles became a full colony independent of Mauritius on 31 August 1903 amid bunting and parades, and to make the change of status a crest was redrawn from the tortoise motif proposed by General Gordon more than twenty years earlier. A brief visit was made by the Governor of Mauritius, who had pressed for continued association because of the advantages Seychelles drew from combining its public service with that of his Island. The Administrator of Seychelles, now Governor, E.B. Sweet-Escott, had argued to the contrary that Seychelles gained nothing but delays from the Mauritius link, and should no longer be seen as a stepping-stone for Mauritius officials on the way to better posts in their own Island.[99] A separate identity for Seychelles was part of Sweet-Escott's policy for making the place a loyal British colony, as he put it. Mahé in particular was one of the most beautiful Islands he had ever seen; this was his impression on arriving in 1899, a welcome contrast to his last post in British Honduras.

The unBritish nature of society in Seychelles drew a refugee from that most proper of English provincial towns, Cheltenham: Miss Emma Wardlaw Best. Not only did Miss Best practise free love with Mr Arthur Westall but, far worse, she published what Sweet-Escott called her foul and unpardonable beliefs in a pamphlet stoutly entitled *A Marriage Protest and Free Union Declaration*. Not that the brave lady found Seychelles much more congenial than Cheltenham, so strongly did the double standard operate even here against her sex, so tolerant was Seychellois society of the adventures of the 'male harlot' – her terminology for husband – and so censorious of those of the female.[100] The first Administrator, T. Risely-Griffith, had made Government House itself a brothel; now Sweet-Escott saw it as his duty to inculcate backbone and grit. His job now was to anglicise Seychelles and make it 'loyal'.[101] Strong, efficient administration was a necessity, and some good public buildings would help further – like a handsome new Governor's Office in town and, as Victoria's centrepiece, a miniature clocktower, modelled on one in London, to commemorate the old Queen. Above all, education was to be the vehicle for change. With a third-class degree from Oxford, Sweet-Escott had been classics master at Royal College in Mauritius but he knew that Britain was the Greece and Rome of the modern world. The school curriculum needed new priorities. French history would be replaced by drawing: if British history were intelligently taught, the young of this British colony would pick up all they needed to know about Joan of Arc and Napoleon.[102]

They should be taught in English too, not French, and still less Créole. That proposal had been advanced as far back as 1881, when the Chief Civil Commissioner, distributing prizes before 340 girls at the Convent, announced his dissatisfaction with the state of education in Seychelles. Not with the Convent itself, where no-one ever found fault with the teaching – this may have reflected lower expectations for and of girls. As the Convent's manager, the Roman Catholic Mission, put it, the fundamental doctrine on female education was that to educate girls beyond their place in society was to flout Divine Providence and expose them to moral danger.[103] Girls should not be taught English, still less in it. They needed only French, the language of religion and the family. Boys were always a different matter. In 1881 the Seychellois had agreed that boys were scarcely taught at all, the College having fallen on hard times since the Brothers left in 1875, driven away by their debts. When Bishop Mouard, first Bishop of Seychelles, arrived in 1882 he found Seychellois actually lobbying for a Government College, which would inevitably be secular and so represent a danger to religion. The Bishop, himself formerly an educator in India, left at once for Europe and returned early in 1884 with a new staff from the fine teaching order of Marist Brothers.[104] They saved the Islands from that abomination, a neutral school where God did not breathe in every squeak of the slate-pencil. St Louis College now became a very good school, particularly for those who could afford its secondary schooling, though in practice the paying classes took in Seychellois boys whose parents could not pay but would not have sent their children to school at all if they were to be put with the Créoles in the free classes.[105] In oblique recognition of its quality, perhaps, the mostly Créole boys of the Protestant St Paul's School took to ambushing the St Louis boys, and once followed a blameless priest up the road shouting '*Voilà St Rock et son chien !* '[108]

The point was that they shouted French and not English insults. The Colonial Office itself was stirred by the reflection that after more than seventy years of British rule the cock was more readily understood than the lion. It directed that a government secondary school should be established that emphasised English.[107] It wondered whether the education grant paid to primary schools at large – the Catholics' many schools, the Anglicans' few – should not be made conditional on the use of English as the teaching medium (that grant was little enough – Rs 4–8,000 a year). The Bishop additionally received a subsidy from Propaganda Fide in Rome and a small grant from Alliance Française about which he did not speak, even in French. He risked losing all his government grant under rules of 1886 which proposed to discontinue fee-paying schools; and he complained that this was no less than a favour to the Anglicans who charged nothing. It was equivalent to equality of rich and poor before the blackboard. And anyway, if the better class of people – meaning the whites, or those whose land now enabled them to pass as white – wanted to buy secondary education and separate classrooms so that their children need not rub shoulders with the offspring of their servants, what had God to say against that?[108]

God must reign in the classroom. The just rights of race, conscience and the Catholic Church must be respected, which they clearly were not in 1890 when government bought out St Paul's School in order to turn it into the long-planned government

college. There was no need for such expense, in this poorest and
least important of British possessions, protested the priests; their
own school was open to all who would learn the catechism and
attend mass.[109] Battle was joined. Convent girls were brought
forward to thank the devoted fathers who willingly laid down
their lives to make them good and holy.[110] At the Government
School, a well-qualified Colonial Office appointee presided over
primary and secondary classes, with one other master and four
monitors, their object being to turn out English-fluent citizens
not quite so conscious of the devil as the Convent girls were
taught to be. Two bones offered themselves here for the Church
to worry. First, because it was well known that God preferred
to be addressed in French, how were children to learn their
catechism and make their confession if they were not taught French
at school? Secondly, everybody also knew that household usage
was nearer to Créole even in some of the most prominent families,
and even the mother-tongue itself had undergone changes in the
Seychelles climate. As a Whitehall wit commented after reading
stirring passages about prize-day at St Louis in the local paper,
Le Réveil Seychellois, they were magnificent – but were they *French?*

The language problem was felt in Legislative Council where
discussion in French was held to be inappropriate, Créole was
unthinkable, and British residents who represented no one had
to be appointed. The aged anglophone François Hodoul, soon to
be the first real Seychellois honoured with the C.M.G., was besieged
by Anglo-Saxons when the language question was discussed there.
For them there could be no question but that English should be
adopted as the primary language and the language of instruction
because French was not in reality the language of the country.
This was Créole, but it was regarded as no language at all, and
dictation-exercises seemed to show what an obstacle Créole must
always be to intelligible French. Hodoul was not so sure, and
later linguistic opinion has similar doubts over the degree to which
Créole had to be an obstacle if French were well taught. Also,
it was clear from the beginning that French was the more appropriate
medium, the language of local commerce as well as of religion
and at least some families, and many more people were acquainted
with it than with English. However, according to Sweet-Escott,
imperial policy decreed English. He had a wider motive too, for
Seychellois were commonly not over-eager to see even their own

brand of French actually taught to the black majority. Nor were the priests very different from *grands blancs*, and seemed content to communicate basic truths in Créole and leave the highest mysteries under a linguistic veil. For Sweet-Escott, English was to be a social leveller: he intended that it should 'give the black population ...the opportunity of improving their position by reaping the full benefits of such education as we can bring within their reach'.[111]

English became, theoretically, the language of instruction in the interests of the underprivileged. Two English scholarships were decreed, worth Rs 600 a year for three years at Royal College in Mauritius or any school in England. The Government School was renamed Victoria School and then, with great inconsistency, acquired paying sections in order to attract the 'better classes', as Sweet-Escott put it. He was as confused and disturbed as the priests at seeing the Queen's school a preserve of Créoles; it was evidently thought that only the better classes deserved scholarships when the push came, and only they had much hope of reaching the required standard. The winners were Savys, Nageons, Loizeaus – now virtually a *grand blanc* family; and although Fernand Touris, who won in 1906, was a Mauritian–Indian of no local status, he was none the less the colonial postmaster's son from a literate household. What upset the promoters of imperial policy more was that most of the winners were not from Victoria School but from St Louis College – that epitome of the unBritish. One of the brightest pupils, Évariste Collet, recalled that a systematic effort was made there to poison his mind against everything not French or Italian. There was no point in incurring the odium without carrying off the honours, so in 1910 Sweet-Escott's successor W.E. Davidson created King's College in order to compete with the upper forms of St Louis as a miniature English grammar school. At first it had a dozen boys, but in time its numbers reached seventy-seven. Potentially King's was a far better school than St Louis; it was staffed by graduates, while the Marists were already admitting privately to having difficulty in maintaining even their existing moderately qualified Brothers. Old pupils of King's recall its atmosphere of freedom and intellectual curiosity in contrast to what all but the very pious found suffocating about St Louis; all the same, both were aimed at the same social strata. When Davidson tried to make King's especially attractive by restricting the scholar-ships to its pupils, he explained to a surprised Whitehall that without this bait Seychellois would send their boys to St Louis in response to pressure from the priests, and this potentially fine school would then degenerate, as he said, into the condition of Victoria School before 1900: a place for Créole children from whom the colony really should not derive its professional classes. It would be better, apparently, for the latter to remain dominated by Mauritians and the public service by Anglo-Saxons.[112]

Apostles of equal opportunity put up the principle and shrank from its consequences, content in Davidson's case to scatter *sous* to Créole children. He was a robust character in his way, not much perturbed to hear that there was a plan to assassinate him on his regular ride.[113] That was one way to prevent St Louis from becoming just a preparatory school for amoral but well-equipped King's College, as Brother-Director Cyrus told the Bishop it would be unless he were given more staff, more money and a decent chemical laboratory.[114] Another was for the Bishop to plead not only the unrivalled watchfulness and discipline of St Louis, but also the combined firmness and charity with which the Church generally, and St Louis particularly, had safeguarded the social gradations so vital in a multiracial society. A better way was to marshal opinion with a petition and to impose the Church's viewpoint through the confessional. The case of the bare behinds is instructive. It came to the ears of the next but one Bishop of Seychelles, Father Justin de Gumy, that the headmaster of King's encouraged the boys in his boarding-house to take a bath together every morning *without clothes*:

> Well, you must have special reasons to do so. But please, Mr Mackay, from our catholic point of view, the matter takes quite another turn. In all our catholic schools, institutions, seminaries, as well as in every family we teach the children that this is opposed to good morals and the virtue of purity....[115]

In their poverty the Savoyard Capuchins transferred the mission of Seychelles to the rich Swiss in 1922 and Father Justin became the first in an unhappy series of Swiss bishops. Breadth of mind was not included in the deal; the threat of excommunication for attending a neutral school was frequently made, and was usually effective. By 1919 King's College was reduced to a shell, confessional influence having been reinforced due to several of its masters' going off to the war. The headmaster went to Fiji, where he sometimes adopted a racist stance that might have pleased the priests but shocked some of the Marist Brothers back in Seychelles. King's was closed. When the Catholic Governor Sir Joseph Byrne handed Victoria School to the churches in 1923, government's belated foray into education had ceased for another twenty years. Cyril Bishop of Mauritius enthused about the moral uplift this return to the arms of the Church would produce, but left it to be provided by the Catholics. With a clear field, they went to sleep. Marists and Capuchins were on the worst possible terms; the brothers resented the poverty in which they lived under their ungenerous contract with the Bishop, while the priests spent their Swiss money adding acre to acre of land and actually had bicycles to ride. Almost forgotten by their own mother-house, footsore Marists grew old at their blackboards; Brother Cyrus, who had arrived in 1894, was still Brother-Director in 1933. In that year diocesan visitors brought about the resignation of Bishop Justin de Gumy by expressing horror at St Louis' old-fashioned and repressive air, its examination-oriented system of rote-learning, and its obvious colour prejudice.

At the start of the First World War, agriculture in Seychelles was on one of its upswings. Cinnamon bark had suddenly acquired great value at the beginning of 1907. A profit of up to £10 could now be made on a ton of bark cut from the wild trees – an industry eminently well-suited to the Seychellois way, a godsend to small proprietors and for Créole women and children, who went out from their precarious shacks while the dew was on the trees and for a few hours collected on the mountain-sides with a gunny sack over their shoulders. Capital was coming in, for other people. The London-based Seychelles Rubber & Coconut Co. took over some 6,000 acres on Mahé, joining the Mahé Syndicate which was interested in the guano on St Pierre. More guano came from Providence, Alphonse and St Denis. Vanilla was recovering from the slump of 1904, but copra was always the mainstay, its position strengthened once Davidson got Messageries Maritimes to reduce their freight-rates. Between 1904 and 1911 the copra exports increased tenfold in weight and twenty times in value, with potential for more if only proprietors could be induced to improve drying methods. With copra as the ballast,

vanilla provided some of the sail now that it had recovered its
markets; but tropical products always fluctuate, and the economy
was like a ship carried through calms by intermittent gusts of
wind.

In a good year like 1911, exports were worth £7 per head of
population or £1,000 per square mile. Roughly, the trading position
was always that each year Seychelles bought rice worth 4 lakhs
of rupees from India and 6 lakhs' worth of manufactured goods
from Europe; upon this cost to the consumer were added 2 lakhs
in import duties, with about 3 more in traders' profits. To meet
the resultant living-costs of 15 lakhs of rupees, the community
sold 6-8 lakhs of coconut products, 1-10 of vanilla, another lakh
of minor products like soap, tortoiseshell and calipee, together with
one more for calling ships, and perhaps made 3 from guano. The
resulting income varied between 12,000,000 and 23,000,000 rupees.
As it usually worked out, for three years out of four the vanilla
crop was poor and people were in debt; in the fourth vanilla
flourished, and the Seychellois – as distinct from the Créoles – paid
off their creditors and spent the rest on pleasure trips to Europe.

This was a homespun economy. The post office provided money-
orders for overseas transactions. Although the Commercial Bank
of Mauritius opened in Victoria in 1911, it withdrew within five
years. Seychellois resented its demands for sound security against
loans and saw the difference between its buying and selling rates
for foreign currency as intolerable extortion. They were happy
enough with the money-orders, and with drafts from the obliging
Treasury to cope with larger transactions in Europe. As for loans,
there was a lively local market in mortgages among Seychellois
themselves. Professional moneylenders like Said & Co. would make
larger sums available to the rash – one moneylender was said to ask
30 per cent. Government began to make long-term loans available
to planters at 6 per cent from revenue reserves in 1904, when the
first fall occurred in vanilla, after a period of years when proprietors
spent hugely, paid dear for land on credit and saved nothing – this
was when the ebullience from the 1890s made people bankrupt
and put their land into the hands of the trading firms. The Seychellois
felt that this was their own money from taxes, and it was therefore
proper that it should come back to them for development purposes,
even if some of them put it to more enjoyable use holidaying in
France. A closer look at the tax structure would have convinced

an outsider that revenue reserves could more properly be said to belong to Créoles, given the high incidence of indirect taxation and the ease with which the direct taxes could be evaded.

At least government loans were well spent by Edouard Lanier, member of the Legislative Council and Consul for France. He had a passion for the sea – its fish, turtles and terns' eggs on islands in the Amirantes; and possessed an imaginative urge to put them all to commercial use. He borrowed Rs 6,000 in 1911 to develop fishing stations on Mahé as well as the Sisters and the African Banks. His plan was to run salt-fish to Africa by schooner. He had wider interests too in his Mahé estates, in guano as agent for the Mahé Syndicate, in the export of copra and in carrying cloves from Zanzibar to Hamburg. A small empire, enduringly typical of Seychelles, Lanier's was run from a bare office above a store in Victoria; there was a pigeon-hole desk, a sweat-towel over the chair, guano and tortoiseshell samples on the floor, a sail flaked-down in a corner. Outside, Créoles waited for an advance on wages they were to earn in the Outer Islands; they might or might not turn up to fulfil their contract when the schooner left Long Pier. And then home for Lanier by bicycle or chair on Créole shoulders to the beautiful house at Point Conan, Ma Constance, built on the site of Hodoul the corsair's, where a Mlle Savy waited. Part Mauritian and part French in origin though Lanier was, he knew how to do business in Seychelles. Another Mauritian was the recently appointed curator of the Botanic Gardens, F.R. Dupont, whose task it was to inspect the guano Islands in which Lanier was interested – St Pierre, Aride, Flat, North; and Lanier found it convenient to pay him a commission, so that he should, as a *cher ami*, 'understand with us that we have offered to pay you in order to keep you on our side in this country'.[116]

Not all the Mauritians in Seychelles were so accommodating towards Lanier as Dupont, in whose defence it may be said that no one had ever shown him the colonial regulations against bribery. At another office in Victoria, and on the deck of another schooner alongside Long Pier, was Adolphe d'Emmerez de Charmoy; a very large man with a guardsman's step, he would introduce himself as belonging to the *vieille noblesse* in case that ancestry, so obvious and important to himself, should have escaped notice or interest.[117] This former Mauritian finally died destitute with his big estate, Barbaron, in the hands of his own lawyer, but he had once been

rich. As owner of *Le Réveil Seychellois* at the time of the King's
College crisis, he had put up his editor to publish a discourse
that represented the devil upbraiding Governor Davidson in hell
for being a damned drunkard.[118] But he thought even worse of
Lanier, who was trustee for two of d'Emmerez's half-brothers.
Their share in the estate would have been useful to the feckless
Adolphe d'Emmerez *fils* in his dealings with the occupant of a
third important office in Victoria before the First World War.
This was the moneylender Mamode Hossen, who had run Said
& Co. since the death of his father-in-law Abdool Rassool in
1896. He had never rendered an account to the other heirs in
the Rassool estate; indeed he seemed bent upon extinguishing
the major interest of his niece Gowar Sultan Meddy. Opposition
came from her father's brother Mamode Hadee – who, the cynics
said, wanted to make use of the girl's interest in another way, by
marrying her to one of his own sons.[119] The Civil Code had
great and sometimes greatly appreciated defects in its provisions
for the care of minors' estates; and there was enmity between
d'Emmerez, who owed Hossen money, and Lanier, who supported
Hadee.

Always there were abnormal pressures in living and doing business
on a restricted bank of time like Mahé. Only an immature, mad
or corrupted judge was needed to produce an explosion there in
1911-12. Lanier's empire accordingly collapsed under legal attack
from his Hamburg correspondents in the Zanzibar clove business
who apparently found it convenient to saddle him with debts
owed by a third partner, now insolvent; while d'Emmerez conceived
a sudden concern for the welfare of his half-brothers, and accused
Lanier of embezzling their fortune by investing it in his own
firm.[120] With Davidson away, the Chief Justice was Administrator,
and in his place on the bench sat the Crown Prosecutor, Alexander
Williamson. By common repute a *mari complaisant* who shared his
wife in a *ménage à trois* with the Civil Chaplain while he consoled
himself with the ladies of Hangard Street, Williamson found it
convenient to silence *Le Réveil Seychellois* on these subjects by
joining the camp of its owner d'Emmerez. Williamson anyway
had a grudge against Lanier for amending a bill in Legislative
Council. Too many labourers, paid in advance for service in the
Outer Islands, had been in hiding when the schooners were ready
to sail, and proprietors had petitioned for them to be put aboard

by the police at a rupee a head. Williamson had tried to make this impost payable instead to himself. Thus Lanier was bankrupted before Williamson's court and sent to gaol. His was a painful case for King George V to read when Lanier's petition reached him – as his private secretary Lord Stamfordham wrote, 'The King cannot help thinking that if half the statements made in the Petition are correct, Mr Lanier's case is a hard one.'[121] And it all made a pretty puzzle for the Privy Council to sort out – which it did to Lanier's advantage and to its own amazement that even a colonial legal officer should use the law quite so much like a misdirected bludgeon as the acting Chief Justice of Seychelles had done.[122] When the microscope was applied, it revealed that the famous air of Seychelles had gone to the Civil Chaplain's brain too. An excellent manly Christian, the Reverend Mr Newton had seemed better suited to his calling than the poor man sent home within weeks of arriving in 1905 with a lady who was a connection of an altogether different kind from the niece he represented her to be; more useful, too, than his successor, who was moral but mouselike. However, when Newton helped his good friend Williamson to cause a crisis in the Seychelles Club over the showing of lantern-slides of undraped female forms in the Louvre, one of the Whitehall wits was so moved by what he took to be the clergyman's hypocrisy that he was tempted to reveal what he said he knew of Newton's antecedents as headmaster of St Pauls, Darjeeling.[123]

The Civil Code was slightly amended on the matter of minors' estates – although there was no getting around a really determined family council. When Gowar Sultan Meddy died from tuberculosis in Paris in 1928, widowed of her Hadee husband, she left Coetivy, Providence, Poivre and Desroches to the care of councils whose main concern seems to have been to remove them in turn from her equally unwell daughter Hélène Hadee. And along with the frailties of colonial legal and clerical personages, the Williamson affair revealed how large a part credit paid in the running of Seychelles businesses; when Lanier was arrested, his safe contained a mere 275 rupees, 188 francs and 50 German marks. As for his friend in government Dupont, a Colonial Office official commented on the punishment proposed for him: 'When I become bankrupt I shall go to the Seychelles, render "agricultural services" to the Islands; prove myself to be "unsystematic in business and hopelessly careless in accounts"; "un-moral" as well as learned; accept corrupt gratifications; and know that my health will save me from prosecution and my poverty will secure me a recommendation for a compassionate grant to start me as a chemist elsewhere!'[125]

Seychelles had opportunity to make money during the First World War, at least till 1917 when Messageries Maritimes stopped taking copra. Lanier got away one last consignment by sending it off to the steamer in 2,141 packages for acceptance as parcel-post.[126] During the early years of the War, proprietors did well without any need for so much enterprise. With nitro-glycerine being made from derivatives of copra, prices were high, but in the initial war scare Seychellois cut costs by dismissing labourers, and shopkeepers hoarded provisions. Copra-buyers were not interested in coconuts. All the organisation of Mahé, Praslin and La Digue as working communities came to an end. The Eastern Telegraph Company's cable between Mahé and East Africa fortuitously broke soon after relaying news of the war's outbreak and encouraged visions of German sea raiders like the *Emden* or the *Königsberg* bombarding the defenceless Islands.[127] The Germans would have been more likely to send ashore for coal and turtles, putting Governor O'Brien to the embarrassment of imitating de Quincy, as he knew very well he would have had to do – old soldier that he was, O'Brien reckoned he could have taken Seychelles with twenty-five picked men.[128] He did not appreciate being dragged out of bed during August 1914 by officious messages from South Mahé's Justice of the Peace, Dr J.T. Bradley, to say that the *Königsberg* had so far not been sighted. Nor did the constables bearing the messages enjoy the bicycle trip; they started seeing ghosts as an excuse not to make it.[129]

The only Germans to set foot on the main soil of Seychelles during the War were four sailors taken off a Norwegian barque and allowed to roam freely on parole, until they roamed into respectable bedrooms.[130] As for espionage and internal security, on which earnest circulars arrived from London, that was also no problem. 'We are in the happy position of having only one subject of enemy nationality in our midst,' the Governor explained, 'and she is a Sister of Mercy.'[131] More effective in the long term was commercial espionage carried out by two visiting Japanese cruisers in 1917.[132] For the rest, the War personally affected only those from Seychelles who went off to fight. Edouard Lanier's younger brothers put on French uniforms, and one never returned from the trenches. Those who stayed raised money for the Red Cross and adjusted to the difficulties of a life heavily dependent on imported foodstuffs at a time when shipping was occupied elsewhere. The price of rice doubled, and if there was money in the pockets of the proprietors who sold the copra and of the shopkeepers who raised the retail prices, there was little in Créole hands. While profits on copra ranged from £20 to £25 a ton, there was an overall local increase in basic living costs of 147 per cent.

Wages fell, the labour force was cut, and in 1916 the government's contribution was to set up a committee to consider awarding heavier gaol sentences for failure to pay the local rate, which had always fallen more lightly on the comparatively wealthy than the absolutely poor. Caning and flogging were the recommended stimuli to pay up, when gaol held no terror; but it became embarrassingly clear that larceny had only increased. This was the resort of the incorrigible – but also of the hungry. Even people who were employed received only 33 sous a day and had to find 2-3 rupees a month for their rent and pay 10-15 sous a pound for their rice. It was not surprising that they stole fallen nuts for food and cooking oil.[133]

The reaction of the bigger proprietors was difficult even for Government House to swallow. A Seychellois Member of Legislative Council announced that not even the scores of 2-acre proprietors should be allowed to dispose of nuts, for if a small landowner could trade in the produce of his own trees he would surely handle nuts stolen from others. What then, asked the Governor, was he to do with his own coconuts? The answer came pat: '*Ma foi*, but eat them, he and his family, he must be made by law to do this for our protection.'[134] It required Touris, the postmaster, to tell the 1916 committee into wages and conditions how Créoles lived. They lived with difficulty. They could no longer get cassava or breadfruit free, since the market now put a monetary value on them. Calico and dungaree, their basic clothing, were now beyond their means. They were afraid to plant a food-garden even if their employer (when they had one) would allow it, for fear that he would order them off when the crop was ready. The guano Islands had shut down production because of the War. A whaling company set up on Ste Anne in 1914 had gone broke almost immediately. What little employment remained was mainly what the land and inshore seas provided. Idle and sodden with bacca the labourers might be, said Touris, but their drinking had been wholeheartedly encouraged by proprietors in the past, and if the Créoles had not defined their aspirations in terms of a gentle life under the sun instead of material gain, few estates would have remained in the hands of old families. Touris knew what he was talking about: when his son Fernand, the prize-winner ('laureate' in Seychelles parlance) of 1906, returned soon after the war as a barrister, he only had to wait till the Depression to acquire Barbaron, one of the biggest undivided estates on Mahé, from his own ruined client d'Emmerez de Charmoy.[135]

There was no lack of striving among the younger Touris' *petit blanc, blanc coco* and Créole contemporaries. They had few outlets: the only significant one during the War was to enrol as Pioneers in the British Army, which meant digging ditches and raising huts and telephone lines for the campaign against German East Africa. Wages in Seychelles were low enough and jobs few enough to make this attractive to 791 men, mostly Créoles, who sailed off in December 1916 and February 1917. What they sought was a wider world with some sort of opportunity; what half of them found was death from an unaccustomed diet's aggravation of the endemic ills of their Islands – venereal disease, dysentery – worked upon by the outside world's beri beri, malaria, pneumonia and a bacterial dysentery foreign to Seychelles. When only 476 Pioneers, some of them dying, were hurriedly returned amid marked imperial embarrassment in August 1917, it was difficult not to conclude that the Créole constitution was fragile and undernourished. And while the Governor tried to shift the responsibillty on to British Army doctors and the lack of decent officers, his lately-appointed police magistrate, Arthur Brooke, was forming the more rational conclusion.

These deaths held no mystery for Brooke when a ten-year-old Créole boy could be brought before his court by his employer for stealing two coconuts. The employer in the case was Hans P. Thomasset, South African, once a back-up member of the notorious Jameson raid, now manager of the London-based Seychelles Rubber Company, owner of the newly-launched paper *Le*

Petit Seychellois and a regular contributor to London's *Truth*. Thomasset paid no more for his plantation-house in the local rate than his labourers paid for their huts. The boy was a typical Créole child, undersized because underfed; his mother – naturally the bedrock of the household – earned the regular monthly woman's wage of Rs 3, barely enough to feed herself. She had not fed her son that day because she had nothing to give him. As Brooke wrote privately,

> What was I to do? They expected me to send the boy to be whipped by the police. I would rather send the Directors of the Co. to be whipped at home. This is a more or less typical case: one large landowner complained of me to the Governor.[136]

Brooke was a nuisance to Governor O'Brien, who prefered the picturesque reports he received from Dr Bradley. On a tour of South Mahé – where Bradley was a considerable proprietor himself and his daughter, from the vantage-point of the 1970s, was to lament the absence of 'love' from Créoles as she had known it in her youth, meaning warm respect – the Governor found it shocking that so much pilfering went on when there was so little want except among those who would not work.[137] A magistrate was commonly presented with evidence that enabled him to see further: fortunately for governors, colonial magistrates typically grew callous. Unusual among them as a former schoolmaster come late to the law, Brooke was a fancy negrophile and in O'Brien's eyes a socialist aspiring to change the colonial order. According to the Governor,[138] the utopian Brooke made his friends among people who were trying to raise a colour question in Seychelles – that happy place where the question no longer even outwardly raised its head. Seychellois had decided whom to admit to the ranks of the accepted, while the colonial government thought that most families had what Anglo-Saxons at their sundowner parties would have called a 'touch of the tarbrush' and therefore viewed pretty well every Seychellois with the same reserve.

In the flesh, Brooke's friends were Fernand Touris, who was not yet rich, and a youth whom Brooke had helped to obtain employment as a master at King's College, Charles Évariste Collet. Son of a part-Indian master-mason supposedly deported from Mauritius as a labour agitator, Évariste Collet had passed his Senior Cambridge School Certificate examinations at the early age of thirteen. He felt that he had missed out on a scholarship from St Louis to

university because he was the wrong colour, but got his chance
when the closing of government's schools in 1922 gave him a
gratuity that let him study overseas at his own expense, perhaps
with some help from Touris. Collet was to become general secretary
of the League for the Advancement of Coloured Peoples, and
spokesman in London for those he called the 'submerged nine-
tenths' of the people of Seychelles. When widows of dead Pioneer
soldiers threatened to riot, Brooke pacified them, perhaps against
his better judgement.[139] All resented the *grand blanc* hegemony, and
Brooke – known to the submerged nine-tenths as '*Oncle*' – learned
how this worked through a court-case involving the ubiquitous
Edouard Lanier and his labourer Aurelius Alcindor. Alcindor was
one of many Créoles who appeared before Brooke's court charged
with drunkenness. He had bought his bacca from Lanier's shop
with *bons*, or tokens, for which the shopkeeper would have given
only 90 per cent in cash. Content to take his pay as usual in
bacca, Alcindor fell foul of the police, but then found himself
before a magistrate who wanted to know how he came to be
spending his wages on drink in the first place.

As a result the outraged Lanier was dragged into the witness-box
to confirm that he did indeed pay his labourers in *bons*, like all
other proprietors. The Créoles could add to the profits of his
shop and then give employment to the police. That was the way
of the world. And so Lanier went before the Governor to remind
him that *grands blancs* did not pay the magistrate's salary in order
that he should set up as protector of blacks. In reality, as Brooke
said, at least half his salary was paid by the Créoles themselves
through indirect taxes. Lanier felt it his duty as a good Seychellois
to make it known how dangerous Brooke's game was:

> *En supposant même que son socialisme soit du progrès, le noir de ce pays*
> *n'est pas encore mûr pour comprendre sainement ces idées et en profiter.*
> *Il lui faudra longtemps encore notre tutelle qui chez moi et nombre de mes*
> *amis est bien loin de ressembler à la haine contre le peuple noir*
> *laboureur.*[140]

Lanier was so well disposed to Créoles that within a few years he
could in a sense be held responsible for the age of consent being raised
from twelve to thirteen years; a Créole girl four months short of her
thirteenth birthday had complained that M. Lanier raped her one
Sunday morning.[141] But he did not like them enough to favour a bill

which Brooke was drafting to give Aurelius Alcindor and his fellows on monthly contracts security for their crops if the proprietor should dismiss them. Aurelius was a rascal, said Lanier – he had deserted his children, and he owned a couple of rooms in town which he rented out, and was rich again from cleaning around coconut palms in the afternoon when his task-work was done. Proprietors were better-disposed towards legislation making labourers cultivate half an acre each, with no lien on what they grew.[142]

In January 1919 Évariste Collet came one evening to call on his friend Brooke and found him dead in a deckchair from potassium cyanide. Brooke had been dismissed by O'Brien the previous April after contesting fees charged on a vacant estate by Mr Barrister Gellé and Mr Notary Loizeau; they were far too high, said Brooke, as of course they were likely to have been. With no money himself now, and no answer from Whitehall to his appeal against the fees although the Colonial Office agreed internally with all he said, Brooke killed himself in despair, convinced that he could never change what he called 'this perhaps forgotten Colony' of Seychelles.[143]

4

SEYCHELLOIS AND CRÉOLE

1920-1939

Seychelles were not entirely forgotten in Whitehall. They were always good for a joke about standards of probity in the Garden of Eden – although the Colonial Office, in this quietist if not faintly whimsical age of allowing colonies to rub along as they wished, rarely ventured to do more than remonstrate through the Governor with local oligarchs; and Seychelles came to mind whenever human obstacles to imperial policy elsewhere on the globe had to be exiled to a place where they could do no harm. There was the example of Napoleon, and the people of Seychelles were more hospitable to the British Empire's guests than they had ever been to the Jacobins. On 31 August 1877 the deposed Sultan Abdullah of Perak arrived as punishment for his alleged part in the killing of the British Resident at his court.[1] Hardly had he been allowed to move away to more congenial exile in Singapore when Prempeh of Ashanti came with a flock of his subordinate slavers and killers, to say nothing of wives and children; they were followed in 1901 by such different guests as ex-Kings Mwanga and Kabarega from Uganda and over 1,000 Boer prisoners.[2] The ex-Sultan of Warsangli in Somaliland was on Mahé for nine years from 1919, promising never to use his horses and his rifles against the friends of Britain again if only he could return and, even, live under the orders of an Englishman; and, overlapping with him, Watch Tower Society deportees from Nyasaland, along with patriots from Egypt who spent a fortune on cables overseas, champagne and doctors' visits and were moved to Gibraltar before their case began to excite the Seychellois' sympathy. The case of five Arabs deported from Palestine in 1937-8 did so; they won damages against Dr Bradley, the Chief Medical Officer, for libel in his paper the *Seychelles Clarion*, and set the Governor to worrying that they would bribe local sympathisers.[3]

It had been much simpler in the older, more innocent days of empire. The only trouble Sultan Abdullah gave, apart from constant petitioning to be allowed home to Perak, or on holiday to Britain or Mauritius, was his need for more money to meet the costs of the children with whom his three wives presented him regularly in accordance with the will of Allah.[4] And the conciliatory Prempeh accepted baptism into King Edward's Anglican church because monarchs needed to stick together; one of his sons became an ordained clergyman. Others of the Ashanti group got into sufficient mild mischief to indicate that the party was very well accepted in Seychelles by 1922, when Prempeh left the Islands at last with twelve survivors from seventy-one original exiles and a flock of new children. In 1922 the Colonial Secretary, Winston Churchill, even proposed to send from 500 to 5,000 Irish patriots to Seychelles, which argued a certain innocence in him.

As the wits said, only Sweet-Escott had ever found Seychelles a difficult place to govern[5] – but Whitehall had to face only signatures on petitions, not people. Petitioning, according to Governor O'Brien, was a Seychellois pastime. For 5 rupees a man with a bicycle could be hired to hawk a petition around Mahé on almost any subject, with fair success; and with a similar outcome and for the same sum another cyclist could go round in the other direction with one diametrically opposed to the first. This for O'Brien was a good argument for ignoring most of the Seychellois' own attempts at home rule. What they actually wanted, he said, was the regular intervention of Providence, preferably with cheap agricultural loans repayable over a long period.[6] This was the view from Government House, an elegant if inconvenient two-storied building originally erected without a staircase by Évariste Collet's mason father to the design of Mrs Davidson, the Governor's wife, between de Quincy's tomb and Belair cemetery. When descendants of the first d'Offay, Savy, Nageon and the rest passed through its doors, it was with little hope of pleasure or profit from the Anglo-Saxon air within. Governor Davidson had been sensitive enough to Seychellois sentiments to print M. Fauvel's collection of documents on the French foundation years, and at his own expense; but in one of his absences on leave his Administrator, the Chief Justice, had been rash enough to forbid the playing of '*La Marseillaise*' before or even after 'God Save the Queen'.

Grands blancs kept alert for every opportunity, freely given, to assert the identity still most congenial to them – of Frenchmen suffering under foreign rule. They were given a special opportunity when Anglo-Saxon senior administrators proliferated in the 1920s. There was the head of the public works department, the Scottish Major Kenworthy, so stiff in his desire for expensive undertakings, so lacking in *politesse* and the *sympathique* – incompetent too, it was finally admitted – that he was a constant butt for *Le Réveil Seychellois*, now owned by Lanier. Nerve failed at the top before its Gallic outbursts – to the extent that during the uproar caused when Kenworthy was appointed to the Legislative Council, Governor Sir Joseph Byrne read so much into a fairly innocuous sneer that he had the Crown Prosecutor lead an action for libel.[7] It helped not at all that Kenworthy was an intimate of Bradley, the Chief Medical Officer, who had to cope in the 1920s with the able Dr L.C.D. Hermitte, a Seychellois, most distinguished of the English scholarship-holders; on returning to private practice in Seychelles Hermitte could see no reason why the *étranger*, by virtue of his government appointment, should be permitted to monopolise hospital beds to the benefit of his own pocket. Bradley had become a great landowner in South Mahé, having invested his medical profits in mortgages regardless of colonial regulations against such a practice. In contending with Bradley – which he ceased to do in 1933 on leaving the Island – Hermitte said that he was moved by 'patriotism and the desire to protect this downtrodden people from abuses perpetrated by certain strangers who have no sense of fair play'.[8] That was the view of the wealthier Seychellois, from the copra-kilns, the little cinnamon oil distilleries and the deck of Lanier's new schooner, the *Charles Edouard*. From *petits blancs* and Créoles, on the other hand, Bradley elicited a petition supporting him – '*ce brave et vaillant Bradley*' who, they said, responded charitably to the orphans' cries and widows' tears, even while he fought the privileged Seychellois.[9]

Dr Bradley's medical despotism apart, what most struck the Seychellois as an abuse between 1916 and 1930 was the cost of administration by *étrangers*. Prices of coconuts, vanilla and cinnamon might fall or rise with equal ease, but it appeared that the costs of government would never cease rising. Seychellois had been hard-hit at the end of the War, with no shipping to be had; near bankruptcy, the colony had to borrow Rs 100,000 from Mauritius to meet the immediate running costs of administration; and the gaol was full again with Créoles unable to pay their taxes. That in itself was a challenge to Governor O'Brien's sanguine aristocratic successor, Colonel the Hon. Sir Eustace E. Twistleton-Wykeham-Fiennes. He replaced the gaol's comfortable canvas stretchers with hard bedboards and put prisoners in their waking hours to work building the long-needed poor-house, the Fiennes Institute.[10] Soon there was also a Fiennes Promenade along the Chaussée; and the poor would have had their dormitories, and Bradley's paying patients their private wards, in a Fiennes Hospital if that handsome but expensive building had been completed in Sir Eustace's time. Local subscriptions were to have paid for it, and did so to the tune of Rs 69,000; the other Rs 211,000 came in a small grant from the Red Cross and a large overdraft on the Crown Agents; the Colonial Office felt that to leave the hospital a shell would be to set up too grisly a monument to the financial incompetence of Lord Saye and Sele's eccentric relation.[11]

'Sir Fiennes' – as he was known to the *grands blancs*, who deplored him – was a delight to, for instance, a certain small landowner of Glacis on Mahé whose pedigree alienated white families from himself; son of a Créole woman taken from her husband by the owner of the estate, this landowner applauded the British in Seychelles before going off to work for them in East Africa, among the first of many to tread that enterprising path and return in old age. Patronage and humour apart, however, Fiennes was one manifestation of the Colonial Office's disregard for 29,000 people lost in the Indian Ocean. It backfired. In 1920 Whitehall proposed that Seychelles should give customs preference to British goods, but Fiennes argued them out of it with his picture of an entirely French community, trading with Marseilles from sentiment and because the prices were high enough there anyway to attract even the two British exporters; this got Whitehall to agree that a place 'so insignificant and so poverty-stricken as Seychelles' could be left free to trade as its own advantage might lead it.[12] It backfired still more, for Fiennes reckoned Seychelles to be far too small to give scope for the unbounded enterprise, energy and tact to which he willingly admitted – concerning his tact in particular, *Le Réveil Seychellois* had its own ideas.[13]

His successor in Seychelles had better be a tennis-player, said 'Sir Fiennes', 'because he can get some amusement out of it, the only one here, except for the funny side of life and there is plenty of that.'[14] Fiennes, who went next to the West Indies, had been in step with some thinking in Seychelles on the desirability of reunion with Mauritius. About eighty people petitioned for it two months after his departure, claiming unanimity unprecedented in Seychelles. This derived partly from new tax legislation requiring that they should, as one Member of Legislative Council put it, incriminate themselves by declaring their incomes; and they were not much enthused by the expenditure of government money on even marginal medical benefits for labourers.[15] What they needed, the Colonial Office told itself, was a professional administrator as Governor in place of the enthusiastic amateurs who had succeeded Davidson,[16] but in the event they got more amateurs. However, it took two members of the colonial legal service to achieve the heights of public absurdity. The sense of righteousness bred on the bench tends to corrode common sense in judges.

In 1928 the Governor's seat was empty, and the interim post of Administrator was held by Chief Justice de Vaux, a Mauritian, who was due for promotion to a bench elsewhere; his replacement as Chief Justice was to be the Anglo-Irishman de Vere (as Crown Prosecutor in Seychelles years before, he had loudly asserted that the Chief Justice of that time was no gentleman; de Vere's superiors said he himself was a 'gentleman' but little else).[17] De Vere expected to take over as Administrator immediately, but de Vaux wanted to stay on until de Vere had heard a pending murder case; if de Vere were not Chief Justice but lording it as Administrator, the case would have to be tried before the Police Magistrate, who was showing an indecent desire to try a man whose guilt he had already proclaimed. De Vere insisted on being Administrator, and was urged on by Kenworthy, Bradley and others among the lonely Anglo-Saxon clique who found de Vaux too closely involved with the *grands blancs*. Witty and cultivated, de Vaux had a Gallic air calculated to grate upon Bradley whose own notion of how to speak French made him the butt of jokes in plantation houses around the Island. This wit had particularly offended poor Kenworthy; he had joined an irreverent group who put sham gravestones against a curb which Kenworthy had caused to be placed along the deep ditch bordering Rue Royale.[18] Possession of Government House was disputed, rival Executive Councils were called, and a tug-of-war was conducted over the Colonial Office cipher book. For a week Seychelles had two Administrators, de Vere and the near-weeping de Vaux. 'If any of these names should come up for promotion', commented the Colonial Office, with several others in mind too, 'they will be laughed out of court after this affair.'[19]

The Colonial Office had put them there in the first place, however, and Seychellois laughter rang hollow. Very little of the costly, direct, practical assistance which the Seychellois felt they, as possessors of the land, had a right to expect was forthcoming in the 1920s. The Colony was on care and maintenance – not much maintenance and very little care, as cynics said. There was little help for fishing, on which many Seychellois pinned their hopes for increased incomes, except a report by a visiting expert; and not much in the way of colonial development fund money for agriculture, although another expert found a need not only for finance but also for re-education in basic agricultural techniques. It seemed fair enough, then, that most of the score of cars imported in the 1920s to drive along 14 miles of made road between Anse Etoile and Anse Royale should be from France. Some Seychellois believed that they could do better for themselves, perhaps even for their Islands too, if they had more of a hand in the government. There had been demands for election of members to the Legislative Council as far back as 1888, and calls for a majority of Unofficial members in 1901. As the three Unofficials of the late 1920s, still appointed and in the minority, put it to the Secretary of State, 'Unless to give a delusive semblance of participation by the people of the Colony in the government of their country, it is difficult to see why Unofficial Members form part of Council at all.' The Governor, a total stranger, was in the hands of the Official members, the heads of departments, and only saw the Unofficials when Council met for a few hours a bare three or four times a year.[20]

That was the experience of Unofficial members C. Nageon de l'Estang, Marcel Lemarchand and W.F. Stephens. It was left to Stephens to articulate the grievance and devise the strategy – something which the tall Englishman would often do during the next twenty years. He came close to dominating local politics, writing the while to Members of Parliament and occasionally descending on the Colonial Office itself to lighten its darkness about Eden. He had come to Seychelles in 1906 as chemist for the Mahé Syndicate and, when the guano extractors broke up, turned his attention to coconuts on the estate where he lived with his *grand blanc* wife at North West Point on Mahé. He had a genuine commitment to Seychelles, as well as generous impulses. Among other things, he deplored the medical department, failing to see why government doctors on comparatively high salaries should be free to take a minimum consultation fee of 2 rupees from labourers earning 25 cents a day.[21] Appointed to Council, Stephens found his claims to be seen as a minor colossus not much acknowledged; and in 1928 he led a walk-out by all three Unofficials in protest against government's failure to take note of their objections to the budget and, still more, the Colonial Office's having apparently ignored the reservation they recorded. In the aftermath of the de Vere-de Vaux affair, London's polite acknowledgment had not been communicated to them.

The position, it seemed to them, was that their dissent was just as ineffectual in the Colonial Office as in the council chamber. Executive Council was the real policy-making body in the colony. Invariably two of the three departmental heads who sat on it under the Governor were strangers too – 'having little in common, and little sympathy with the planters, merchants and others, mostly of French descent, who form the backbone of the community', as it suited Stephens to please his friends by saying. Administration of this authoritarian sort might be appropriate for colonies peopled exclusively by 'primitive native races'; it was far from being proper in Seychelles 'where there is, beside the illiterate native labouring class, a small educated community which should be given an effective voice in Government'.[22] So the resigning Unofficial members of Legislative Council saw it, expressing themselves in the words of the *grands blancs* and on the busy typewriter of Mr Stephens. Legislative Council failing, they would resort to a pressure group. A Planters' Association founded in 1917 had foundered in a welter of personalities; in 1927 Stephens refloated it, and in 1930 took its recommendations in person to the Colonial Office.

A little money was available from the penurious quarter now. Under the Colonial Development Act of 1929, £1 million a year were to go to the Empire – so novel a situation, after all the financial obstacles in the way of economic development hitherto unless it were done by private enterprise, that official minds confessedly found the change hard to grapple with. At any rate, grants came to Seychelles for road-building and a tuberculosis ward. £14,000 in loans was also offered to planters to buy the fertiliser so much needed by their sun-baked soil, but this was a bad time to try it. With the Depression, copra fell from Rs 40 to Rs 18.11 in 1931 and even to Rs 9.37 in 1934. A mixture of bone-meal and guano would raise coconut production by over 100 per cent –so Dr Bradley's son-in-law, the scientific planter Douglas Bailey, proved at Anse aux Pins; but when copra was so low, even double the price did not pay the cost of fertiliser.[23] The proprietors would rather have had £60,000 lent them at 3 or 4 per cent to pay off their present 8-12 per cent mortgages. As the Depression bit harder, with copra and cinnamon-leaf oil fetching less than they cost to produce in mid-1931, proprietors sought a moratorium on repayment of capital, along with reduction of customs dues and a year's grace in payment of income-tax. Failing this, they said, they would have to dismiss nearly all their labourers. Wages were now so low that it was clear to proprietors that the sale of bacca should be banned, to remove one area of conspicuous expenditure – and of course to enable proprietors to get their estates cultivated through *festins* in the good old way.[24]

As Stephens put their case in Whitehall, they also wanted an agricultural bank to replace the firm of Teemooljee, which had taken over the major credit role from Hossen. Through Stephens proprietors demanded cheaper government in place of the present pretentious aping of big colonies; they sought the appointment of an Unofficial member of Legislative Council to the Executive Council and required that the Planters' Association should itself be authorised to appoint two of the three Unofficial members to Legislative Council. They were dead against elections to it, because a development which in 1888 would have crossed no man's mind was now a faint possibility: the Colonial Office might not be content with a franchise restricted to the planters, merchants and other men of property who, in their own eyes, formed the backbone of the country.[25]

As Whitehall could clearly see, what the men and women of property wanted was a pure plantocracy. Nonetheless the Colonial Office put the proposals to the Governor of the moment, the shy non-French-speaking South African Sir de Symons Montague George Honey – who was about to try flying into the sun on wings of wax by totally prohibiting bacca drinking. Honey replied truly enough that the Planters' Association was certainly representative of the proprietors, but according to its constitution it was a non-political body. As for Stephens, its president, he had the full confidence of members in pursuing free benefits for planters but had never yet dared to test his standing with them by advocating anything as undreamed-of as co-operation with government or improved conditions for labourers.[26] And so, his back to the wall, the Governor was claiming concern for the Créoles – the politically inarticulate black majority who had no leadership, unless it were *grisgris* men like Gros Louis, otherwise Louis Clémentine, or Charles Zialor, *alias* Charles Marove, prominent practitioners of arts involving chicken heads and other paraphernalia, upon whom deep suspicion had fallen in 1923 when Father Théophile broke his neck falling down a cliff at La Misère after preaching strenuously against black arts.[27]

The Governor's concern rang hollow. He had just recommended to his unappreciative masters in London a new Labour Ordinance, drawn up with the advice of a committee of proprietors, recommending penal sanctions for absenteeism, especially where men were tempted away by the higher wages of the port. His concerns rang hollower still when a commissioner came from London in 1934 to look into the taxation and general structure of the whole place. 'Either Dr Bradley's superconscientiousness, about which we have had complaints, or the Seychellois instinct for turning everything into comic opera' was behind it, in the words of one Whitehall comment, when Commissioner T. Reid was quarantined on arrival. To Reid this was not extravagant administration, as Seychellois claimed, but incompetent amateurish administration with feckless hedonism among Seychellois themselves. They showed vociferous interest in politics – expressing themselves with fluency and great courtesy, for *la politesse* still ruled, and St Louis had produced an articulate élite; but the white families had no concern for anyone save their own class. They recognised that if the colonial bureaucracy were dismantled, as they would have liked it to be, its probable successor, representative government, was likely to put power in Créole hands.[28] Créole and Seychellois alike flocked to Reid with petitions. The Praslinois and Diguois told him that they were 3,700 souls remembered by government on Mahé to the poor extent of four police-stations, a few miles of primitive pathways, three dispensaries with a medical officer in attendance once a week, and a small grant-in-aid for their elementary and only schools. The hookworm on La Digue was as bad as anywhere in the world. A deputation of proprietors from the Islands at large required all heads of departments to be Seychellois and demanded drastic retrenchment, along with twenty-year loans at 3-4 per cent enabling planters to pay off their present mortgages; their main spokesman, Stephens, respected among them for being a very straight man, had figures on the export crops to prove how thin the economic bedrock really was. This was the year when copra, the mainstay, hit Rs 9.97 for a hundred nuts; and when it was remembered that a quarter of the copra exported came from Outer Islands which were in the hands of Teemooljee and the Hadee brothers, it emerged that the remaining 3,750 tons of copra sold at Depression prices had to be the largest contributor towards supporting the population of some 30,000 people.

Cheaper shipping was necessary, urged Seychellois; as were an attack on the scale-insects, which at present reduced the yield, and cover-crops to protect the covering of crops against erosion, both of which would necessitate cheap loans. Let them go to genuine developers, urged Alexandre Deltel, a particularly able, slightly cynical Seychellois, an old King's College boy; it was notorious and typical of this government, he said, that loans generally went to the powerful, not necessarily those who would put the money into land rather than trips to Europe. Scenting this unfriendly wind, another Seychellois, a Lemarchand, wrote to clear himself of any suspicion in Reid's mind that he was in this opportunist company. True, he had spent six months in Europe; true, his wife lived there all the year round for her health; but he had repaid his loan, brought his yield from 22,000 nuts to 35,000 in nine years, and again represented a very good investment for more cheap money. Perhaps he would then bring his labour force back to its usual twenty-five from the twelve which were all he could afford now, at Rs 5 a month for men and Rs 4 for women.[29]

The voice of such uncertain wage-earners, now reaching government with some force for almost the first time ever, seemed particularly cogent to Reid (who in later years sat in the House of Commons as a Labour member). The Créoles had found a spokesman: Joseph Eulantin, *Délégué de la Classe Ouvrière* as he presented himself. A former labourer retrenched from the Public Works department and more recently winchman for Baty, Bergne & Co.'s successor the Union Lighterage Co., Eulantin had the respectful nickname 'Captain'. It was no secret to him or, probably, to the

250 who signed his petition that they were exploited. The fall in wages, it said,

> .... is being currently accounted by the proprietors to the fall in produce prices, but we, who are daily following our masters in their whole industrial life, positively assert that we come to the conclusion (and we beg Your Excellency to believe us) that their transactions, mode of living, etc. go far to confirm...that their financial position is being grossly exaggerated. A decisive proof of our contention is summed up in the number of de luxe motor cars, motor cycles, etc. which are being imported and are also in transit and also in the monthly club accounts of our masters.[30]

Thanks to this unprecedented opportunity of addressing an outsider, Joseph Eulantin told Reid in French, he personally hoped his compatriots would see their chains fall off – chains *'jusqu'ici rivées au bons plaisirs de nos exploiteurs sans consciences'*. He cited the engagement of labourers for outlying islands as one example of exploitation; 'boys' were entered at Rs 3 a month long after they had become fathers of families. Payment elsewhere was now by the day and often in kind. *'Inutile de vous dire que nous sommes écorchés'* – to be *écorchés* or fleeced was very often a labourer's lot in life. And the responsibility for much of the economic backwardness lay in the lack of aptitude and drive among proprietors: *'On parle sécrètement entre les propriétaires de nous opprimer pour notre "insolence" de vous avoir addressé cette pétition. J'ai été personellement prévenu. Nous attendons votre geste.'*[31]

Like his precursor-socialist Brooke, Reid concluded that, however much proprietors might complain, Seychelles was run for them if it was run for anybody. Rightly so, Edouard Lanier would have said; the land, the capital and in his case the enterprise off which everybody lived were theirs; it was proper that he should receive an extension of his Rs 16,000 government fishing loan for thirty years, interest free. He could show Rs 60,000 of his own invested in the *Charles Edouard* and fishing undertakings generally; he leased the Lesser Amirantes for the eggs of the noddy tern, which found a market overseas as well as on Mahé; he had Cosmoledo for fish and turtles, and was seeking markets in Africa, Madagascar, Mauritius and Europe for salted and dried fish, sharks' fin and skin, egg yolk, albumen and trepang (bêche-de-mer); he fished Farquhar, Providence and St Pierre, and planned to net

mackerel, for the Transvaal goldmines, around Mahé where the
3–400 registered fishermen would benefit, along with the numberless
unemployed who now looked to their nets and *casiers* or fishtraps
for a living. Close to death, Lanier remained an active and imaginative man.

Even so, proprietors like him built up at least the appearance
or prospect of capital at the expense of the poor. The cheap
government loans came from taxation which, as always, fell dis-
proportionately to the advantage of the monied. Proprietors declined
to incriminate themselves in the matter of income-tax, and declared
derisory sums. Indeed the tax structure was remarkable, so heavily
did it fall on labourers; they paid 3 per cent in flat-rate tax on a
combined family income of 100 Rupees, while payers of income-tax
proper would not pay three percent until their total income reached
at least Rs 3,000. All through, disagreeable taxes were confined
as much as possible to the poor. Members of the middle class
had joined the proprietors in looking after themselves. Advocates
had secured exemption from the tax on professions. Government
servants, hit now by a levy on salaries to help reduce the deficit,
had in the past allocated themselves all sorts of perquisites. The
administration which the Seychellois felt was particularly their
property was, out of all proportion to income, paid for by the
Créoles who used its services least – except the gaol.

None of this tax-structure reflected credit upon an occasionally
watchful, commonly satirical but rarely intervening Colonial Office.
It had allowed *grand blanc* privilege to grow without even winning
much thanks from the *grands blancs*. With some appearance of
remorse and more determination to economise, London sent an
efficient Governor, the first for twenty years, but in less than two
years it moved him on to a more important Colony. 'The Colonial
Office do that sort of thing, unhappily,' commented W.F. Stephens,
now firmly re-ensconced in Legislative Council. He was a member
of Executive Council too, and greatly in favour with the successor
Governor, Sir Arthur Grimble.[33] A man of tender conscience in
some things, solemn and humourless – lugubrious even, according
to his exasperated Whitehall superiors[34] – Grimble had begun his
career in the Pacific Islands, and often wished he were back there.
He had a fondness for the ladies, which the experienced Seychellois
readily detected; with solemn hypocrisy, they held this up for

public viewing as a scandal when welfare schemes that he was both instructed and personally inclined to introduce, in the light of Reid's findings, promised to curtail privileges and advance what now became known as social justice.

Among other things, there was to be an agricultural bank, along with income-tax reform. The bank did eventually open, but it was not much used; and the whole question of tax evasion was too explosive to handle with confidence. When it came to the point, London balked at legislation that would allow inspectors to look at books, and Grimble hesitated to put up the tax-scales. He hoped that the newly-appointed Chief Inland Revenue Officer would find the apprehensive rich sufficiently forthcoming with honest declarations in future to increase the revenue from the present scales. Not till 1939 did he plan to exempt incomes below Rs 500 and remove the annual Rs 2.20 levy paid by every male over eighteen. But he talked a good deal, saying in private that he found the ratio of cold-blooded profiteering in Seychelles to be incredibly high, while susceptibility to bribes reached 'into what is (locally) regarded as the better kind of society'.[35] In public his words, while more restrained, were still revolutionary in the context of Seychelles.

As Grimble put it to his first Legislative Council in 1936, the labourers, the unassuming Créoles, had aspired to change little in their way of life since they became free four generations back; therefore, they must be educated to aspire, and it was the obligation of the Seychellois to create a reasonable demand on life in the Créole, to awaken in him a consciousness of his deep need for better housing, playgrounds in Victoria for his children who now played in the streets where dirt, congestion and degradation ruled; for a chance to acquire property, and to enjoy a full social life in place of the present atomised existence. Grimble went to the Colonial Development Fund seeking playgrounds, community centres, and canteens where labourers could drink in decent surroundings the bacca he thought harmless; and he asked for model housing and small-holdings to give Créoles a stake in the country. While the Colonial Office was chewing upon these requests, the *grands blancs* chewed upon the Governor.

There was now another newspaper in which to do this. The arrival of Grimble's predecessor, the reforming Sir Gordon Lethem in 1934, had followed hard upon the retirement of Dr Bradley.

Not wishing to waste the insight he had acquired on the hidden undercurrents pulsating in the Islands, Bradley had founded his *Seychelles Clarion* soon afterwards. He made it a platform from which to attack his successor as Chief Medical Officer, Edouard Lanier's son Maxime, and generally stirred up mud in whatever sink-hole offered itself, as Grimble put it.[36] A restrictive press law succeeded only in closing down an Anglican church news-sheet, the *Seychelles Cathedral Magazine*. Its publisher, the Venerable J.A.F. Ozanne, was well aware that the law was aimed at the *Clarion* and *L'Impartial* but pretended to believe that he might otherwise involuntarily put himself in court. Set down as an ass for this in the Colonial Office, the Archdeacon had his Bishop rushing to his defence soon afterwards when he was guyed as the bibulous Reverend Saul Angel, Archdeacon of Seychelles with a barmaid wife, in the ephemeral novel *Isles of Torment*.[37] This was written under a pseudonym by Captain H.A.D. Mackay – one of the occasional tourists who stayed at the new Hotel des Palmes to enjoy its water-closets, provided for it by the Colonial Development Fund and almost unknown in Seychelles, while they waited between one monthly British India steamer from Bombay and the next on to East Africa. Ozanne himself soon broke into print again, with his uncharitable but amusing view of Seychelles, *Coconuts and Créoles*. It was banned in the often humourless Seychelles (which, even as an independent state, is not a place much given to ready laughter at itself). It has two self-confessed members of the aristocracy – the Marquis de Chocolat de Bonbon and Monsieur Caffait au Lêt – preparing to fight a duel at the end of Long Pier, each in despair lest the amused police should not arrive to stop it in time.

The élite were happy to support the ban, which the Catholic Church imposed for reasons of its own. Ozanne was a better writer than Bradley. The Anglican clergyman – Guernsey-born, a former Royal Marine and war-time member of the Royal Flying Corps – had been educated for the Catholic priesthood, like his predecessor of the 1880s the Reverend Mr Grandjean, but joined the Church of England in order to marry. Bradley had his moments, even so. The regular Créole letters in the *Seychelles Clarion* were very funny, professedly written beneath the flaming sangdragon trees bordering Port Victoria's Gordon Square where straw-hatted philosophers gathered to watch the world go by. And he had a good contributor in Captain H.T. Munn. This retired Arctic sea-captain developed a nice line in satire with his regular column, 'Grandfather Says'. Grandfather once said or broadly implied that that Olympian God, the Secretary of State for the Colonies, might more appropriately have been styled 'Olympic Goat' for his stupidity. The Goat had to intervene to stop government prosecuting Grandfather for libel, so rattled had his representative Grimble become.[38] Humour stayed in old Captain Munn to the end: when he died at the age of eighty-eight he was buried at sea but his coffin floated up to the surface in fulfilment of a promise to return, and landed on Long Island.

Impartial administration demanded that government should redress a generations-old imbalance by leaning towards the labourers, as Grimble saw it. Creation of a decent standard of living and the inculcation among them of the conviction that their interests were regarded seriously, seemed to him essential to the social health of any community. He tried demanding sanitary housing on estates. And some Island owners, like the Hadee brothers, had to be convinced that their habit of retaining good labourers beyond their contract-time, while letting unruly ones get away, could be redressed by the law. 'Rather than run the island at a loss, or if hard conditions are imposed on us, the number of labourers employed will have to be reduced,' the Hadees threatened in the usual vein.[39] Grimble assured Legislative Council, on the contrary, that if proprietors had bestirred themselves more when prices rose again in 1936, they would have been able to pay labourers decently and still buy motor-cars for themselves –but, as he told his own superiors privately,

> .... even the elementary regulations which do exist here for the protection of the labourer have suffered from a long neglect. [...] The ruling opinion here, quite blatantly expresed, is that the negro worker is an animal and must not be allowed to forget it. Employers who hold this view are not necessarily oppressive to their labourers, but even those who are most kindly inclined grant justice as a favour, not a right.

Landowners could not now say that Britain had done nothing for them; the Hotel des Palmes' lavatories apart, an entomologist was saving the coconut palms by spectacular control of the scale-insects, paving the way for a steady increase in copra exports for fourteen years after 1940, in recompense for the Depression.

As Grimble put it, reflecting on the tendency to leave much in the hands of God, 'The willing coconut and the industrious cinnamon, starved or ruthlessly hacked though they generally continued to be, none the less succeeded of their own proper virtue in heaving the Colony once again out of its financial morass.' And then in 1938 when copra fell once more and cinnamon-leaf oil was unsaleable, a country whose export revenue was down to Rs 900,000 squandered Rs 310,000 on importing rice and other staples when it could have produced the equivalent itself.[40] When Grimble looked at social attitudes he thought revolution was their logical result. He was mocked when he said so to his friend Stephens' Seychellois wife. She wrote to disabuse him of his philanthropic notions, breaking into French to do so more effectively. Revolt was not at all in the nature of these blacks she knew so well. The Governor's community centres, for instance, would only give them a false idea of their importance; moreover, '*cela les encouragerait aux plaisirs et aux repos qu'ils prennent déjà trop*'. And they would get together in the centres to talk politics; discontent would arise, even communism! '*Je connais la mentalité de ce peuple*'. They were stupid, '*crapule*', but not wholly bad; it would not be proper to expect the same from them as from the superior classes. Nor could they be compared with the 'higher blacks' of other countries, born with qualities developed by civilisation. And to push them up from the station in which it had pleased God to place them would be no kindness at all. Give a black a bit of land, and he would no longer work for *blancs* on what little wage the copra and essential oils could afford. Why anyway should Créoles need possessions?

> *N'avoir jamais rien possédé, ne peut pas démoraliser une race, un peuple.* [...] *Ces noirs d'ici, qui ont des biens, sont-ils meilleurs que leurs semblabes qui n'en ont pas? Non, ils sont plus turbulents, plus mécontents, et surtout, plus insolents.*

Let not the history of our Islands be lost sight of, said this *grand blanc* lady who in practice was kindly. These scraps of granite were colonised by Europeans and them alone. The blacks of Africa had come as inferiors. They were happy. What more could Seychellois give Créoles than they already provided – liberty, equality, justice, free schools, free treatment in the hospital, and free refuge at the end in the Fiennes Institute? In these latter days, the country had gone so far as to exempt them from paying direct taxes to support a place which gave them so much. If a disaffected newspaper like the marginal *L'Impartial* thought they deserved more, if – part-owned by Dr Bradley for its nuisance-value and edited by Mr Calais for historical reasons – this paper was actually trying to stir the Créoles up to demand a minimum wage, let the Colonial Office set maximum freight rates for what they helped produce and minimum prices for it on world markets; and then think about a wage not controlled by supply and demand. *L'Impartial* with its bolshevist opinions was the breath of Satan; but let Satan blow in Spain, here in Seychelles his servants were of no account. These opinions were voiced merely by a dozen people – '*quelques "peaux-rouges" enragés de n'être pas des Blancs*'.[41] Calais was one *peau-rouge*, from his Ramalinga heredity. Another was the barrister Fernand Touris, owner now of Barbaron estate – Grimble made him a Member of Legislative Council in the hope that his genuine concern for the poor could be put to use. A third – so dark in pigmentation that, though not African, he could never have passed for anything but one of '*ces noirs*' – was a correspondent of Calais in London, Évariste Collet.

He was Charles E. Collet now, an able but bitter man. He demonstrated resentment at all the years of stratagem and striving he had had to devote to educating himself, while for Dr Hermitte, say, it had plain sailing on scholarships. After leaving for Europe to study for the priesthood, Collet had become a Quaker – he was said to have fathered a love-child and the Bishop of Seychelles had intervened. A medical student for a time, married now to a French lawyer, he was reading for the Bar himself, eating his dinners at Lincoln's Inn (he was called in November 1943). He was also General Secretary to the League of Coloured Peoples and in 1937 he approached the Colonial Office with a list of reforms for Seychelles. They might have convinced Mme Stephens that Satan had landed, but the Colonial Office, roused from slumber and bad jokes by Reid, would have been delighted to adopt them.

Collet wanted an immediate rise upon the labourers' Rs 7 a month, or fourpence-ha'penny a day, an independent wages tribunal, and an end to government loans which so many so-called planters squandered. As he said, echoing Lieutenant Sullivan across 126 years, 'the majority of these "planters" think of the English as "FOREIGNERS" and consider it fair game to plunder the FOREIGN Government'. Land left uncultivated should be taken over, he urged; most of the proprietors after all had not the slightest notion of civic duty – which again was a phrase Anglo-Saxons had been throwing around in Seychelles for some five generations. Medicine should be free for the poor, and venereal hygiene taught in schools. And since so much of the social malaise could in his view be traced to the narrow vision of the Swiss Capuchins, let them be put under stringent control; ideally, replace the monks with Mauritian secular priests.[42] If the Capuchins' former acolyte, young Evariste, had seen Governor Lethem's private characterisation of them as 'a bad set of narrow-minded Swiss peasant bigots',[43] he would hardly have sprung to their defence – which did not mean that he thought much better of the Anglican Church when Ozanne was its shepherd. But Anglicanism could hardly fail to seem more liberal in education while the Roman Catholic Church had the upper hand. As Collet saw it, his own old school, St Louis, 'is responsible for the propensity to untruthfulness and dishonesty and absence of civic responsibility, and for the incurable laziness and crapulous ignorance of the "white" Seychellois who is its principal "beneficiary", and his intolerable and intolerant Bigotry.'[44]

That was the breath of Satan indeed. To combat its local sighings in the Seychelles press, that staunch son of the Catholic Church, Marcel Lemarchand, had launched the monthly *Action Catholique*. It was dedicated to the glory of God and the safety of souls. To protect them, Lemarchand's brother had drawn his revolver against a group of Anglicans and newly-converted Seventh Day Adventists who doubted too loudly that God was a Roman Catholic.[45] The beauty of woman's role in the home was a theme of *Action Catholique*, and the Red terror in Spain did not go unmentioned. Caution was advocated in the choice of reading matter, for instruction did not in itself make a man moral, and faith was easily damaged. Certainly the faithful should not read *Le Réveil Seychellois*. Its current proprietor and editor Sydney Delorié, *peau rouge* that some said he was, actually called on his countrymen to throw off clerical domination. He particularly wanted freedom from that domination in education, and an end to teaching inspired by the mysterious anxieties of religion; and he was joined by the current head of the St Ange family, Kerseley, in calling for the eclipse of this 'powerful and relentless foreign priesthood'. It was all too uncomfortable for the Church. *Le Réveil Seychellois* was put on the local index and the Governor was importuned – in vain – to close it down. All the world knew, said *Action Catholique*, that *'celui qui veut séparer religion et éducation a cessé de penser catholiquement '*.[46]

If that were so, twenty-one of the thirty prominent Seychellois who attended a meeting at the Carnegie Hall in July 1935 had ceased to think catholicly. They sent a deputation to the Governor demanding a new government secondary school, 'completely free from dogmatic and theological bias'. It should be controlled by a liberal-minded Director of Education from England aided by a board of 'virile' local personages. The school must include sports in its curriculum and have absolute liberty of conscience; there must be no more of St Louis' daily catechism and mass, no more communion twice a week, and an end to prayers for obtaining a priestly vocation, at least in school hours.[46] At Government House the virile deputation met absolute agreement in principle but difficulties in the matter of money. The Church paid for its right to lead the youth of Seychelles – not handsomely, as the poverty-stricken Marist Brothers told their own superiors and the sub-standard primary schools declared to any observer, but enough to meet the gap between what schools cost and the Rs 22,000 or £1,650 which government granted. Money apart, Sir Arthur Grimble worried whether the Seychellois would really dare to stand by a government school – he foresaw a greater probability that they would give way again to anathemas on any parent who countenanced what the Bishop's educational secretary, Père Olivier, called '*un funeste et coupable libéralisme en matière d'éducation*' when he himself ascended the Bishop's throne.[47] It was agreed, though, that an extra Rs 9,000 should be paid to St Louis in return for its obtaining five new qualified teachers from the Marist Brotherhood; but the long-standing disputes between Mission and Marists came to a head before more than two had arrived.

Capuchins and Marists were both the worse for their long isolation in Seychelles. A visitation by Cardinal Hinsley as Apostolic Delegate in 1933 had led to the resignation of Bishop Justin de Gumy. The schools in particular horrified Hinsley – the College and Convent especially, since nobody seems to have expected much of the country primary schools, exclusive as these were to the poor. The Mother-Superior was very conservative, as well she might be at nearly eighty, and had no English. Brother-director Cyrus had ruled the College for over thirty years. Worn out in the chalk-dust, neither of them, so far as Hinsley could see, had any ability to promote education. His opinion was shared by a Capuchin with educational qualifications who came to report on the College the next year. Its teaching was slavish rote-learning geared to passing the somewhat irrelevant Cambridge Certificates and London Matriculation; and the Capuchin found that the College made a distinction between paying and non-paying pupils, between classes and colours, which he thought inconsistent with Christian principles.[48]

One of Hinsley's recommendations was a recipe for disaster. He recalled that under their original agreement the Marist Brothers were simply to teach, while the Roman Catholic Mission administered the College; in practice, the Marists now ran it and this he felt should be stopped, his loyalty to his order perhaps overwhelming his sense of what was practical for a teacher. So in future the Bishop must run the College and be seen to do so. The Brothers felt humiliated and resentful. They were already at loggerheads with the Bishop, since they sought an increase in their small allowance, at which he expressed pained astonishment that they should crave worldly goods. Now they were, in effect, being threatened with being put under Père Olivier: pious, intelligent and capable they said they acknowledged him to be, but also authoritarian and even a bit brutal.[49] He had been sent to London for a few months to study English and teaching methods. This was an amateurish way of getting partly qualified, and only served to enrage the professional teacher Brother Gérard – Adam Meister in his former life, an American with an M.A. from Auckland University who arrived in 1936 via the South Seas and later took over from Brother Cyrus. A lonely man, Brother Gérard was also much disappointed, even in the Seychelles themselves. He found the Islands sombrely beautiful but with none of the dazzling atmosphere of his beloved Samoa. The Brothers' house and school, so ramshackle after what he had known in the South Seas, were in curious contrast with the shining palace lately built for the priests. Known to the irreverent as the Stable of Bethlehem, this towered among the shacks of Victoria and symbolised the spirit of this Mission to others besides Brother Gérard. As he saw it, the priests wanted control of the College because through it 'they expect to recuperate the Goodwill and Favour of the white and black population, they have lost through their own bungling and non–savoir faire'.[50]

Children came to be at risk through the squabbling of these celibates. They quarrelled over the additional Rs 9,000 subsidy; the Brothers accepted two–fifths of it but apparently did not tell the Bishop so until 1938, encouraging the recurrent suspicion that they were not averse to an unsanctified partnership running the school with the government as paymaster. Nor were they averse when their professionalism as teachers got the upper hand of their religion; but suspicion was anyway second-nature to that Père Olivier, who became the insecure and over-reaching Bishop Maradon in 1936. 'Mean-spirited and distrustful', Brother Gérard finally called him to his face. Let him seek another order to run his school, advised the sorely-tried Marist – 'men more to your liking, perhaps more of the type of the doormat and the lickspittle, cheaper ones you won't find'.[51] It was all very difficult for Bishop Maradon. He had great power in Seychelles – greater than the Governors', he was prepared to say, for they came and went while the Church went on forever. The spirit of Satan was blowing from unlikely quarters, all the same. His laity were not yet quite so disenchanted with him that, as later, he felt it wise to remind them in *Action Catholique* that the priest was another Christ, quite infallible; but they were restive, and government remained deaf to his hints that *L'Impartial* with all its bolshevist attacks on the Church was also a danger to the State.[52]

The State was moving too. A qualified Director of Education came at last in 1938, and a new Board of Education was established. It had church representation, despite the efforts of Fernand Touris to exclude both Catholics and Anglicans, but it still over-represented the laity in the Bishop's eyes. And the question of what language should be used for teaching was up for discussion again. Let it be English in practice, as it already was in theory, concluded the Director of Education. His grounds were that Créole was an obstacle to learning grammatical French and that French was not the language of the country; in the Anglican schools, where English was used, the children's French was no worse than that achieved in the Catholic schools, and the English was a great deal better. The laity agreed, on the grounds that the Islands could not much longer contain their growing population, who would need English in order to migrate to East Africa.[53] With French the language of religion, the prospect of English as the teaching medium was a blow to the Bishop. Consequently, he was to be heard at education board meetings assuring everybody that all his communicants – and were they not the bulk of the population? – had adequate French, even while he was saying elsewhere that Créoles did not understand a word of it.[54] However, his greatest immediate difficulty was over the staffing of the College and the Convent; the mother houses were failing him in his need for more, and professionally trained, teaching religious, without whom it would be still harder to resist the rebirth of amoral King's College. A secular school was his nightmare: '*Quel désastre ce serait pour la formation religieuse de nos enfants....*'[55] Something else was threatened too. He must have more nuns, he told the Sisters of St Joseph de Cluny in 1939 – and let them be French-speaking, for '*Je vous dis que le Gouvernement cherche à angliciser de plus en plus les Seychelles, mais comme c'est au détriment de la religion, je dois nécessairement mettre un frein à leur ambition.*'[56]

5

GRANDS BLANCS TRIUMPHANT

1939-1960

Government would willingly have 'anglicised' Seychelles if it could – meaning an education system giving scope for equal opportunity, social welfare schemes like settlement of labourers on the 3,000 acres purchased in 1939 from the Seychelles Produce Company, model villages, the rebuilding of picturesque but squalid Victoria, and a living wage. Plans had been laid when war came again in 1939. Grimble had even discussed with the Colonial Office whether Charles Collet might be asked to direct education and social welfare. He had been very sympathetic to Collet's aspirations for reform in Seychelles. 'What a glorious Income Tax Officer he might make,' Grimble wrote, with prophetic but imperfect insight.[1] Meanwhile it was agreed that economic advance through agriculture, ideally with fishing and some tourism too, must go hand in hand with educational and social reform. The Colonial Development Fund was to be invited to provide the money required. With war intervening, a distracted London had to content itself with the pious hope that Grimble would somehow manage to get a few bricks made in spite of the prevailing shortage of straw.

Some straw was promised in the shape of Rs 251,000 to initiate the first scheme for cheap town-housing and rural resettlement ever attempted in Seychelles, but the fall of France in June 1940 threw all the burden of the war on to Britain, and it seemed unthinkable to accept the money. In Seychelles war experience had been superficial up to that point. Essentially it consisted of petrol-rationing, which sent people back to whaleboat and bullock-cart for moving produce but was fairly well accepted – 'though only one class rejoiced quite openly, the rickshaw men', as the compiler of the War Diary for 1939 commented dryly in order to relieve his yawns. On 3 September, when the declaration of war was announced, the unlucky choice of a bugle to mark the event by the Officer Commanding the newly-raised Local Defence Force reportedly gave one old lady a heart-attack and drove more nimble people helter-skelter into the mountains. Bugle-calls were the air-raid warning. Two days later a suspected German raider was sighted at sea, but when it vanished, the ship was set down instead as a smuggler – which raises the question of how much smuggling went on in peacetime, when eyes were not so attentively turned toward the sea. And on 17 September the telephone line between Victoria and the Beau Vallon defence-point was cut, leading to fines for sabotage being imposed upon two Seychellois. Countrymen of theirs were soon winning the D.F.C. and Bar as airmen, or being Mentioned in Despatches as soldiers.[2]

In the original perception of imperial war strategy, the Islands themselves called for no detailed consideration; they had minor strategic importance as a connection-point on the telegraph-cables between Zanzibar, Aden, Mauritius and Colombo. Cable and Wireless's installation on Mahé became more important after the Mediterranean cables were cut. As the war progressed, Seychelles became a focal point for monitoring shipping on passage 200 miles to the north between the Far East, Ceylon, East Africa and the Cape; and 6-700 to the west, traffic converged between the Cape and the Red Sea, and ships returned to the Far East. Hence there were a seaplane refuelling depot on St Anne; a pair of old naval 6-inch guns on Pointe Conan – appropriately christened De Quincy Battery to protect the harbour from what, at worst, would have been hit-and-run attack from the sea, since the enemy could have gained no conceivable advantage by occupying Seychelles without command of the surrounding ocean; and a garrison company from Ceylon to cover landing-places with rifles and bren guns.[3] None was ever required to fire in anger. The closest the War of 1939-45, as expressed in explosion and local death, ever touched the Islands was on 5 March 1941 when a Walrus amphibian plane from HMS *Devonshire* carrying the garrison commander caught fire while flying low to inspect De Quincy Battery's camouflage. What the real war meant outside Seychelles was brought home to families who lost members in the fighting services overseas; or when, in 1944, the administrator of Alphonse went over to Bijoutier islet in pursuance of his orders to keep copra production at around 17 tons a month and there found seven survivors from SS *Tulagi*, a Sydney-registered ship named after one of the Solomon Islands in the far Western Pacific where war was raging; she had been torpedoed by a Japanese submarine off Chagos, sixty-six days away by drifting lifeboat. By the end of the war, eighty-six Seychellois had served in the fighting services overseas, while some 854 Pioneers from Seychelles had been at work for the British Army in the Western Desert and in Italy, often under fire.[4]

The fall of France had nonetheless caused acute Anglo-Saxon apprehension in Seychelles. When the Vichy government made its decision for Hitler in June 1940, it was feared that many *grands blancs* might have liked to follow Marshal Pétain into the Führer's camp. Seychelles now had no very close connection with La Réunion, which rallied to de Gaulle; rather more with Madagascar, which followed Vichy. The French Consular Agent avoided any definite commitment. Among French citizens, only Ernest de Coulhac Mazerieux was quick to declare himself for Free France. Then fifty public servants from the old Seychellois families, led by M.-C. Nageon de l'Estang, offered an assurance of support which enabled Grimble to say gracefully that he had never doubted their loyalty:

> You have said that the France of the Pétain Government is not the France of your ancestors. I say in reply that the Pétain Government is not of France at all, and no more represents the country of your ancestors than a disease represents the victim upon which it has fallen. France will arise again, if we remain true to her.[5]

Even so, the view from Government House remained troubled on the internal security front. The Créoles were easily excited, said Grimble secretly to London, and their economic situation was deplorable. They were generally pro-British – from distrust of their employers, if from no other cause – but their lot was so hard that an agitator who cared to espouse their cause could easily work them up. The only reason why class struggle had not been politicised so far was that agitators, of whom Seychelles had their share, happened to be *grands blancs* proprietors or Anglo-Saxon exiles, all intent on attacking the government and keeping Créoles suppressed. Even that situation had its dangers, as the local government put it in a secret memorandum: 'A widely held view is that, as the "negroes" (i.e. the labouring masses) would be kept under by the Nazi régime, a German occupation of Seychelles would be an improvement upon government by the British.'[6]

Almost as blunt in Legislative Council, the Governor told members that no intrigue they could think up would make his administration recede a step from the programme of social improvement – which amounted to readjustment of taxation, small efforts in housing and some land-settlement. These efforts were the commonplace of British colonial administration in places less reactionary than Seychelles, and he warned Seychellois that they fell far short of what postwar enlightenment was going to require as a matter of course. Otherwise revolution could be expected. For instance, proposals to reintroduce the poll-tax on the poor were as politically stupid as they were inhumane. 'To these reactionaries who can devise for themselves no worthier War activity than the attempt to sabotage Democractic reforms', said the Governor, 'I have only to say that my Administration will do its utmost to protect the community against them.'[7]

This warning was directed at a new pressure group that had appeared just before the war – the Seychelles Taxpayers' Association. Its objects were to get taxation shifted from cigarettes and alcohol back on to the stock-in-trade of development like building materials and agricultural implements – and to put elected representatives into Legislative Council, with nominated members to represent those who could not aspire to the franchise because they were mostly black, poor and uneducated. No one was rich here, said this long-enduring association, except the labourer who now paid no direct taxes at all. To tax liquor was anti-social because the only social life in the Islands hung around occasional sundowner parties. As this vocabulary suggests, the original moving spirits in the Association were expatriate British, a couple of retired army officers and a remittance man or two who found the Governor without morals and the Créoles damnably idle; but the Taxpayers' Association thrived nonetheless.[8]

Although it might invite a Biblical parallel with the Lilies of the Field, if ever they had formed a Toilers' and Spinners' Guild, the Taxpayers' Association outgrew its more comic origins to become the first effective political party Seychelles had seen. Before long it comprised a great many proprietors. They were still intent on redressing what they saw as the imbalance of post-1934 policy by pushing the burden of taxation back upon the poor. Colonel

Fulton was succeeded as President by the very enterprising Seychellois entrepeneur Sydney Delorié – 'one of the bitterest enemies of liberal reform in Seychelles', according to Grimble.[9] Delorié wanted the introduction of flogging for praedial larceny; he believed that the good fortune that helped an industrious man to become well-off was bestowed by the Creator.[10] And in 1942, as though to mock Grimble, he won a vital court decision in an income tax case: even when a proprietor claimed expenses against income which were evidently disproportionate to the cost of running his estate, the learned judge ruled, the claimant's word must be accepted unless it could be proved false. Returns of income made by proprietors could often be seen at a glance to be false, but proving this was another matter.

By then the Taxpayers' Association embraced about half the larger landowners and, in all, about a quarter of the élite – but not W.F. Stephens, now Senior Unofficial Member of Legislative Council. Stephens enjoyed his open entrée to Government House. He liked to see himself as an old campaigner who had learned to know his Seychellois, and affected to find difficulty in taking the Association very seriously; the fun of sniping at government was what brought people into it, he thought, not the desire to keep government up to the mark by constructive criticism. He professed amusement when innocent Labour Members of Parliament in London allowed themselves to be put up in the Commons to beat Ministers with an anti-imperialist stick provided by the slave-drivers, as Grimble's successor Sir Marston Logan called them.[11] However, this was not funny to Grimble. The Taxpayers stalked the Governor in his nightmares. Lugubrious to the end of his seven years in Seychelles, but as a rule perfectly clear-sighted, he saw the Association as a grave social danger, 'the embodiment of every reactionary force in Seychelles', and he knew it was prepared to use any weapons to discredit an administration seeking a fairer distribution in the Islands.[12] If the Taxpayers were to be allowed elective Legislative Council seats, election must, in his view, be on adult franchise with a literacy test – but not before far-reaching educational and social reforms had produced an informed Créole electorate too. Secrecy in ballotting was impossible, and as things stood Créole votes would be bought by the Seychellois to Créoles' ultimate disadvantage, given that *grands blancs* were labelling social welfare schemes as anything from fascism to bolshevism:

I do not think that there can exist anywhere else in the British Empire an employing class so riddled with graft and corruption as that of Seychelles, or so callously determined to maintain its own privileges at the expense of the labouring masses. To introduce universal suffrage at present would be to betray the working man into hands which would use his ignorance without scruple, and his helplessness without pity, to scuttle his own chances of progress.[13]

'This mole-hill, or dunghill, of an Assocation' was what the Colonial Office accordingly called the Taxpayers,[14] but they were still a force to be reckoned with. Yet parameters in society were less firmly drawn than Grimble imagined; there was none of the outcry he expected when he appointed a Créole to Legislative Council in November 1940, for this Créole was a formal member of the Taxpayers' Association himself, the king of the Long Pier, Joachim Arissol. Born in 1888 at Anse Boileau and educated there in the nuns' primary school, he had walked across to Victoria at the age of eighteen looking for a future. Now he was chief stevedore for the Union Lighterage Co., a commanding though not big figure in a khaki suit. He would take his stick to erring labourers and spoke Créole with sharply enunciated consonants, not slurring his speech in the usual way. A cynical post-independence generation of workers remembered him in the 1970s as being like a Cabinet Minister, with the difference that help might be got from Arissol in case of need, but nothing tangible from a Minister. Arissol's membership of the Taxpayers' Association was actually not much more than window-dressing on both sides. He had not left his class. When one of his much-renewed terms on Council was up, he asked to be allowed to continue witnessing passport applications for Créoles off to seek work in Uganda:

The reason is: I am a coloured man and know the needs and mentality of the people (in a word, they do understand me), they come either to my Office or at my home and at any time to have their papers signed without waiting for long hours and same free of all charges.

His request granted, Arissol thanked the Governor for 'thereby enabling me to be always closer and closer with my Class'.[15] He was a Nominated Member of Executive Council when he died in 1953. He was needed for so long because he was almost unique in Seychelles – pure African, as the great bulk of the population still were, for all the mixing, but fluent in English and owner of a house and some acres of coconuts. He knew the limitations of his position. He was only an employee of the lighterage company, he once reminded government; ultimately, he was in the hands of *grand blanc* directors.[16]

Democratic reform was still government policy when Grimble left for the Windward Islands in 1941. Seychelles was sadly more backward in social and welfare services than any West Indian colony. The comparison was valid. So far as social make-up was concerned, Seychelles were part of the West Indies lost in the Indian Ocean. Justice and policy both demanded rapid social reform. The problem for the Colonial Office and for Grimble's successor Sir Marston Logan was how to keep the re-styled Planters' and Taxpayers' Association in step. It would have been impossible to ignore them, as the dominant minority who owned 90 per cent of property, without causing a revolution in a way that would have been outside all Colonial Office tradition.

The Taxpayers, with their desire for elections on a narrow, property-based franchise, were told that elections would not yet be in the interests of the people – meaning Créoles; they came back to ask that the *principle* of elections be recognised at once and put into effect after the war; and Logan, no fire-eater as a Governor, could not well see how they could be denied this. The present quiet meetings of Legislative Council twice a year for two or three hours in a morning, with all three Unofficials sitting on the Finance Committee, might reasonably be taken as indicating cordial concurrence with the colonial government but were actually interpreted by Seychellois as subservience on Unofficial members' part, the price of their nominations. Denial of elected representation for the often undoubtedly sophisticated Seychellois families was deeply resented.[17] The spirit of the age did not approve it. Unofficial membership should at any rate be increased to five, the Colonial Office agreed, with one of the new members to be if possible a Créole. Decision on the principle of elections had better await a visit from the permanent Under-Secretary of State, Sir Cosmo Parkinson. Accordingly this most bland of mandarins spent fifteen days between steamers in October–November

1943, listening to a dull sermon from Archdeacon Sole and canvassing the opinion of notables.[18]

Parkinson found it a gloomy scene. Where were the leaders? Stephens had paid for his intimacy with governors by isolation from most other people; the voice of Touris was always expected to be heard on the labourers' side but he had virtually retired to Cerf; and Arissol seemed to represent nobody, although his views were cogent. He wanted education for the Créoles before constitutional changes were made, five members all nominated, close government inspection of schools while retaining church control, development of a fishing industry geared to export so long as a canning factory went with it; and on the question of union with racist Kenya, for which the Taxpayers led by their British contingent were significantly agitating, Arissol wanted it only as an outlet for surplus population.

It was the Planters and Taxpayers who, having the St Louis-educated leadership, wielded the political clout. Led by Paul Lanier, Edouard's younger brother, 140 of them met Parkinson claiming that they represented 7,000 people, although the actual electorate they foresaw was only 2,000 on an income-based franchise. They lived up to Grimble's image of them by attacking the estates purchased by government for labourers' settlements; such valuable land would be better in private hands, they said. Besides, the estates were competing unfairly with proprietors by providing cheap food and amentities for labourers out of profits.[19] This all confirmed what the Colonial Office had heard on 30 June 1943 when that indefatigible lobbyist Charles E. Collet called, in company with a fellow committee member of the Aborigines' Protection Society and a Member of Parliament, to present a programme for Seychelles: redistribution of estates in order to break the proprietors' monopoly of labour-opportunities; use of Colonial Development and Welfare funds to buy more land for smallholdings; and rejection of the scheme to fuse Seychelles with Kenya. 'It will not be for the benefit of the 29,600 dumb black people of Seychelles that the 400 others are clamouring for this union,' said Collet who plainly led the delegation. As was soon to be amply demonstrated to Parkinson too, the Créoles' dumbness was a particular concern with Collet. According to his experience, the poor could only make their way in the world with education. This would never happen through the Church, and therefore he wanted a model government school, with all teaching in English.

> In spite of the highly vocal *small minority* strongly supported by the priests, who speak French, mostly debased French, the French language is *not* the language of the people, i.e. of the 29,750 (out of 30,000) who speak a very limited patois with a vocabulary which scarcely exceeds three or four hundred words. The only practicable solution is to make *English* and English only compulsory in the primary schools.[20]

Collet wanted sex education too. The Church now forbade it, drawing away from the idea of advising treatment for the venereal diseases so prevalent in Seychelles, and still more averse to instruction on the means of avoidance. As things now stood, the first infection was regarded by boys as a badge of initiation.[21] If there were to be constitutional change at last, said Collet, let enough power be reserved to the Governor to prevent control passing to proprietors until Créoles, through education, were able to fend for themselves.

Even so, pressure from *grands blancs* in favour of immediate elections was hard to withstand. In cabled exchanges between Logan and London, it was agreed that there should be three Elected and three Nominated members in Legislative Council, with the Governor holding the casting vote from among the ranks of his own six Official members. However, when the franchise was determined, the Colonial Office insisted on literacy being made alternative to a property qualification; the expectation in Whitehall was that literacy would become the sole condition for a vote when the revolution now projected in education had begun to show its effect.[22]

Education itself would have to undergo a very real revolution. This had just been re-emphasised in private letters to the Colonial Office from the first Director of Education, C.B. Smith. The Marist Brothers had lost touch with trends in education and gone in for simple cramming, he wrote. 'There is a strong colour bar. The native is only what the French settler element has made him and the contempt of the latter for the former is really shocking.' Only promising pupils received attention; with 400 boys at St Louis, a mere forty reached Junior Cambridge standard. Only virtual certainties were allowed to sit the examination, after intensive coaching with trial papers.[23] None of this meant that St Louis' best ex-pupils did not do well overseas; it was a far better school than any of the Anglican ones. But the boys at St Louis were nearly all white, whereas those at the Anglican Victoria School were mostly black, with little hope of studying abroad. This colour question was raised by the Bishop and not the Brothers, who did not care what colour their pupils were. When government made scholarships to St Louis available to Victoria School boys at the beginning of 1944, Brother-Director Gérard was attacked by the Bishop's educational secretary for filling St Louis with Créole boys. Quite untrue, replied Brother Gérard; he had taken only four black boys; but what if it were true?

> For the Government there does not seem to exist any colour-bar. At least it does not show it. We have to accept any boy, no matter of what colour, the moment he wins the scholarship. Before God all men are equal no matter of what colour their skin is. I wonder why some of the Mission have always to find fault with the few dark-skinned boys that are at the College?[24]

They remained few, the Bishop forcing the Brother-Director to discover that he had no room for the scholarship boys, in much the same way that, as Bishop Maradon did not mind announcing, he had taken care that nothing should come of Smith's aspirations towards modernity in education. A Catholic himself, Smith had been open to threats of excommunication, but from the safety of Oxford he felt free to call the Bishop 'a very proud and pompous young man' who was not above abusing the power of the Church to achieve his own ends. The Bishop might have replied that his ends were those of the Church; and he did often say that the Church had done much for education. He held it to be an unjust disregard of the Church's rights that it had only an equal two members on the education board when it owned twenty-one (four-fifths) of the schools. Each of the primaries was under the management of the parish priest, and if a nun was not actually the head teacher, it was at least in the care of a pious lady who regarded herself as the priest's servant, and did not know what short skirts or nocturnal picnics were, but sedulously gave her pupils an hour's religious instruction every school-day and would never promote them to Standard Three until they could read French fluently. The older children, or a selected few, were in the care of the Brothers who had educated almost the entire

Seychellois élite. And all this at an expense to the Church of Rs 51,908 for primaries alone, to take 1941 as a specimen year. The Government, with its Rs 38,276, was paying less even than in 1915.[25]

When the Bishop was asked whether bad relations between Marists and Capuchins did not damage education, he replied that this was purely a domestic matter. He was angrier still when he learned that Cardinal Hinsley's damning reports of 1933–4 on the College had been leaked to impious laity. And when it was put to the Bishop that more primary children, Créoles, might get to Standard Three if they were taught fluency in English rather than French, when it was even hinted that Créoles identified French as the language of oppression, he replied that the Catholic faith to which most of the people belonged was too closely linked to the French language for English to replace it. He seemed proud of his rundown primary schools with their bored children and untrained, underpaid, browbeaten teachers. Let Holy Church's great sacrifices for education no longer be recognised merely with kind words, he demanded in May 1943; let government pay all the primary teachers, giving the Church a quarter of the rental value of its schools and a grant for each child. As for the Teachers' Training College that government wanted, holding in its modern fashion that teachers' piety should cease to outweigh their ability to give intelligent instruction, government must assuredly pay for such a college but the Bishop would naturally keep so formative an institution under his own control. As the Secretary to Government summed up his view, 'There seems to be an impression that a splendid job of work has been done & all "*nous autres*" need do is: cheer, wave our hats, & pay!'[26]

That prospect also did not appeal to many of the Bishop's flock, who were doing some of the paying. Even *grands blancs* were in revolt against the Church's stranglehold, the men at any rate. A government secondary school was needed now as it had been for years before, as R. Morel Duboil, a member of the Legislative Council, insisted. It should be for every class and creed, a manly school without piety. Why had government not acted? 'It took years for Mr Smith to do ... nothing? Nay: he filed a report.' But even without being pressed, M. Morel admitted that the King's College debacle might easily be repeated. If government went ahead with a neutral secondary school, there was still no guarantee that children would not be barred from it by 'clerical domination' over mothers. These ladies' exemplar, the gentle Mother Superior, told a meeting of the Education Board in October 1943 that with government money she would like to start one of those useful homebuilding things, a domestic centre – for white children, of course, although it ultimately proved that such a centre was regarded as an insult to white Seychellois.[28] That meeting had been called to enlighten an educational adviser on one of those flying visits from the Colonial Office. He received a petition, redolent of views held by a few old King's College boys among *grands blancs*, demanding the Church's complete withdrawal from education unless it would accept secular control, secondary teaching entirely in English, and safeguards to prevent victimisation of children whose parents spoke out against the Church. The Colonial Office man heard the Bishop in his turn, and then sent an urgent cable to London. Everything that had been said against education in Seychelles was true, he reported. A new system of education, humane and universal, would be essential if post-war Seychelles were to be part of the modern world. For this money would be needed, and it would have to be administered by a senior educationalist full of ability and tact.[29]

In June 1944 a communist arrived instead – this was how the Church saw the new Director of Education. In fact W.W.E. Giles, who held the post in 1944-8, became president of a local branch of the Conservative Party after retiring to his native Norfolk to open a prep school, bruised from his efforts to provide Seychelles with democratic education. Giles was an Oxford graduate, and his wife had been Gilchrist Scholar there in French before studying in Lausanne and at the Sorbonne; they were the best-equipped couple the Colony had ever seen, theoretically sophisticated but very practical educationalists. Their viewpoint was much like that enshrined in the British Education Act of 1944, with its emphasis on free-ranging, rounded learning. And when, as government censor, Mr Giles opened letters sent overseas, he did not fail to note when he intercepted a Capuchin writing to a fellow priest abroad that echoes of this unhappy statute were finding too willing ears in Seychelles.[30]

On his own professional ground, Giles was not patient or tactful. He knew very well how much the Marist Brothers themselves disliked the priests, and had no opinion of the Brothers' own scholarship. He saw no good reason why he as Director of Education should wait, cap in hand, upon the Bishop to discuss staffing or curriculum, or why he should listen unmoved to the Bishop as he congratulated himself on his evident victory over Smith. The primary schools with their exploited female teachers saw no further than grammar and arithmetic, taught by the most antiquated methods. Children left in droves. There were no handicrafts, no physical training, hardly any games. Unless the colonial government was prepared to go in for improved modern education, effective social welfare schemes and an articulated plan aimed at the total modernisation of society in Seychelles, it might as well shut up shop. Plainly education was being denied to the great majority of the population in order to maintain a plentiful supply of labour. St Louis was visited by Mr and Mrs Giles in unconciliatory tandem –' *une affaire familiale* ', the affronted Brothers termed this, in derision –and was found wanting in its staff's professional qualifications to teach, in its method, in its devoting six and quarter hours a week to religious instruction in addition to the daily mass, and above all in its élitist philosophy.

For Giles a school did not exist for the sake of a few selected pupils;[31] his aspiration was efficient modern education for all classes and colours. The schools were to act as community centres too, with play centres for children under six, primary schools for the six-to-twelve age-group and modern schools for those aged twelve to fifteen. The College and Convent were to be brought up to grammar school level. All was to be under the control not of the Bishop but of the Director of Education, whose particular weapon was going to be a Teachers' Training College with a secular atmosphere and professional standards. Couple all this with English as the teaching medium, and the picture became at least as gloomy for the Bishop as he could ever have anticipated. Secular secondary education apart, his worry was the Training College – he was capable of employing a pious housemaid in preference to the only trained teacher at his disposal. Certainly a government training centre would not produce Catholic teachers in, as he said, the true and full meaning of the word. As for the language, he saw no merit in teaching English to labourers' children who would never find any use for it in their predestinedly narrow world.[32] And he could talk of little else but the rights of his Church and the need to respect them under the new education ordinance being drawn up by Giles, who could see fewer rights involved than duties, mainly secular ones.

The Bishop especially insisted on his managers' right to dismiss a teacher for deficiencies in the giving of religious instruction, without reference to anybody but God. He agreed in the end to the ordinance with its provision for the Director's wide-ranging control, but only because he wanted government's development funds, and knew that ordinances were so much paper while the Church was eternal. Shy and uncertain in the eyes of his friends, the Bishop was adept at agreeing face to face and then announcing by letter that he had not understood, had made a mental reservation, and wished the whole matter reopened. Giles concluded after a few months' experience that neither black nor white would get a fair deal in education so long as Bishop Maradon remained in Seychelles. The Islands were a religious colony, so far as the schools were concerned, yet verging on the degenerate. Giles had seen exasperated nuns in the primary schools cuffing small Créoles. Nuns were driven to depair because they did not understand what a decent school could be, and yet they held all but two of the highest-paid posts in the primary schools. No Seychellois at all was employed teaching in the College or the Convent. The bursaries had failed to put Créole children from the country schools into either of these unwelcoming white preserves. Even when Créole children could get the necessary testimonials from their parish priests, once at College or Convent they received none of the extra coaching that bright white children could expect.[33]

Let the Capuchins be packed off home, urged Giles at the beginning of 1945; they were a commercially-minded Mission who by virtue of ecclesiastical privilege were exempt from income tax and had used their profits to carry even further their domination over the Colony. The education ordinance was flouted. Petty obstacles were invented. The sisters, inspired by their spiritual fathers, had begun the 1945 school year by finding it necessary to throw parents' arrangements into disarray by turning their boarders' dormitory into a classroom. Parents were fighting back; a petition was circulating among the Planters and Taxpayers themselves for the removal of the Mission. Surely that would get the Secretary of State to act?[34] The Secretary of State was being urged to do this by Giles and the Chief Justice, who was Administrator in Sir Marston Logan's absence on leave; but Logan, consulted from

Whitehall in the natural course, plainly wondered whether he could ever dare to go on leave again. The Swiss monks might be bigoted, seditious, over-wealthy and on bad terms with many of the leading families – they had never had many defenders; but one supporter they could count on was among the ablest of the *grands blancs*, the manager of Outer Islands, mainstay of the widely circulating *Action Catholique* and sometime President of the Tax-payers, Marcel Lemarchand.

'Monsieur Marcel' was too formidable to be taken on by Logan, a gentle old fellow who had been promoted Governor near the end of his career. After less than a year in Seychelles, Giles himself was not aware of how volatile opinion there could be. A few months more and he began to realise that, whatever they said, a good many Seychellois would support the Mission for the sake of preserving their own supremacy at the expense of the Créoles.[35] As Logan saw it, a better way than frontal assault would be to get the Holy See itself to replace Maradon with a more worldly British bishop. This had been suggested by the Catholic Primate in Britain, who accordingly paid a call on the Apostolic Delegate with Logan and the Colonial Office's resident educational specialist, who had not forgotten what he saw in Seychelles two years before, and these two came away with the feeling that both prelates would be glad to see the Swiss Capuchins as far away from Seychelles as the Director of Education could wish them to be.

Actually to achieve this through papal channels was another matter; it was not achieved, although the hierarchy did toy with the idea of sending Anglo-Irish Capuchins in place of the Swiss. Meanwhile the Primate did not doubt that his brother in Seychelles had received a rap over the knuckles from Rome.[36] Bishop Maradon left Seychelles in a flurry in June 1945, then unexpectedly came back a week later by flying-boat with Father McCarthy, Acting Apostolic Delegate to Tanganyika. Giles had known him there and had a favourable opinion of him. And before they left again on 29 June, Bishop Maradon signed an agreement with Giles – with such emotion that he left his own copy behind at Government House. Time devoted to religious instruction was to be reduced; an English priest qualified in education was to replace the Bishop's present rather sinister *éminence rousse* as education secretary; English was to be taught from the start and made the medium of instruction as soon as possible; the Mission was to rebuild school-buildings on the education department's model, with government meeting half the cost; government was to build and maintain all new schools, the Mission being free to establish new ones at half its own cost; the Mission was to raise no objection to government paying all the salaries of teachers, who were to be appointed by the Director on the recommendation of a board composed of himself, the Bishop and the Anglican Archdeacon; the modern schools and play centres were to be established by government, the Convent to be rebuilt at joint cost on land provided free by the Mission, with British nuns qualified to teach, and freedom of admission without distinction of religion or race; and government was to build a new boys' secondary school – a tree having fallen on ramshackle St Louis. The new St Louis would be run by the Director, the Bishop, the Archdeacon and three nominees, and staffed by Marists or a similar Brotherhood so long as its members were British subjects and qualified to teach. Religious instruction of any approved persuasion was to be permitted at both the Convent and St Louis.[37]

'Thanks God Father McCarthy could come over,' wrote the Bishop in his faulty English to Giles before leaving to find better-qualified Marist Brothers or an entirely new Order to teach the Seychellois élite, as he put it. Certainly Father McCarthy had done pretty well. Giles indicated as much to the returned Sir Marston Logan, who was horrified, easygoing as he was, to find his Director of Education not really satisfied with the compromise. Giles would have preferred full public ownership of the schools, with the boys' secondary school staffed by secular, graduate masters from the Colonial Education Service.[38] Having given way to Holy Church's alleged rights in these fairly vital areas, Giles found points actually conceded by the Bishop being contested by his coadjutor Father Maurice. In this rearguard action, Father Maurice secured a triumph of discipline over conviction in Brother-Director Gérard by getting the Marist to tie himself up in logical knots to help save the Church and the Bishop.[39] For Brother Gérard now hated the Bishop as much as a good religious could hate any man. Gérard was tired of teaching at St Louis anyway, tired of the monotony and poverty – he even had to justify to his own superiors the possession of a bicycle. He was lonely and miserable, and seized on the agreement between Bishop and Director of Education as a pretext to get himself and his fellow-Marists away from Seychelles.[40]

Their pride prevented their remaining to teach primary children only, as they were qualified to do; and their mother-house could find no educationally-qualified British Marists to augment them in the secondary school in the way the agreement required; nor could the Marist congregations in Australia and New Zealand, who were appealed to by Maradon.

The Bishop was desperate to make sure that the new boys' secondary school remained in the hands of a Catholic teaching order – he was not so desperate to keep the Marists, whom he suspected of treachery. That suspicion can be seen as a natural defence mechanism against the implications of his recognition that the Brothers were greatly loved in Seychelles even while the laity found their educational services wanting in many ways. In public, though, the Brothers like all of the Mission found it more convenient to go along with the inspired propaganda of *Action Catholique* which found it necessary to blame the Bishop's co-signatory, the Director of Education. The success of this manoeuvre showed that Logan really knew his Seychelles. Sixty-seven years of devoted service by the Brothers was being rewarded with their expulsion at the whim of the state – such was the accepted but untruthful refrain. '*C'était jolie, ça!*' The Brothers did not leave at the behest of the Mission, said *Action Catholique*, adding the following in italics to remove all doubt: '*Les chers Frères quittent la Colonie à cause des exigences irréalisables du Directeur de l'Education.*' Even so, when Brother Gérard called to ask the Bishop for his fatherly blessing, Maradon gave it but said he hoped it would not turn out a curse.[41]

The Marists left early in 1946 amid lamentations from Seychellois, who were told by the Church that it would have been better if the Director of Education had been sent off to England instead, preferably in a leaky pirogue. A new King's College had to be started in the Brothers' wake, and it would have been kept going indefinitely if people like Charles Collet could have made their preference prevail, with British graduates from the Colonial Education Service to run it until there were educated Seychellois to take over.[42] However, the Church still knew its rights, and sent the Apostolic Delegate from Mombasa to negotiate the arrival in Seychelles in 1950 of another teaching order, the Ploermel Brothers, not all of whom would have met the high professional standards required by Giles. His standards were more than Seychelles could afford. As Giles saw it, Seychelles College – as the new King's was renamed in deference to Catholic feeling – was to be the principal motor for social and economic progress in association with the Ten-Year Development Plan launched in 1946. Education aimed to achieve all-round spiritual, mental, physical and moral regeneration through the schools – not such a visionary aim, since 35 per cent of the population were under fifteen years old – at an estimated cost of £162,496 in capital expenditure and £349,810 recurrent over the ten years. Government proposed that Seychelles would find £35,000 for buildings and £100,000 of the running costs, while the rest would come from Colonial Development and Welfare funds.[43] This was too much for both the funds and the Colony, the Colonial Office objected; so ambitious an educational scheme would cost the Islands £40,000 a year to maintain unaided after the ten-year period till 1956, which would probably be beyond their resources. Reluctantly Giles cut back to £71,641 in capital costs and £163,360 recurrent for the first ten years, £100,000 of the total to come from Development and Welfare funds. The cuts were significant, and the decision to do away with the Training College in favour of pupil-teacher training went a long way towards wrecking the plan. The Education Department found itself faced with teachers who could not construct accurate simple sentences in either French or English, put a question or express an idea, and neither knew anything of the world outside Seychelles nor realised how dismal their predicament was.[44]

It was not difficult to foresee the objections even to this much expenditure on education that Sydney Delorié was to voice in *Le Seychellois*, organ of the renamed Taxpayers' and Landowners' Association, on 24 January 1953. As he saw it, expensive provision had been made for the education of Créole children who would otherwise have been at work for the proprietors – and when the black children did finally leave school they were as incompetent as they were insolent. To force education on them was to oppose the design of the Creator, who had expressly made them to serve the higher classes; to do this at considerable cost with no result was to compound the sin. Nor was it surprising, in the shorter run, that when Giles unexpectedly descended on Cascade primary school he should have found the timetable upset, with parties of little Créoles being carted off to church for confession; and that the Bishop should find the idea of the sexes sharing the same

classes in the modern schools inconsistent with the Catholic viewpoint. Sex education by the Education Department was clearly a
plan to sully the pure minds of the children.[45]

An improbable but revealing row erupted over the department's
attempt to teach domestic science to convent girls. In May 1948
nine of them suddenly refused to attend after being told by the
étrangère from England who was teaching them that they were
better fitted to cook in a garden than a kitchen; this unhappy
comment brought down the wrath of parents, who resented the
insult of their daughters being taught servants' work anyway. The
Mother Superior agreed with them, and objected to her girls
going off to the amoral Education Department to be taught who
knew what in addition to how to clean fish. In face of her meek
insolence and quiet stirring among the parents, the Director of
Education rather lost his head. And the Bishop discovered that
he had made a mental reservation when he agreed the course
should be compulsory; he was worried lest some of the truths
taught at the department might be subversive of Scripture. Parents
gathered; Captain Voss from Yorkshire shouted that Giles was
trying to turn these fine white girls into natives, and another
father, from a minor Seychellois family, explained to the Governor
himself that his own daughter might become a housewife or a
nun, but either way, having servants, she could make no use of
'domestic science'. If the unfortunate subject had to be approached
at all, Church and parents agreed, let it be done quietly, within
the decent confines of the convent, by a nun who would respect
class feeling.[46] So it was agreed and Giles left soon afterwards,
hustled away by a new Governor who had his hands so full with
the Planters' and Taxpayers' Association that he preferred to conciliate the Bishop with cigars, apples, a propelling pencil and a
sacrificial departmental head.[47]

Dr Percy Selwyn Selwyn-Clarke, who succeeded Sir Marston
Logan as Governor in 1947, knew well that Giles was no communist
but a good Conservative. Selwyn-Clarke himself, by contrast, was
a Fabian and an emissary of the postwar ruling Labour Party. Sent
to press on with restructuring social values, he had ears for only
one adviser, a fellow-Quaker Charles E. Collet.

A Soungoula had come back to instruct as well as entertain, and
professionally he was well trained, but he came with far less goodwill

than Soungoula the trickster of pre-emancipation days, as well as being much better equipped. Collet, as we saw above, had been called to the Bar in 1943, and with his French wife, also a barrister, he opened practice in Seychelles late in 1946 and made his presence felt. As a Quaker, he offered the local Carnegie Library a subscription to the *Friend* to offset Catholic journals there – 'among them a well-known cryptofascist paper', as he said. He wanted the monumental Bible removed from the table on to the shelves in its proper place alongside the Koran, and demanded the sane ecumenical journals so much needed 'in this superstitious, priest-ridden country'.[48] However, he had little talent for alliances, and savaged Wilfred Giles, who agreed with him wholeheartedly about the priests, over an imagined slight. Collet was painfully thin-skinned, and he resented *étrangers* quite as much as might any *grand blanc*. Middle-aged, hungry for power and full of resentment against Seychellois who he believed had robbed him of his right to scholarships in his youth, he was easily recognised as a legal bully.

Big cases meant big fees, for which after the lean years he was hungry too. As counsel for merchants he appealed successfully against revised income and excess-profits tax assessments; and he acted for the Chamber of Commerce when it sued Arissol for saying in Legislative Council that merchants had imposed slow agony on the poor by following their usual practice after a war – closing their shops in protest against price-control, they said they did this in the interests of the consumer. That case went to the Privy Council where Collet lost it – as he lost many of the cases he appealed;[49] in his eyes Arissol was no doubt a compromised establishment figure. Collet amused himself at the expense of others of the old guard. His car – and he had more than one, with a driver too, although he had once rightly said that cars should never have been allowed on the Island – was inconvenienced by a badly contoured corner near the house he rented at Beau Vallon; and so he proposed to sue the President of the North Mahé Local Board, who happened to be W.F. Stephens.[50] When the Ten Year Development Plan was being drawn up, to spend £250,000 of Colonial Development and Welfare Fund money on roads, health, and fishing, as well as education, Collet organised a question in the House of Commons on the composition of the planning committee.

Effective representatives of his submerged nine-tenths were needed, Collet felt, when the Planters and Taxpayers, whose own representatives thronged the committee, had just resolved to demand a head-tax of Rs 6 for every estate-labourer and Rs 12 for every Créole *out* of employment.[51] Collet sought recognition and money for himself, but also opportunities for others of his own colour, and he found Governor and Colonial Office of the same view. For Seychelles the time of postwar reckoning promised by Grimble was at hand. It came like a whirlwind because the new Governor was an inspired amateur with a dream of fast social and political progress. The fact that Selwyn-Clarke had never governed a Colony before but only run colonial medical departments freed him from some of the constraints which career governors were prone to feel. His experience in Hong Kong during the war, when he had outfaced the Japanese to maintain essential medical services until they jailed him, made him feel that he could deal with almost anything that came his way. Certainly no Seychellois could frighten him, when the Japanese had failed even though they twice made him face a firing-squad. 'Forty-four months under the heel of the Japanese, much of it in a dark cell in solitary confinement when not actually being "interrogated", is something of a testing time,' as he said.[52] Perhaps it was not the most relevant of experiences for his present task, all the same, although the more open-minded of his opponents among Seychellois remembered him long afterwards as a man of merit personally.

As much subtlety as straight courage was needed in Seychelles. Selwyn-Clarke intended to bring Seychellois and Créoles into the modern world as he, a socialist, thought the post-war world should be, even if that meant reciting to Legislative Council what the American Declaration of Rights had to say about the self-evidence of inalienable rights in all men. Who better to help him than a particularly distinguished son of Seychelles who happened to belong to the underprivileged majority? On the evening of 15 July 1947, the month of his arrival, he had the Collets to Government House and outlined his programme. Next day Charles Collet confirmed his support. He was willing to be Chief Justice if the salary were increased, he said – which was cool for a barrister of less than four years' standing, however much his example had transformed the easygoing local Bar. He became Acting Attorney-General instead. His wife was nominated to Legislative Council so that they could sit there together *pour épater les grands blancs* with Europe's advanced views. Charles Collet emphasised that he was coming into government only so as not to let Selwyn-Clarke down; he was giving up independence achieved through years of hard struggle; so conscious was he of this that he could not quite bring himself to make the sacrifice but laid himself open to attack by keeping up private cases.[53]

New and progressive legislation was one result of Collet's appointment, startling to what Selwyn-Clarke with uncharacteristic restraint called 'this beautiful but old-fashioned little country' when he addressed his first Legislative Council meeting in September 1947. His new Attorney-General was going to transform Seychelles with splendid modern laws giving married women property-rights, for instance – in the teeth of (in Collet's phrase) 'the Corsican woman-hater', whose sacred Napoleonic Civil Code vested property a woman brought to marriage in the husband unless a separate contract was drawn up.[54] There was a bill providing for a public notary, and proposals to buy out the existing notaries at a price computed from their income-tax returns – a good bargain for government, said Collet, since they had all been cooking their tax returns magnificently for years.[55] A new Penal Code was proposed, to replace the present patchwork derived from the French Code of 1804, bits of English law, and importations from the British Indian Penal Code. 'There is no reason why Seychelles should not be a pioneer colony in law reform!', said Selwyn-Clarke when he saw Collet's draft. It reduced incest, sodomy and indecent assault to what Collet thought was their proper perspective as pathological manifestations rather than crimes.[56] But all this was rather advanced for the Seychellois, who did not want to be pioneers in these fields. Mr Stephens was startled, and the Planters and Taxpayers felt that any rejection of Napoleon was an insult to their heritage, a threat to their French personality.

'Seychellois', they called it now, but its roots were in France of more than a century before 1945. On married women's rights, the very foundations of society were being undermined. Identities were reasserted in the manner of a hundred years before, as the postwar constitutional pace down the socialist path quickened. There was talk of tradition and the rights of property; there were assertions of the right to continued supremacy which proprietors, quite without foundation in history or constitutional law, somehow felt they derived from the articles of Mauritius's capitulation in 1810. Slaves had not been prominent except as legal property. With the principle of elections to Legislative Council agreed, but drafting held up by Britain's preoccupation with the negotiations for India's independence, the Planters and Taxpayers were declining to accept nomination. They would not sit in the council chamber until they could do so triumphantly as elected members on a carefully limited franchise.[57] Selwyn-Clarke thought that they should aim at universal adult suffrage, with self-government a short distance around the corner. For the moment four members should be elected and two nominated, as he got London to agree; elected local bodies should be rapidly set up to serve as the base of the self-government triangle – nurseries of politicians for Legislative Council, which was the apex. The franchise would currently have to be restricted to those paying tax on income of Rs 500 and able to write their name. He counselled patience, when Collet's newly-launched Seychelles Progressive Association protested that this would mean only 1,800-2,000 voters in a population of 36,000. Any radical change in the Bill would postpone electoral reform still further; little by little, Selwyn-Clarke believed, universal adult suffrage would certainly be achieved.[58]

Paul Lanier insisted on behalf of the Planters and Taxpayers that at least two members elected on the existing franchise should sit on Executive Council. Let people educated to Standard VI vote, even if they paid no direct tax; let French be allowed in debate; let the Legislative Council not be dissolved by an outflanked Governor without first obtaining the consent of the Secretary of State himself. At a joint meeting of the Legislative and Executive Councils, Unofficial members in panic pressed for an elected Unofficial majority in both councils under a revised constitution at the earliest possible time. This was in reaction against the appointment of Collet, whom they wanted to muzzle. Collet agreed all the same – provided that this step toward immediate self-government was accompanied by universal adult suffrage, so that the Legislative Council would cease to be the preserve of the propertied.[59] His known aspirations and the horror of propertied people at what they believed would result were one cause for alarm; another was that he was making people pay their taxes.

Very few had ever taken income tax seriously before; that was no part of Seychellois identity, when the government was still essentially a foreign one. In 1945 the simple Anglo-Saxon W.F. Stephens paid a tenth of the total income and excess profits taxes received by government, although he generated only 1 per cent of produce exported.[60] Seychellois proprietors declared their incomes on the dishonour system and paid a pittance as an act of grace while the Seychellois Chief Inland Revenue Officer conveniently lost many returns. He was retired, and an elderly man of straw appointed in his place. Effectively the post was taken by Collet, who delighted in smiting those he regarded as his class-, even his race-enemies, hip, thigh and in pocket. He went so far as to claim twenty years' back taxes, in defiance of the specific legislation, on the grounds that taxes were a simple debt recoverable under the Civil Code; and backed it up with promises of ruin at interviews with proprietors, during which he confronted them with their known style of life and browbeat them into offers to compound their debt to the public purse. Sydney Delorié was among the first to come to grief. In recompense for the tax case of 1942 whose outcome had in effect allowed him to pay as much or as little tax as he pleased, his pockets were searched in the street and his property was attached. He promised that before he let himself be ruined he would literally blow Collet up – and complained that Collet was so proud that he was not frightened. In the end he agree to pay Rs 40,000 if another Rs 58,757 which Collet's guesswork reckoned to be due were overlooked.[61]

This became the pattern, and most proprietors and professional men submitted to it. A gleeful notice posted all over town announced that in two months eight big proprietors had been forced to pay out Rs 140,000. Their signed acknowledgments of guilt were on file. One of the notaries complained miserably that by the written confession extorted from him he was 'a self-confessed deceitful fellow and a cheat'.[62] An Island owner, renowned for the heroic fruitfulness of his widespread amours, as befitted a son of Edouard Lanier, offered a compromise while pleading his many innocent dependants and the false sense of security into which he, like so many others, had been lulled by the incapacity of taxgatherers in the past.[63]

When people less philosophical, or with more to lose, demanded time to consult lawyers from overseas, Collet solemnly referred them instead to his own wife. Hers were the only professional services available. Lawyer Loizeau was suspended on charges of professional misconduct, laid by Collet to avenge his long-dead friend Arthur Brooke; and the other barrister, who was to be the first Q.C. of Seychelles, had paid over Rs 35,000 and then discovered an urgent need to take a holiday by one of those steamers that only stopped in Seychelles with 'fretful reluctance' – this was how British India's timetable struck the London *Daily Express* foreign correspondent James Cameron on his arrival in 1949. Cameron was thus marooned for much longer than he had originally intended to spend looking into Charles Collet's *règne de terreur* – as the Seychellois long called this era – and he went fishing a good deal with Harry Savy of Frégate. Cameron's reports were too strong for the *Daily Express*. He captured the atmosphere of Seychelles beautifully – the interminable miles of ocean making up Mahé's world from the top of Morne Seychellois; the straw-hatted men drifting back for endless talk under the sangdragon trees at Gordon Square in Port Victoria when the steamer had gone; the endless chewing upon stale news – 'I feel I am constantly on the verge of being given the news of the Battle of Waterloo'; and all around, the social pyramid typical of small tropical island colonies.

Labourers, at the bottom, were now on Rs 12 or twenty-four shillings a month; and at the top, selling copra for £50 a ton in the postwar boom, were the *grands blancs*, 'a quaint name for these simple, narrow French Bourgeoisie'. In them the ingrown parochialism and intense selfishness characteristic of colonial élites seemed to reach apotheosis. To the well-travelled Cameron, the *grands blancs* were 'a charming and hospitable people, insulated so long and by such vast distances from every liberal trend, every humanistic development, that their political attitude is almost medieval'.[64]

Neo-medievalism, as some parts of the postwar world saw it, was maintained in 1948 as the first Legislative Council elections approached. The Planters' and Taxpayers' Association actually watched the electoral roll to ensure that no illiterate, unpropertied people managed to get on to it. This involved visits to Praslin where young Arthur Savy, a tennis professional in France before the War and concentration-camp inmate during it, had so far forgotten his inherited obligations that he had joined the Progressives, rubbing shoulders with the Indian, Chinese and Persian merchants who mainly composed its active members, and wangling votes for Créoles.[65]

An eye had to be kept on government too, for it was swelling the roll through broadcasts and speeches, and by giving Seychellois civil servants a half-day's holiday to register. Some of them testified to the resentment in the community by remarking that they could not answer for their wives' registering, now that these former chattels were no longer subject to marital discipline.[66] When the question of elections to the Praslin District Council came up, the Association recognised a matter of life and death. This, the first of the local councils set up under a local government bill designed by Collet, was elected on adult suffrage with only the simplest literacy test. *Grands blancs* had, as they said, to face the danger of the labouring population coming to power[67] and Praslin becoming a nursery for radicals.

Radicals did badly in the Legislative Council elections, as the nerve of the few prominent people among the Progressives seemed to fail them. Only the Taxpayers' able secretary, Gustave de Comarmond, was given a run for his money in an 89 per cent poll on Praslin and La Digue, by Arthur Savy; in South Mahé Alexandre Deltel was returned unopposed; so were Jean-Baptiste Beauclerc Benoiton for North and Marcel Lemarchand for Central. All four were Planters and Taxpayers, all had campaigned as being '100 per cent Seychellois', dedicated to the maintenance of '*nos traditions et nos coutumes*' – among which was certainly not the trades union that Collet was suspected of planning to set up on his return from a trip to Europe. They also wanted a produce-stabilisation fund, improved inter-island communication, a doctor back at Anse Royale to cure the monied instead of Selwyn-Clarke's emphasis on preventive medicine for everybody; they sought better teaching of French in the schools, preference for Seychellois in every post except that of Chief Justice, reduced taxes....[68] And while they prepared fiery patriotic speeches to reaffirm Seychellois values during the opening session in November 1948, government was beginning to lick wounds resulting from a monumental backfire in Collet's income tax crusade.

Absolutely secure in Selwyn-Clarke's confidence, a living symbol of wrongs to be righted, Collet had prosecuted proprietors who refused to compound. In court before the weak Acting Chief Justice J.V. Homer-Vanniasinkam (from Ceylon), Collet behaved in the manner that the cur had proposed to adopt towards the mouse in *Alice in Wonderland*: ' "I'll be judge, I'll be jury", said cunning old Fury, "I'll try the whole cause, and condemn you to death".' And when poor, bullied Vanniasinkam, not long for this world, began finding instead for the defendants after they brought in the redoubtable Maître Gellé from Mauritius, Selwyn-Clarke protected Collet from the consequences of abusing Vanniasinkam. Concerned to the bitter end that Seychelles should not lose Collet's great ability, Selwyn-Clarke even wanted to give the Collets the benefit of a barely-existent doubt when Joseph Albert claimed that he had retained Mrs Collet to intercede with her husband to get his Rs 58,000 of unpaid taxes reduced to Rs 21,000, and paid her 10 per cent of the money saved.[69] Collet came under orchestrated attack in London too. W.F. Stephens was there with the Planters' and Taxpayers' banner again after resigning all his prized government appointments over tax-collecting methods. The old gentleman was nursing private grievances too; the autocratic Dr Selwyn-Clarke would not accept his valuable lay advice to pursue curative rather than preventive medicine. And so Stephens had turned a somersault to rejoin people on whom he had been pouring scorn in the recent past.[70]

Even now they embarrassed him, overjoyed as they were at winning tax appeals. He was sorry to find P. d'Offay compounding for Rs 20,000 when in his original return he had declared only Rs 1,500 as due; and E. Nageon de l'Estang Rs 8,000 instead of Rs 676. Stephens could well see that he would have to keep this from the Colonial Office. It was a disappointment because in flights from reality he had hoped to portray the sufferers as wholly innocent.[71] Nonetheless he pressed Whitehall hard, and through the Conservative Parliamentary Secretariat the Planters' and Taxpayers' direct representations reached Captain L.D. Gammans, M.P., vice-chairman of the Conservative Imperial Affairs Committee. Collet, much in London, was as well supported by the Colonial Office as by Government House. In Parliament Gammans was firmly answered by the Parliamentary Under Secretary for the Colonies, Rees-Williams, who joined in the name-calling by portraying the Seychellois as feudal exploiters and would-be slave-owners. When some of the Seychellois' near-ancestors owned slaves, retorted Alexandre Deltel in the Legislative Council chamber, they treated them better than factory serfs were treated in England during the Industrial Revolution, which was taking place about the same time. Collet for his part wrote inviting Gammans to come and

see Seychelles for himself but, as Hansard records, could not forbear
to add that the Honourable and Gallant Member was an undeflatable
gasbag.

Collet was promising to come home and stop the mouths of
the *couyons* – word had got about that this was what he liked to
call the *grands blancs*, turning back on them the local argot for
'sons of bitches'.[72] He was confident that he could take over the
Islands, and the better to do it he resigned. He planned a death
duties bill which would break up big estates and drive capital
away from land used unproductively; he envisaged an Agricultural
Trades Union, the hint of which had already got him labelled a
communist.[73] He was not at all worried by the Planters' and
Taxpayers' success in the Legislative Council elections, as he wrote
to Selwyn-Clarke from the solid comfort of the Hyde Park Hotel;
the results could not have been better if he had planned them,
he said, dropping a hint that he intended to mobilise the Créoles
by harping on their exclusion. Meanwhile he expected Selwyn-
Clarke to nominate him to Council so that the authentic voice
of the people could be heard. He had been flexing his muscles
in the Colonial Office too, hinting that the 'fifteen' people who,
as he said, made all the trouble in Seychelles would have to be
dealt with – and that he was the man to do it. He was resentful
to learn that the new Chief Justice, just promoted from a district
magistracy in Kenya, was one of the usual run of Colonial Office
legal misfits, and his hackles rose when he got nice words without
evident substance behind them from the Whitehall wits. He promised
to use a little blackmail in the form of unwanted publicity about
low wages, for instance, if they did not stir themselves. However,
in a meeting with the Secretary of State himself, Arthur Creech-
Jones, on 2 November 1948 he felt he had got all he wanted.
Rather as though he were the patron and the Governor the protégé,
Collet assured Selwyn-Clarke that Creech-Jones understood all
that was being done to socialise Seychelles and had promised full
support.[74]

It was needed. Apprehensive of Collet's return, his *couyons* made
the opening meeting of the first elected Legislative Council a
shambles as a way of showing their strength. Planters and Taxpayers
had planned to form up at the clock-tower and then proceed
behind their elected representatives with photographers and a brass
band; but a procession became unprofitable when the chamber

was moved from the education department to the Carnegie Library, only a stone's throw from the clock; instead they crowded straight on to the balconies to deplore Selwyn-Clarke's lecture on the necessity of ending privilege for the few.[75] He was not in conciliatory vein – a doctrinaire man impatient with the forces of reaction which he identified in these representatives of a few hundred voters. He was infuriated by their attacks on Collet for whom, as they suspected, he had indeed reserved the empty nominated place down the table. His talk about universal adult suffrage was not what elected members wanted to hear. They required two of themselves on the Executive Council as a cast-iron assurance that Collet would never be allowed into the chamber again. They challenged the legality of all measures enacted by the present Council while this seat was unfilled; in this they were upheld on appeal, and a validating ordinance had to be passed.[76]

On 9 January 1949 Collet arrived back to be welcomed by a deputation ranging from Suleiman Adam of the firm of Adam Moosa to Créole bacca-sellers; some of them declared him a David come to fight Goliath and all were duly shadowed by an enthusiast for the Taxpayers, a spy who subscribed himself a Christian Democrat and member of the party of the Right.[77] A couple of months later a visiting Under-Secretary of State received a petition from labourers and artisans about wages, housing and racial attitudes, which they reckoned were about fifty years behind the times; they declined to be slaves any longer, and complained that the new education plan was under especial attack from the *grands blancs* 'as if they always want to keep us in the dark'. Then the elected members had their say. Those who lacked breeding, civilisation and intelligence entitling them to go on to secondary education must do manual work, they observed, yet the blacks felt honest toil to be dishonourable if they could read and write a little. There had never been any racial question in Seychelles at all, said these four elected *grands blancs*, meaning that their class never allowed obvious questions to be raised. They would only admit that some families might not receive certain others in their houses, which was a purely private affair.[78] Seychelles were now divided as they had not often been since the 1850s. On Praslin, after the success of the Progressives at the District Council elections, Arthur Savy as President declared the day of its first meeting, 4 February 1949, to be the dawn of democracy, the first step toward self-government,[79] and the elected Legislative Council member, Gustave de Comarmond, secretary to the Planters and Taxpayers, said bitterly in the Council chamber that since the introduction of the double franchise and double representative organs, Praslin and La Digue had been rent by open class hatred as never before.

In the month of the Progressives' triumph on Praslin, the Taxpayers found an unexpected ally in the new Chief Justice, M.D. Lyon. 'Dar' Lyon was a cricketer of genius and an eccentric. The only colonial judge ever to have played in a first-class match, he was one of the few to sit naked on the bench beneath his robes in protest at having to wear wig and gown in the tropics. A writer for Charlot's Revues in his youth, he liked to deliver puns from the bench before retiring for refreshment to the Seychelles Club. The bar there knew him so well that in 1956, the year before he was hustled away to be puisne judge in Uganda, the Secretary of State was asked in the House of Commons whether it was true that the Chief Justice of Seychelles was drunken, incompetent, vicious and corrupt.[80] Probably these adjectives were provided by Collet, and most were unfair, but Lyon was not judicial; in one of his overturned cases, the appellant judges were staggered by his hostile cross-examination of witnesses.[81] From the first he let himself be ruled by his dislike of 'Septic Selwyn' as a socialist – the Governor had eccentric views on sewage disposal too – and still more by his aversion to Collet as a black man tricked out as a British barrister.

In Lyon's view a former railway clerk had no right to be a Minister of the Crown even under a Labour government. How much less was a man without proper training, background or tradition fit to be a barrister? This was how Lyon described Collet when giving judgement in favour of Joseph Albert for recovery of Mrs Collet's commission. Power, said Lyon privately at his mildest, had gone to Collet's head.[82] 'Blackmailer' and 'liar', Lyon called him in February 1949 when he awarded Louis Lemarchand Rs 6,330 as a refund of taxes for 1930-42 which had been screwed out of him by threats. The irritated Parliamentary Under-Secretary, Rees-Williams, was understating the case when he commented in the Commons that for a judge Lyon was too extreme and flamboyant in his strictures – which resulted in the Chief Justice getting press coverage for his speeches defying the executive's right to question the findings of his court – which was not quite what Rees-Williams had done. Whenever the shadow of executive pressure fell on the judiciary, the door was opened to tyranny, declaimed the Chief Justice, whom the Secretary of State's continued defence of Collet only encouraged in his determination to get the upstart coloured man disbarred. Collet had laid himself open to it all, of course. And Selwyn-Clarke, his fairly frequent lapses in diplomacy a puzzle to those who admired him, did nothing to deflect Lyon by forcing him to accept a dinner invitation to Government House during Collet's cross-examination in Lemarchand's tax appeal and seating the Chief Justice alongside Collet.[83]

The pity of it, to borrow from James Cameron, was that the ethics of the whole matter varied in infinite degrees between black and white, like some of the population. Collet was genuinely progressive – which Seychelles needed, as later generations would argue. And most *grands blancs* made unconvincing martyrs. Louis Lemarchand, a test-case, was lucky to get his favourable judgement; the case went his way on a technicality which the government lacked the nerve to challenge. It did consider basing an appeal on Collet's view – the basis of all the blackmailing – that under-payment of tax in 1930-42 could be regarded as a debt repayable under the Civil Code, which Lyon denied; but Collet was dis-credited and his successor as Acting Attorney General was too timorous to advise risking it. The only alternative was what Sel-wyn-Clarke had sworn he would never do – to repay all the money. Only Delorié got nothing back; charity was strained in his case because he was accused of tax-evasion again for 1948 and 1949. Collet himself was away for most of 1949, when the pigeons began to come home for him. With car and driver, he left for London via Bombay soon after Lemarchand won. Lyon's first salvo of incriminating papers to Lincoln's Inn followed him. Action for slander would lie against the Chief Justice, so Collet assured Selwyn-Clarke privately; but possibly his meetings with the dis-ciplinary committee of his Inn dissuaded him from bringing one.

He had other cases to fight and lose. Back in Seychelles early in 1950, he survived threats from the father of many innocents, Harry Savy, to kill him in his ship's cabin before he could even set foot ashore, and applied himself to union work; the Stevedores' and Lighterage Union wanted higher wages and were trying to force the manager J.B.B. Benoiton, M.L.C., to use only union men. Although Collet had given up his nominated seat on the Legislative Council, this did not lessen his determination to work for the submerged nine-tenths who he believed had put their trust in him. Even so, he formed no viable political party; the Seychelles Progressive Association might be the people's joy, in Arthur Savy's words, but it had no real organisation. Collet's intellectual arrogance was such that he did not seriously recognise the need for organised popular support, but there was none for him to invoke when Lyon drew the net tight, and in 1954 he was disbarred. Income tax was his downfall throughout – he had failed to declare fees he received in October 1947 and January 1948 for representing M. André Delhomme against the brothers Hadee in one of the last in that long line of lawsuits for control of the dead heiress's estate.

It was a curious and sad combination of coincidences. For Mme André Delhomme, née Hadee, at one time owner of the Outer Islands of Coetivy, Providence, Poivre and Desroches, life had begun on 3 August 1917 and ended in July 1947 by death from tuberculosis – a family legacy, like the islands – after years of negotiation with what the British called wicked uncles. Orphaned, she had run away as a girl of seventeen from her guardians in Paris to her godmother in England. Her valuable hand had reportedly been sought by Dr Lanier. Her uncles had offered her a home and a pittance in return for absolute control of the islands which, under their management, had already somehow contracted large debts – to themselves among others. With the help of the Official Solicitor in London and the rise in copra prices of the late 1930s, she had brought Coetivy and Desroches to her marriage with a radiologist from France, Delhomme, who took up residence in Seychelles. And then, when she was dead, the temptations still offered by her estate helped to ruin a man who, in half of his nature, would have wanted to see the law of succession so altered that her legal troubles would never have occurred.[84] Collet died from a heart-attack in December 1961 while on holiday in Cannes, at the end of a decade in which reaction returned to rule Seychelles. The keynote was struck in 1950 when Bishop Maradon, advised by the watchful Marcel Lemarchand, wrote to warn the government against screening of films that neither had seen but both knew must be subversive of faith because they were called '*Helzapoppin*' and 'No Orchids for Miss Blandish'.[85]

The socialist sands ran out with Selwyn-Clarke. Denied his second term as Governor by a startled, contrite and henceforth very cautious Colonial Office, he was succeeded in 1950 by Frederick Crawford. Knighted in Seychelles, as Governors almost without exception were, having never before quite earned their 'Colonial K', Crawford established an image as a good businessman before going on to Kenya in 1953 to help deal with Mau Mau. He was later a sympathiser of Ian Smith's Rhodesia; and he showed no great sympathy in Seychelles with 'so-called labour' – as he called Créoles.[86] Selwyn-Clarke had hoped to the very end that universal adult suffrage would come within the life of the first elected Legislative Council, but Crawford readily decided that all constitutional advance could be postponed indefinitely. In London his newly-returned Conservative political masters approved. Members of the Legislative Council elected on the restricted franchise were soon, with one talkative exception, placed on the Executive Council as well.

Amply consulted now by the Governor – except for one member whose sense of confidentiality was particularly suspect – they were well enough satisfied to regard themselves as the voice of the people, to deliver set speeches about Seychellois tradition and urge economy. The cost of establishments had increased, was increasing and ought to be diminished – the incessant theme of the South Mahé thunderer Henri Gontier, successor of Alexandre Deltel. The burden fell especially on the planter regarded as Gontier's rival for loquacity, Dr Hilda Stevenson-Delhomme, who had her husband's islands Coetivy and Desroches to consider. A spendthrift colonial administration was not merely providing basic necessities for the population at large but was catering to refined palates and capricious appetites: this was the complaint of the second Mme Delhomme when government in 1956 abolished income-tax for 2,400 people on low wages, reduced licence fees, ceased charging for hospital beds in third-class wards, and made stationery free for children in the primary schools. The school system bequeathed by Giles was an obvious point of attack. The education plan was far too costly in the view of those who could afford to pay fees and rarely used it. So much money had been spent and so little in the way of literacy achieved, said Mme Delhomme at the Education Advisory Council in March 1956. She and the Bishop agreed that there should be more concentration on French in the first three years in the free primary schools. It might be the case that the British Army and Navy offered ordinary people their best prospects of employment, but even so 'you don't need much English to understand "Come here, go there, do this, do that"'.

Given the poor training of the teachers themselves, there were sound objections to the effort to teach two languages, but the old political dimension still remained. As Collet told the Director of Education, a return to French was dubious enough when the poor quality of the French then current in the Islands was considered; and still more so when it was remembered that for most of the people 'French' would in practice mean Créole. Either way, the result – and the object, according to Collet – would be that 'a black British people groping slowly towards democratic freedom is successfully deprived of future leadership coming from its own ranks, a knowledge of English being essential for that leadership'.[87] Beneath it all lay the uncomfortable old economic realities. Over-population and a fragile tropical agricultural economy led – inescapably, it seemed – to poverty for the great majority.

Copra production in the mid-1950s fell significantly below the earlier postwar average of around 6,000 tons a year. Melitomma beetle ravaging the palms was one cause. Another was that as the population increased by 1,000 mouths a year, so did the local consumption of coconuts. Nor were there enormous profits accruing to proprietors, all of which would be ripe for redistribution if income tax were increased to British levels. On Mahé there was a proliferation of small, often very efficient estates with plainly limited potential – 619 of them up to 5 acres, 340 up to 25 acres, 145 between that and 100. There were eighty-six estates up to 1,000, and only seven bigger than that. The most substantial proprietors had certainly made money while copra sold well, and the small ones had been able to increase their rate of expenditure as well as accrue cash reserves. The bulk of the population were no better off, and their lot could not be much improved by redistribution at the expense of those who in fact were rich only by the modest standards of the Islands. A reasonable subsistence could be maintained, with heavy dependence on imported rice, but no more than that.

By 1957 Seychelles were importing Rs 18 more per head of population than they exported. The gap was filled by the government's expenditure on development works, funded partly from London but twice as much from revenue-reserves. Elected members and *Le Seychellois* saw this as spendthrift dissipation of proprietors' money, in wicked competition with them for 10 per cent of the labour force at higher wages than proprietors would ever pay. The government felt some reluctance about turning a predominantly subsistence Créole economy into a monetary one, but decided that it was worthwhile to increase productivity through money incentives. That, again, met with scant sympathy from *grands blancs*. Elected members complained bitterly when the House of Commons was inaccurately assured that they had opposed a 50 per cent increase in the minimum wage to meet a cost of living rise; but when the wages committee sat again the following year, 1957, to look into the effect of an admitted 10 per cent rise in living costs, elected members lived up to Westminster's image of them by recommending no wage-increase at all. The government, horrified, put wages up by 12 per cent but still reckoned that the wage-level could not have been publicly defended anywhere except in the Seychelles Legislative Council. Increased productivity, the obvious solution, did not commend itself to the typical proprietor, who seemed to prefer a quiet life and a reduced labour force.[88]

However, government had to cut back its own labour force, and Seychellois could fairly say that funds spent maintaining it had not gone into revenue-yielding projects. Nor had land-settlement schemes produced even the social benefits expected, for settlers were often slow in learning to live together. The failure of the Colonial Development Corporation's grandiose fishing venture between 1947 and 1952, with unreliable engines, the wrong gear, few local contacts, and some North Sea skippers with elevated ideas about standards of living due to them in the tropics, only confirmed Seychellois disrespect for Anglo-Saxon attitudes.[89] Local attempts to develop an export fishing industry were no more successful, though less costly; the technical expertise to maintain diesel engines and cold-rooms was lacking. By 1958 Seychelles were in deficit again, and as economic experts arrived, as it were on the heels of the banished Archbishop Makarios of Cyprus, to plan an economic rescue operation, the Islands became grant-aided. This meant a tight leading-rein from the British Treasury, which was rarely broad-minded and never lavish or fast-moving, and it was resented accordingly. Even so, their disgust at Treasury control did not lead those Seychellois with profits to invest to put the money back into Seychelles. New capital tended to find its way into havens overseas. There were parallel resentments at Westminster too. If these Islands must always be run at the behest of a French-speaking plantocracy, said an exasperated M.P., better they be given back to France.[90] It was more likely that social and economic relations in Mahé and its sister Islands would at last give birth to the radical politics which had been in British prediction if not in local gestation since 1939 at the latest. Even Seychelles could not forever postpone their days of reckoning.

6

DAYS OF RECKONING

1960 TO THE 1990S

As the 1950s came to an end there was a sense around Victoria's streets and even on Outer Island beaches that time was pressing on at last for Seychelles. It was not news of the Battle of Waterloo that was awaited now in Victoria but word of decolonisation processes in the sometime imperial world at large. In different forms, word was soon to be carried back by young Seychellois educated in Europe, and became intertwined with all those inherited, sedulously cultivated prejudices and acquired enmities of a small enclosed society whose members at large were quite unaware that some of their leaders might embrace significantly different strands of the political thought that descended from the eighteenth century when human society in Seychelles began. One set of leaders accepted the pragmatic approach which assumes trial, error and compromise; the nucleus of the other set based its eventual actions on the assumption that it possessed 'a sole and exclusive truth in politics'.[1] Rhetoric was in the end to take command of reality, and totalitarianism resulted along with several violent deaths.

Meantime, on the night of 4 December 1960 flames lit up Victoria harbour and so added point to the warning the Governor, Sir John Thorpe, was just conveying to the Colonial Office about the potential for violence in the Islands and the need to advance social welfare both for its own sake and to head off social conflict. The labour-lines at the Admiralty fuel depot on St Anne had been set on fire, and on La Digue animosities waited only for Christmas Day to break out in an attack on police. The Chairman of La Digue's Local District Council was Karl St Ange, who was among the little Island's biggest landowners and in his youth had been ordered to be dismissed from the agricultural department. He was understood by the government to have become dissatisfied lately with its sudden interest in his buying of vanilla without a permit after a long period when the police had considerably averted their eyes. Such factors may become the stuff of radical politics in small societies. St Ange became Vice-President and a financier of the new Seychelles People's United Party, whose barely subterranean Leninist assumptions were eventually to take Seychelles through a coup into fifteen unprofitable years of one-party rule ending in 1992, with the St Ange family being jettisoned on the way. In the society of Seychelles at large, entirely centred on Mahé, determined attacks on upper-class privileges were certainly expected by 1960. As Thorpe told London, 'When the time comes for people to get really interested in and worked up about political issues, the Police Force are going to have their hands full.'[2]

Quite apart from the rhetorical anticolonialism that was drifting in through Africa without sufficient depth of thought for the morrow, and quite apart too from the certainty of more personal animosities within the Islands such as had always found political expression in words if not much in action, actual hunger in Seychelles was also likely to sharpen people's interest. The coming generation of Seychellois was not showing much greater willingness to cope with longstanding problems than its predecessors. Population continued to outpace the economy while church and influential laity still expressed horror at any hint of family planning. Opportunities for emigration were closing as the former British colonies in East Africa became independent. What good land the restricted plateaux did afford was not always put to full use even now. Visiting economists had no doubt that the Islands would become derelict without massive capital development funds injected by Britain through three main arteries – the coconut industry; land-settlement and domestic food supply; and tourism, with improvement of communication with the world an indispensable prerequisite. A chartered cruise-ship might be a good start. '*Nothing* would do the place more good, in every possible way,' said Thorpe, thinking of the, to him, archaic social attitudes which still prevailed in the wake of the Progressives' defeat but might even yet yield to tourism.[3] In the Executive Council he alarmed elected members particularly with the provision in his comprehensive new *Plan for Seychelles* for land development under compulsory orders with even the possibility of forced sales of unused land. The estimated cost of rejuvenating an economy in which, as with St Lucia in the West Indies, and as from the beginning of human occupation of all these sometime slavery-run islands, praedial larceny remained a national pastime, was some £3 million. No more than £1 million could be found by the Colonial Office, where officials could not readily follow Thorpe in recognising tourism as the immediate vital money-spinner; they preferred concentration on agriculture, and had to be told what unemployment really meant when they questioned the use of Colonial Development and Welfare funds on public works primarily as a form of assistance. 'One wonders', Thorpe protested to them privately, before drowning while saving two boys at Mahé's Grand'Anse, 'whether the Treasury forgets that to be unemployed in the society of the type that exists in Seychelles is not merely a matter of drawing the dole but is at worst near starvation and at best eking out a miserable existence on the mere pittance which Public Assistance can afford.' As it was, cash-strapped government went hand to mouth from month to month, narrowly escaping major protest marches from workers who had to be laid off until the Public Works Department had the funds to take them on again.

What really awakened political interest was a proposal by the élite in the early 1960s to assume control of government. They were prompted by London's evident desire to see a step towards internal self-government, and supposed that, if there were to be any devolution of power from officials, it must come to them, the natural leaders of society.[4] When the Planters' and Taxpayers' Association issued a manifesto for the 1963 Legislative Council elections calling for independence (it turned out that they meant internal self-government), Seychelles in general and Créoles along with unpropertied *peaux rouges* in particular became politicised overnight. People responded to the presuming Taxpayers with the cry: 'The *grands blancs* want to enslave us all over again.'[5] Ever since administration from London had begun more than a century earlier, said 3,700 signatories led by a former Collet supporter, the Créole public scribe Uranus E. Bibi, 'we have enjoyed the inestimable advantage of having justice in administration and the position of dignified freedom secured, and we have had always confidence and respect to Her Majesty's Government.' They wanted no change, they said, until the franchise had been broadened and they could elect their own representatives.[6]

The memory of slavery was still very much alive in the minds of people who, as they would have put it, had white people's names but were slave-descended themselves. On 28 April 1963 nearly 300 men and women gathered in Gordon Square to see Harry Hockaday Payet, organising secretary for the newly-formed Seychelles Islanders United Party (SIUP), hold up a picture of a black man trying to get free from chains while a *grand blanc* stood over him holding a whip. They heard Payet say that the poor had no interest in self-government when, through control of internal affairs, proprietors 'want to put us back 153 years, back to slavery'. Cats and dogs were better fed by proprietors than labourers on their Rs 60 a month, said Payet as he toured the Island shadowed by Special Branch. Taxpayers' Legislative Council candidates were singled out for virulent attack as exploiters – Parsons, Gontier, Dr Maxime Ferrari, the surgeon T.M. d'Offay; and particularly hostile attention was given to the Indian merchants, who were unpopular for their exclusiveness and for draining the Islands of capital which they were understood to repatriate to India, as well as for their prices. It was strong enough stuff for one of those held up for public hatred to call on the Colonial Secretary, in company with the current leading humorist and crank Major H. Tindale-Biscoe l'Estrange, and complain that Payet should not be allowed to say things that might lead to rebellion.

They got little sympathy since government felt that *grands blancs* and all their allies had it coming to them.[7] Even so the candidates supported by SIUP were themselves from the establishment: Dr Hilda Stevenson-Delhomme with her husband's formerly Hadee-owned Outer Islands to protect and her apparent preference for the briskly personal rather than structural alleviation of poverty; the lawyer Robert Frichot; and James Richard Marie Mancham, future Chief Minister and President, then just returned from studies in Europe to practise as a barrister. The twenty-four-year-old son of a leading merchant in Victoria who was himself half-Cantonese and half-Seychellois through descent from the Tirant family, Mancham had returned with much to reflect on from Harold Macmillan's speech in South Africa in 1960 on the Winds of Change – the speech, as Mancham like others saw it, 'which committed the British government to an overt policy of decolonisation, of dismantling the Empire and getting rid of Britain's responsibilities as fast as possible'.[8] He could not see how Seychelles, conceivably a strategic prize in the Cold War world and certainly strategically placed in relation to Middle East oilfields, could secure meaningful independence for itself on the basis of its own internal resources.

And although Dr Delhomme was still reckoned to be the most powerful political personality in the Islands, that palm passed to Mancham soon after his election in August 1963.

Since adolescence he had been aware that the present concentration of representation in the élite meant that a power-vacuum was growing below and around them. Selwyn-Clarke, friend to Richard Mancham the father, was mentor to J.R.M. Mancham the son. Ebullient, extrovert, growing increasingly handsome, amiable, a poet and in personal retrospect admittedly naive – 'immature but engaging', the Colonial Secretary of Seychelles described him in 1965, and the same could perhaps be said of his verse[9] –James Mancham had been founder, president and financier of the Seychelles Students' Union in London, and was always self-confident. 'Astute and fun-loving...a formidable combination' was how the anti-communist mercenary Lieutenant-Colonel Mike Hoare, who had known emergent post-colonial leaders from Nigeria to the Congo, where he acquired fame in 1961-4, later summed him up, adding: 'It is not, however, a combination which produces great leaders.'[10] As a student in London, Mancham gave cocktail parties for the Governor when he arrived on leave, and did not fail to report his own speeches for publication in *Le Seychellois* –'his audience sat paralysed at his dramatic style', an admiring fellow-student once reported.[11]

'Tough – democratic-to-the-core James R. Mancham', according to the *Seychelles Weekly*[12] which he began publishing on the old *Clarion* press in October 1963, he was greatly concerned to define a 'Seychellois personality'. Essentially he wanted it to be multi-racial, with an end to the established Seychelles-Créole-Indian-Chinese distinctions. His own personality, which was vital for Seychelles in the next ten years, was very much that of the small-island youth looking for recognition in the world at large. His hankering after a film-star version of the good life emerged with his description of his 'first smell of VIP treatment' while travelling to the prophetic Zanzibar independence celebrations in December 1963.[13] His apogee was to come through friendship with the millionaire arms-dealer Adnan Kashoggi, who with his motor yacht made Seychelles his holiday retreat after they became independent in 1976. Mancham was made the subject of a BBC television documentary; one of the few British newspapers to resist his charm, the *Evening Standard* quoted in Seychelles, commented that the film revealed him as 'native boy become Stuyvesant International Man'.[14] But he had imagination, presence and a sense of occasion. His style caught the local imagination; funeral parties felt honoured when he graced them with his sober presence and old ladies were glad to have their hands shaken, as Seychellois observers recall; assiduity in attendance at such rites of passage assumed electoral importance.

Essentially a pragmatist, Mancham had genuine ideas of social justice which most previous elected members had been glad to reject on the rare occasions when such inconvenient notions had been thrust by government within their ken. The fifth issue of the *Seychelles Weekly* had an article by him depicting seven children in a house in Hangard Street, hungry and half-clothed, with the same mother but different fathers, while the Church went on insisting that birth-control was unnecessary because world resources could feed many more millions yet. 'The Bells of the Cathedral are ringing again,' Mancham concluded. 'We must go to Church....'[15] The next week he commented on another kind of suffering, the risk of being blackballed at that antithesis of Hangard Street, the Seychelles Club: 'If you have a white skin, a French name and over 75 acres of good coconut land then you have nothing to fear.'[16] The *Weekly* mocked *Le Seychellois* for continuing to insist that there was no colour bar in the Islands, the ancient defensive illusion of the élite.[17] In Mancham's eyes the problems of Seychelles were bigger than the Islands themselves – overpopulation, rising unemployment, continued illegitimacy leading perhaps to instability of personality as well as of family life, malnutrition. And all these were compounded by complacency.

A few years later, in office as Chief Minister and showing signs of complacency himself after electoral victories for his new Seychelles Democratic Party, Mancham felt that a fairly high level of multi-racialism had now been achieved – 'so that you are a Seychellois irrespective of where in the world your origins started'. To the extent that this was true by about 1970, it owed something to his own assiduous image-building; but he gave the credit to his father's friend Sir Selwyn Selwyn-Clarke for his 'age of clairvoyance' which 'shook the privileged ones into an awareness of the way the future was shaping'. As for Charles Collet, 'Will an objective historian with an appreciation of the spirit of the time really conclude that Collet was a wicked man? I do not think so....'[18] Mancham's

own view of the future centred on a tourist-based economy served
by an international airport and with even closer political links to
Britain to maintain the internal stability necessary to attract investors.
Winds of change were at last beginning to rattle even the coco-
de-mer. The revolution in Zanzibar along racial lines but under
a Marxist umbrella a month after independence there had a shattering
impact in Seychelles. Mancham's promotion of integration with
Britain along much the same lines as that of France with its nearby
colony La Réunion had wide electoral attraction. The Planters'
and Taxpayers' Association itself, still vigorously alive, petitioned
for Her Majesty's continued protection; like any group of Créoles
gathered at Victoria market, *grands blancs* and their allies now resolved
that Seychelles should after all remain a Crown Colony 'until the
political institutions of the colony have gained sufficient experience'.[19]
Mancham himself proposed a motion in the Legislative Council
calling on Britain for an unequivocal assurance that the Islands
could remain British for all time, preferably by a form of integration.
The contemporary world, he said in October 1964, was like a
field on which adults were engaged in a hectic rugby match. He
welcomed Britain's typically guarded reply – that it would certainly
not wish to take the initiative in suggesting any change in its
relationship with Seychelles.[20]

'Nobody but a bad father would let go of the hands of his
handicapped child,' said Mancham in the chamber, while from
his true-blue-painted headquarters in Royal Street, a shack called
'Progress House', came statements of support for a joint British-
American naval base which was currently being proposed for the
area. On Christmas Eve 1964, the *Seychelles Weekly* reprinted with
approval a British journalist's apocalyptic vision of Seychelles taking
their place in the age of Polaris, the commando carrier and the
long-range bomber as a vital link in global strategy such as Aden,
Suez and Trincomalee had been in the past. There was a great
fibreglass golfball on the top of Mahé to show that this might be
more than rhetoric – the rent-paying US satellite-tracking station,
built in 1963. Mancham had been retained to do the main
contractors' legal work for this, 'more because of the US State
Department's perception of the role I could play politically to
defend this controversial development', as he later ruefully concluded, 'rather than my proven expertise as a lawyer'.[21]

The cost of living and of loving too had risen, following the influx of well-paid young servicemen and technicians from America to compete on unfair terms with the local Don Juans in a market where sex had its price. Americans, accordingly, had been popularly invited to go home, and in the end Mancham and his majority party were to see that they had been wrong to believe that in agreeing to this station, with its ability to track Soviet military satellites and place American ones, they were guaranteeing Seychelles' right to democratic freedoms against totalitarian forces within the Islands themselves as well as outside. Strong feelings were stirred for and against the prospect of a much larger installation, with its promise of jobs and as a sure shield against the cold socialist breezes from places in Africa like relatively nearby Tanzania; in the 1960s the government's information sheet, the *Seychelles Bulletin,* tended to be tediously British in tone and content for local tastes – and with somewhat militaristic overtones about the Cold War when not trumpeting, say, the merits of the Standard Vanguard motorcar. The promise of Polaris (the nuclear missile) was a fine evocation of the spirit of Christ's coming, answered an office down the Chantier where the Seychelles People's United Party (SPUP) was embarked upon what it (at least in rhetorical contrast to the Seychelles Democratic Party-the SDP) represented as its own historic struggle to free Seychelles from the British colonial yoke. All this was in the name of a democracy in which the SPUP was ultimately to prove that its leaders did not at all believe (in that concept's Western sense) when democratic processes failed to get them into power.[22]

Party politics had come like a whirlwind, and as the years passed violence erupted. A lorry belonging to an overseas construction firm went up in flames; Progress House was mildly dynamited; a bomb lifted the floor at the Seychelles Club so that visiting members of the House of Commons should not go away believing that all was well in the Garden of Eden; an explosion wrecked Radio Seychelles. At first, there was a game-element in it all. Mancham, who was above all else an individualist, had found it advisable to form the SDP in mid-1964 to answer the SPUP directly – although whether he ever got around to framing a constitution for the SDP was another question. The parties organised rival trades unions, and were rude about each other in the *Seychelles Weekly* and the

SPUP's less well printed but sometimes rather more thoughtful organ, *People*. They painted rival slogans on walls, organised rival gangs of unemployed youths or 'hooligans' to support them, and altogether behaved in what most of the more sophisticated among the British colonial officials thought a fairly mild and thoroughly stereotypical fashion.

The more insular Seychellois, by contrast, were convinced that the day of judgement was at hand, and here perhaps they did not lack foresight. The gamesters were playing with dynamite, after all. The games could become serious, the rhetoric meaningful, and the totalitarian streak perceptible in the SPUP overt, unashamed and violent. In the end Davidson Chang Him, brother of the then Archdeacon and later Archbishop of the Anglican diocese of the Indian Ocean, was to be called on to fulfil the pledge wildly made for him by *Seychelles Weekly* and die for the Democratic Party. The rhetoric of the SPUP had actually presaged some such outcome right from the beginning, if not quite from the moment on 10 December 1963 when from Luton, outside London, the twenty-eight-year-old France Albert René, as President of the SPUP, wrote the Colonial Office a somewhat schoolboyish letter deploring 'certain political and economic policies' of the British Government in its administration of Seychelles and demanding the machinery for independence on the basis of universal suffrage along with the immediate introduction of a fishing and canning industry.[23]

He was not known in Whitehall and his party was still un-registered in Seychelles, where René had been born in 1935, son of the overseer of an Outer Island, Farquhar. The young René's early life was at any rate that of the poverty-stricken majority; his education overseas was first pursued at the expense of the Church, as a postulant for the priesthood; after he discovered atheism and went in for the law, rumour had it that the *grand blanc* Harry Savy had helped to pay the cost. However, on René's return to Mahé as a young barrister in 1958 his intimate was Charles Collet, from whose example he learned that one man could not stand alone or virtually so. And René shared one thing with Mancham from whom he differed in most other ways, being the reverse of flamboyant, badly-off, and reputed to row out at night to the occasional visiting Russian 'trawler' bristling with radio aerials; this was a penchant for telling a favourite story about his formative years. Mancham's story centred on the ill-fitting suit in which he landed so self-consciously in London as a young student and the speed with which he obtained a replacement for it from a West End tailor. René's was about an incident in the Seychelles Club soon after his return in 1958 when Harry Savy tried to establish a position of public dominance over the young barrister, at the same time commenting sneeringly on the likelihood of Collet and other blacks who did not know their place being allowed membership. René resigned on the spot from what he called the 'Seychelles White Club'. One point of difference between the two party leaders was that although Mancham attacked the Club, he remained a member.

René returned to Seychelles in June 1964 from a second period in Britain, during which he studied economics while working for the Midland Bank, and at that time the Seychelles Club's back door served as a vantage point from which people with white skins, French names and the specified acreage could heckle populist meetings in Port Victoria's usual public forum, Gordon Square. On 21 June that year René was under the sangdragon trees observing responses to the mercurial Harry Payet, who had launched another short-lived party, the Seychelles Archipelago Action Group. Payet was haranguing Sunday promenaders about the expatriates' salaries on which – as he claimed, borrowing from Henri Gontier – the whole of the British Treasury's famous and begrudged grant-in-aid was wasted; and about the need of Créoles for decent villages and tarmac roads. From the Seychelles Club Georges Savy mocked Payet for his spell in gaol, tormented Payet's supporter Desaubin with reminders that he had lost his family land, and developed the latest *Seychelles Weekly* joke.

According to this, when independence came next year René was going to be Minister for Birds' Eggs, Tortoise and Goats' Affairs, with headquarters at Desnoeufs in the Amirantes; there he would probably write a book entitled *How to be Independent – a Thousand Miles from Anywhere on a Birds' Eggs Economy*.[24] Independence by 1965 had been René's theme on his way home when he consulted some of the many Seychellois still in East Africa and affected by the decolonising process there. Interviewed there by the press, he said that the Seychelles Legislative Council was the puppet of rich planters. He had sought help from all the world's socialist movements before embarking on the struggle for

freedom: 'No matter what methods we use we must have independence next year.'[25] As he explained it when he got home, his
justification was the usual rather highly-coloured rhetoric about
the immorality of the colonial system: 'Anyone...who supports a
system which has brought chaos to our economy and poverty to
our small landowners is himself responsible for such chaos and
poverty. In advocating that we remain a British Colony one must
accept the responsibility...for the evils created and maintained by
Colonialism ... .'[26] As usual, in Islands now so educated by St
Louis College and the Convent as to have lost all track of their
human history, and with hardly a book capable of helping them
toward an understanding of past reality, that was to give far less
than their due to nearly eight generations of Seychellois and Créoles;
they, or their leaders, had applied themselves to creating what
René identified as evils despite all that the 'colonialists' had occasionally attempted to do to the contrary. René was on firmer
ground in arguing how vain it was to think that after 153 years
Britain would manage to bring about an economic revolution
overnight, still more that she would go in for practical central
planning; but he lapsed back into rhetoric in implying that the
objects of the rather loose planning that was all Britain seemed
capable of would not be general welfare, full employment and
higher living standards.[27] Responsible analysis was hardly René's
object, for all that his party's paper *The People* was to go in heavily
for what the SPUP called 'education'. As an emergent politician
in the rhetorical mode familiar in small colonial societies taking
at least some inspiration from the Eastern side of the wall in the
Cold War, René's methods of course came readily enough to
hand.

First, the strike for impossible demands. With a mail steamer
in harbour on 31 July 1964 the Stevedores, Winchmen and Dockers'
Union struck for a 100 per cent wage increase and moved to
make René the union's general secretary in place of Mancham's
lieutenant D.G. Joubert.[28] 'Handsome David Joubert' of the *Seychelles Weekly* was a former schoolteacher who wrote about the need
to develop a Seychellois personality of nobility, stability and excellence: a small man, often to be seen with a swagger-stick under
his arm, he may occasionally have struck observers as rather con-
spicuously concerned to project his own personality. On the whole,
he appeared to belong more naturally in René's camp along with

personalities such as the SPUP's organiser in East Africa, the gigantic Guy Sinon. Joubert had actually written René a bitter letter, typical of the underprivileged, attacking *grands blancs*, Indian shopkeepers, expatriates standing between his own tub and the sun, and Mancham himself, before going along with the SDP as its most prominent Créole leader.[29] Then, in April 1965, the SPUP contested the Victoria District Council elections, entertaining voters with ridicule directed at the Council's long-term chairman Dr Stevenson-Delhomme for her maternalistic approach to workers' needs. It won four of the nine seats. While existing Legislative Council members were putting up proposals to limit election contests – proposals which the government rightly anticipated that London would find more amusing than acceptable[30] – René stood in a Praslin by-election and won, despite what the watching police inspector secretly described as 'Mr Mancham's brash arrogance' in trying to shout him down with the help of a well-liquored contingent from Mahé.[31] René moved at once to deplore the lack of democracy in Seychelles and, when the Colonial Secretary expressed surprise that the honourable member for Praslin should have bothered to stand, replied with the dazzling René smile: 'Sir, the honest answer is that I thought it would be easier within the Legislative Council to destroy it than from outside, because I do not believe that this Legislative Council in its present form reflects the wish of the people.'[32]

Nor, of course, had the British ever thought so, either. They had merely been waiting for a local lead. Now they had sent to Seychelles a constitutional adviser, Sir Colville Deverell. He could see no general desire for unqualified independence, and recommended universal adult suffrage, taking what appeared to be a mature view of party conflict; any responsible government in Seychelles must concentrate on improving the living standards of the people at large, and it would be deplorable if the concerted effort which this objective demanded were to be deflected to a preoccupation with meaningless artificial issues concocted to lend party strife the appearance of genuine meaning.[33]

So far as the people were concerned, commented *Seychelles Weekly*, the only constitutional changes needed were what would bring the Islands closer to Britain[34] – the more so when the SPUP was looking for support to liberation movements in Africa, that dangerous reef. A second bloody Zanzibar or a second affluent Hawaii were the choices for Seychelles, according to Jimmy Mancham. He had just tasted the good life in America's pineapple, sugar and tourist island state with its multi-millionaire immigrants and its relatively poor indigenous Hawaiian remnant; following this partial personal revelation, he discovered Taiwan too – that 'major show-case for democracy and free enterprise in Asia', as Seychelles would be for the Indian Ocean if only René's alleged communism could be excluded.[35]

It always amazed and angered Mancham that the British should insist on trying to stay neutral between him and his rival,[36] for there was more reality to the party strife than Deverell supposed. F.A. René, for all his unostentatious liking for material comfort, was at any rate a little more than merely a theoretical Marxist. As events developed, he seemed to have been, at heart, more of a patient Leninist. Personal antipathy between the two leaders was, or became, real, but on the surface there was ample room for simple co-operation. With René's essential Leninism not always evident, it truly seemed that only vote-catching split the parties. While Mancham pressed for an airport, tourism and an end to capital gains tax, René spoke for housing, education and care for the aged and, like Sir John Thorpe before him, remarked that most people in the Islands kept going on sheer courage.

Conscious that the electorate was conservative, René dropped independence from his platform for the first election on full adult suffrage, held in December 1967, and called instead for the As-sociated State status which Britain was currently arranging for small West Indian islands, with internal self-government but with Britain retaining responsibility for defence, internal security and budgetary needs. René was, of course, offering a sop. As Mancham did not fail to point out, Association left the option of independence open, and so Mancham went on pressing for integration with Britain, on a model similar to that of the Channel Islands. La Réunion, with ten times Seychelles' population, was booming under a similar relationship with France – the budget subsidised, the people free to work in the metropole, and with internal security and freedom from international attack assured by the availability of French troops. Let René insist that integration would extinguish Seychellois identity, said the SDP; let him argue, as he was doing

with some success among the Créoles, that the Islands had more
of a shared heritage with Africa than with any part of Europe.
In reality René was prepared to change the genuinely Western
European, ardently Catholic nature of the Seychellois heritage by
seeking help at the Soviet, Chinese and Ghanaian embassies in
Kampala. Electioneering was enlivened by the trial of the SPUP's
former General Secretary for abstracting from the party files a
letter which proved these Marxist connections – the shock of the
disclosure had made him change sides.

Independence meant famine, said the *Seychelles Weekly*, but only
a little over half the electorate seemed to believe it; a bare 301
more votes were cast for Mancham's party than for René's; and
several *grand blanc* families were reckoned to be selling land to
invest more securely in Switzerland or Jersey. The parties had
three seats each in the Governing Council; but Dr Delhomme's return
as an Independent enabled Mancham to claim a majority in the
Council set up under Deverell's unpopular constitution –
unpopular, because it had been designed to check party politics,
and in consequence seemed to blur lines of responsibility. *'Je
l'appelerai tout simplement une constitution faite par les Anglais ,'*[37] said
Karl St Ange, Vice-President of the SPUP. Support for the radical
party from such a supposed *grand blanc* quarter and his choice of
language were indications of the way threads had become crossed
and identities restated since the advent of more developed party
politics in the 1960s, and Britain had only opened the door to
confusion by losing the political initiative.

Whereas Selwyn-Clarke and to a lesser extent Thorpe had urged
constitutional progress forward, the Governor who succeeded Thorpe
– the Earl of Oxford and Asquith – was a Catholic peer, inclined
as he said to err on the side of conservatism.[38] The Earl concurred
with others in thinking Mancham immature, but nonetheless cau-
tioned his Colonial Secretary against appearing to sympathise with
the perhaps more sophisticated René. He had to be reminded by
London about the tactical advantages of domesticating the radical.
We do not want another Mintoff, said Whitehall, which was then
struggling to contain the Prime Minister of Malta.[39] René of
course did not want to be domesticated politically by being put
on committees in areas where his views coincided with expatriates';
but the conservatism and lack of sensitivity to the times shown
at Government House threw the government much further than

was necessary into the reactionary colonialist role in which René would anyway have cast it.

He partly inherited and, under the guise of modern anticolonialism, seemed largely to have embraced the old French hostility to the British, which owed so much of its origin to the emancipation of the slaves whose descendants, or their best interests, René now claimed to represent. Certainly, for a modern radical party the SPUP sometimes took on an odd appearance. Among René's lieutenants were 1960s-educated scions of *grand blanc* families such as Jacques Hodoul and in the end Danielle Jorre de St Jorre. Incorporating stock *grand blanc* mythology, the SPUP even contrived to regard Selwyn-Clarke as a class enemy, perpetrator of a reign of terror against the liberties of the Seychellois people; and its hostility to tourism, partly genuine on social grounds, partly political but in the end evanescent, led a party official to attack the British for allowing the vigorous agriculture which the French had maintained to run down.[40] He overlooked slavery, although his own forebears appeared to have been slaves. Corsairs were recalled with enthusiasm, but not the Mahé slavers whose activities were probably largely unknown.

Let Seychelles be restored to France, urged one writer in the *People*; this would 'restore and develop our superior and advanced culture, which through jealousy the British Colonial Government has always tried to obliterate'.[41] Planters and Taxpayers could scarcely have said it more emphatically. And when a constitutional conference met at Marlborough House in March 1970 to admit the failure of Deverell's attempt to neutralise the parties, Sir Selwyn's non-taxpaying opponents of old could not have failed to approve the emphasis Albert René laid on the need to respect 'our French language and heritage'.[42] The French language was under government attack again, but chiefly, as before, in the hope of making everybody literate in one tongue. After twenty years of using English as the medium but teaching French as well, 82.7 per cent of pupils were found to be illiterate after their six years in primary school. With overwhelming support from teachers, it was decided to drop French in the first three years, then introduce it for the last three with more sophistication.[43] As a result, the lay organisation Union Chrétienne Seychelloise went to a Caritas Internationale seminar in 1974 carrying bitter complaint about '*l'impérialisme du colonisateur* ', this '*colonisateur anglais*' who, '*en imposant sa langue de force*', had deprived the Church of much care of souls.

How some others saw the whole language issue – and they the people for whom the SPUP claimed to speak – was revealed when Sir Colin Allan, a Governor who was accustomed to the confidence gained by Pacific islanders from speaking their own languages, proposed that Créole, the actual medium of communication in Seychelles, should be regarded as a language in its own right. An anonymous spokesman for 'the Downtrodden', who misunderstood the Governor to be advocating Créole as the medium of instruction, countered that the small France-oriented group which advocated this step was an élitist clique engaged in a clever, well-known manoeuvre. The French had had their own unhindered opportunity to spread their language generations ago, under slavery, but had preferred to make the slaves speak a patois that labelled them as inferior. Even within very recent memory whites had continued to insist that slaves' descendants should speak only Créole. There should be no going back on Giles's reforms, said this writer, since they had enabled 'the ordinary working class child to learn a language in which he should feel to be LIBERATED'.[44]

Although the population figure of 54,000 in 1970 represented almost a doubling since forty years earlier, liberation from excessive child-bearing was still denied to the working-class woman by people whom it sometimes suited the SPUP to regard as Seychellois patriots. Contraception remained an emotional issue, barely to be hinted at as desirable by a colonial government in despair at the population projections. The Catholic Church stood pat on the rhythm method, one step from abstinence but not so reliable. Clinics proposing more certain methods were tolerated by the Church only as long as they remained discreet. When the International Planned Parenthood Federation issued sample sheaths from its stall at a national show in Gordon Square, the dignity and personality of the Seychellois people were deemed to have been insulted.[45] And as the prominent lay Catholic Seychellois ear, nose and throat specialist in charge of the obstetrics ward at the hospital in Victoria said quite accurately, his moral objection to sterilising women even where there was extreme danger to life was the reason why government replaced him.[46] In the government's view, a more fully qualified, non-Catholic gynaecologist was needed –one prepared not only to perform hysterectomies in cases of direct surgical necessity, as Dr Ferrari, a property-owner married into the ranks of the *grands blancs* through the Nageon de l'Estang family, and founder of Union Chrétienne Seychelloise, was thought by government to be, but one willing, say, to sterilise a woman in her forties whose eighteenth child had been born dead and who was likely to die herself if she had to bear a nineteenth. The Scottish gynaecologist who replaced Ferrari soon resigned in face of hostility from the Irish nun who ran the operating theatre and, as he said, interference from ignorant and fanatical priests.[47] The former Taxpayers' candidate Dr Ferrari, a sea-captain's descendant and to his friends a Seychellois *par excellence*, became a leading member of the SPUP on the spot, underwent 're-education' as his fellow party leader and sometime prospective son-in-law Jacques Hodoul later put it, and was set up on the spot by the *People* as a Seychellois martyred by the colonialists for his love of the masses. Less than three years earlier Dr Ferrari had commended Dr Delhomme's evanescent ultra-conservative Parti Seychellois to the 1970 electors as the only party for '*tous les honnêtes Seychellois*'.[48] The *Seychelles Weekly* observed him marching for the SPUP on May Day in 1973 and wondered: 'What has a capitalist and rich man like Ferrari got to do with a workers' procession?' The *Weekly* at any rate often had a more developed sense of history than the *People*, which made an anti-colonialist hero of Prempeh of Ashanti, and might perhaps have made more subtle use of the example of the banished Greek Cypriot leader, Archbishop Makarios. His period of comfortable detention high above the sea at Sans Souci in the mid-1950s gave him respite, he said. Even so, there was little lasting respite for Cyprus after his return, only war and partition. As the SDP organ said, Dr Ferrari came 'from that section of our population which always regarded the British presence here as a hindrance to them'.[49]

While the SPUP was increasingly drawing inspiration from an improbable French past coupled with an expressed admiration for decolonised Africa, the SDP was swearing that although the sun might have set upon the British Empire in general, Seychelles would remain British for ever. When the United Nations resolved that Britain should give the Islands self-determination and independence, Mancham stoutly replied that in this unique part of the world 'self-determination' meant 'integration'. Sanguine to a fault, he tried to convince the SPUP's allies in Africa of this. He and his frequent travelling-companion Joubert had some success with conservative, free-wheeling Kenya, but none at all with the Organisation of African Unity, which responded to a descent which the pair made upon a general meeting in Algiers in 1968 by hustling them out of the country. Contacts in the otherwise rather blasé Foreign and Commonwealth Office were concerned enough for their comfort and safety to send couriers to look for laundry they left behind.[50]

Britain would not force independence upon anyone, said British press releases issued in that year. The wishes of a people were her main guide, the British mission at the UN repeated the following year when Joubert called in to express unhappiness about the dogmatism of the Committee of Twenty Four on Decolonisation. It was agreeable for the British delegates to see Joubert trounce the UN ideologues over lunch, pleasantly unmoved as he appeared to be by the Ghanaian representative who, with the superior insight of relatively brief but sometimes violent experience of statehood, believed that what Seychellois did with independence was their own affair but, for good or for ill, they must have it.[51] Britain's strategic interest in Seychelles, almost entirely dormant since 1794, had re-awakened as the result of withdrawal from the Middle East. Riots along racial lines followed by the emigration of apprehensive individuals from minority groups had preceded Britain's departure from Mauritius in 1968-9 where, by force of numbers, descendants of indentured Indian labourers had inherited political power and seemed disposed to use it, as elsewhere, for the advancement of their own majority in government office. In the Cold War a foothold in the Indian Ocean still made strategic sense to Britain and her ally the United States – not a full-blown base on Mahé, but an Anglo-American staging-post in the Outer Islands. Secretly, that had been under discussion since 1962. Aldabra, Desroches and Farquhar were resumed or purchased, detached from Seychelles and, with Mauritius's Diego Garcia, made that year into the separate British Indian Ocean Territory (BIOT).

This was an obvious affront to those in Seychelles and elsewhere who for a variety of reasons wanted these seas to be neutral or at any rate not effectively patrolled by the West. The Governor tried to stop Seychelles College Old Boys from debating the legality

and morality of this removal of territory, and the SPUP found
still more interests in common with the Soviet Union. It was not
clear that BIOT was any safeguard to the Democrats either, since
Britain had told the UN that she would certainly keep the detached
strategic atolls but might give up the more populated Islands; this
piece of cynicism led the *Seychelles Weekly* to question whether
Britain had after all lost its last trace of morality.[52] Association
certainly became less attractive to Britain from her experience in
the West Indies, where Anguilla's secession from St Kitts involved
an embarrassing fire-brigade intervention with troops and frigates.
In Seychelles the Earl of Oxford and Asquith called in the Royal
Navy to maintain internal security during a strike – an equally
embarrassing precedent that could be ignored even less easily under
Association. And integration of Seychelles with Britain on the
lines of the Channel Islands and the Isle of Man, like that of
Réunion, Martinique and Guadeloupe with France, was something
to startle Whitehall. It was not something which had ever had a
place in the British decolonising tradition.

Yet when Mancham had talks at the Foreign and Commonwealth
Office on 7 July 1969, he was still not denied outright what he
wanted. The Minister of State, Lord Shepherd, would not completely rule out integration, and wanted to judge what support
there really was for the idea in the course of a week he was to
spend in Seychelles in September, a month before an Anglo-
American survey team came to assess the strategic potential of
Farquhar. On that visit he said what he was to repeat at the
Seychelles Constitutional Conference in 1970. On both occasions
it was inconclusive:

> There were still some five million people living in British depend-
> ent territories throughout the world. A decision of this kind
> cannot be taken without considering all the territories and the
> implications for them. We as a government recognise that there
> is always scope for development in any constitutional arrange-
> ment. We appreciate that it may be necessary and desirable at some
> future date to consider afresh the relationship of the metropolitan
> country with its remaining dependencies. But that time has not
> yet come.[53]

The notion was that before final decisions were taken, political
stability must be introduced through economic development, helped

by the new Westminster-style Constitution agreed at the conference.

All was cheerful and peaceful during the November 1970 elections that gave Mancham ten seats for 52.9 per cent of the vote and René the other five for 44 per cent, or so the occasionally optimistic Governor described the atmosphere in his initial cable to London.[54] Under proportional representation, however, Mancham's SDP would have won only eight seats to the SPUP's seven; the defeated party convinced itself that it would have won anyway but for expatriates' votes along with SDP intimidation, tampering with voting-cards, and hand-outs of beer and bully beef provided by the merchants. The most visible engines of the SPUP's own external support had been a couple of Landrovers provided by the Organisation of African Unity. Expatriate votes apart, the SPUP's accusations did not seem to stand up to police investigation[55] —which did nothing to decrease the bitterness now more than ever apparent in the party's utterances.

Given the undoubted conservatism of the electorate, the SPUP had done remarkably well; its emphasis on brotherhood with the emergent peoples of Africa, for instance, had appeal among Créoles. The next five years would be crucial, as Mancham himself could easily see. As Chief Minister he was in Britain during February 1971 to remind the Foreign and Commonwealth Office that Seychelles were not far from the coast of Tanzania, and Whitehall's reminder that the OAU was after all pledged not to interfere in the affairs of member countries did little to pacify him (Seychelles were anyway not yet even within that doubtfully protective pale). The Islands were to be opened up to tourism on a massive scale when the airport became operational at last in a few months —3,175 tourists came in that year, 15,197 in 1973 and over 30,000 in 1975. Strains would be unavoidable, and the SDP looked far beyond Africa for the future, but not at all toward Eastern Europe. Closer association with Britain, in Mancham's persisting view, was still the best if not the only antidote. This was the main issue on which he had won the election – for most Seychellois 'look upon Britain, not as an exploiting colonial power, but as a benefactor and champion of human dignity and freedom'. He claimed that his opponent René, having dropped the expedient Association mask which he had worn for this election too, was now preparing a mere disruptive campaign on familiar anti-British lines. Economic development would transform the lives of Seychellois, and the first essential was going to be that stable government which in the past Seychelles had been too isolated – and was now too vulnerable to anti-colonialist forces – to maintain unassisted 'without recourse to illiberal measures of the kind adopted by so many newly-independent countries but foreign to the nature of our people'.

Mancham therefore asked Britain 'to remain our benevolent protector', ideally in a relationship similar to that she had with the Channel Islands,[56] and it seemed to emerge from the Foreign and Commonwealth Office's reply that she was jealous of her rights in Seychelles. Britain was willing to let him approach France for education aid – mainly, as he said, to placate the small but influential French-oriented group; yet she was a little discouraging about his proposal to ask the United States for substantial aid to offset that mixed blessing of a tracking station with its hundred or so Americans 'who lived off duty-free imported goods, but chased the girls'. Whatever approaches were made should be through Her Majesty's Government. For the rest, the Office was not lavish with offers of benevolent protection in the long term. After a period of rapid and generally successful decolonisation, officials said, Britain was now being met with continued requests for help and protection. She could not devise a status for Seychelles or anywhere else without looking at implications for all the remaining territories. And although Anguilla had given Association a worse name than it deserved, ministers in future were unlikely to adopt any system giving them responsibility without authority. They would certainly not see the Channel Islands as providing any model at all. In short, self-determination was Britain's recipe for Seychelles so long as that did not mean what Mancham's majority wanted it to mean, namely integration.

Meanwhile, 'stability' was the desired commodity which everyone talked about, except perhaps Albert René whom it did not necessarily suit. And stability was to come through the input of tourism, Jimmy Mancham's particular political offspring. When the inaugural British Overseas Airways VC-10 landed on 4 July 1971, Mancham appeared from within as the door opened. When Prince Bernhard of the Netherlands, ostensibly acting on behalf of the World Wildlife Fund, arrived the following month aboard his own aircraft, in company with his friend the Dutch representative of Lockheed and Northrop, the stage was becoming set for Seychelles' opening to the world of colossal undercover commissions and underhand deals, of millionaire middlemen, middle-aged playboys, film-stars, jet-set popsies and package tourists.

There was other construction in hand besides hotels to accommodate these visitors. With British funds, massive reclamation took place at Victoria for a new port and dock area, and by 1974 the construction industry was adding 50 per cent more than tourism to the gross domestic income, while agriculture was yielding twice as much as tourism. Even so, the Islands were rapidly being remade after the self-image of the small island youth. Mancham now spent much of his time overseas, but his presence was maintained by the press. 'He is a king among kings', enthused the captive *Seychelles Weekly*, 'and a common man among common people, but above all he remains a great Seychellois leader preaching love and unity.'[58] Abroad the *Daily Express*, charmed to find one grateful young Commonwealth leader at last, celebrated his descents upon London night-life: 'Dancing with one gorgeous girl, sipping champagne with another, the happiest Premier hits town.'[59] A serious projection for 1985 put the tourist-target at 124,000 – more than the total Seychellois population was likely to be, even given its extraordinary fertility; more rational counsel prevailed in thinking that this was far more than the Islands could handle, certainly without harm to conservation-oriented policies which were among their major selling points. How much of the tourists' money actually stayed in the country was open to doubt; much of the food they consumed was imported, and it was not difficult to follow the *People* in thinking that the rich were getting richer and the poor poorer. Agriculture had not been successfully encouraged to expand. 'The tourists will not lack food, the merchants will not lack clients,' said the *People*. 'The people will dance in the streets on a diet of rice and – and tourism.'[60]

In tourism-supported small economies the general amenities may increase, but so does the cost of living; and the political backlash from those not benefitting directly or indirectly from construction or hotel employment can be expected to be extreme, not least when there are leaders covertly promoting dissent because consensus is not at all in their own interests. A particularly intellectually-muddled news-sheet, apparently written or published by the SPUP's own Kenya-born public relations officer who was deported for it, gave or pretended to give vent to some of the underground feeling in 1972, just before Queen Elizabeth II came on a visit and a year before the Foreign and Commonwealth Office let Mancham know definitely that he must stand on his own feet entirely. The short-lived *Seychelles Black Tortoise Epoch* complimented the pioneer French on their agriculture, attacked the British for their slave-driving, complained about tourist-introduced mini-skirts, and deplored the unnecessary deaths of the Pioneers in the First World War.

Bombs again revealed political frustrations or politicians' opportunism. In January 1972 the Government Workers' Union pressed for a 40 per cent wage rise, to meet a somewhat smaller rise in the cost of living, and after prolonged negotiation workers were offered 15 per cent, with the possibility of doubling income by doing two of their relatively light tasks in one day. In the early morning of Monday, 14 February, bombs went off at a petrol-station in Victoria and in a room in British Overseas Airways' Reef Hotel at Anse aux Pins – where in 1976 more than half the waitresses were reckoned to be pregnant by package tourists. A security guard was charged with planting the Reef's bomb, and eventually gaoled for twelve years, and it surprised nobody to find a confession entered in court by the police on his behalf crediting Albert René with providing the gelignite. Nor did it cause surprise that the guard's ordeal should turn into an indirect trial of the SPUP leader, whose alibi was nonetheless watertight. Thus René was given another political platform – the witness-box.

All means short of violence were legitimate, he declared, in this struggle to convince the British government that the Seychellois people had a right to govern themselves and were not inferior to the British. What he had said in his many speeches was not incitement to violence; he was simply saying that unless government listened to the people, violence would surely follow. He was attempting to avert violence. Certainly on 13 February he had told a crowd that the war would soon be on; by this he meant the war to keep out foreigners whom development was bringing in – and rising social inequalities with them. According to René's estimate, there were 600 foreign residents' votes in Mancham's 1,300 majority at the last election. 'One of the main purposes of many of my speeches', as he put it, like Enoch Powell on racial issues in Britain, 'has been to prevent a situation arising in Seychelles where violence will come, because I believe that violence comes by itself as a result of conflicting forces where there is no way out.'[61] Presumably it was in this same pacific spirit that on 12 April 1972, half way through a general strike, he informed a crowd that he was not *telling* them to call upon the Chief Minister at the New Secretariat down the road. However, 2,000 strikers did call, and eventually had to be dispersed with tear-gas.[62]

To add further insult in Mancham's eyes, as he surveyed the shattered windscreen of his white Triumph 2500, five of the younger Swiss and Seychellois priests had been encouraging the marchers with their sympathetic presence, while a comment in *Action Catholique's* successor, *L'Echo des Îles*, indicated support for men wanting to live like men and not like slaves. That prompted a special issue of the *Seychelles Weekly* in which the Chief Minister noted the implication that for a century the Church itself had been dreaming and had systematically neglected workers' interests. Arbitration eventually awarded a 35 per cent wage increase, but there was evidence to suggest that tasks had actually been so light and so quickly done that it was difficult to believe in any genuine exploitation model. By now Mancham felt that he had cause to wonder whether Britain's benevolent protection was not protection of strikers and bombers anyway. Tear-gas was as far as the Governor was prepared to go, along with some mild prison sentences for actual violence. When Tanzania's obliging UN delegate painted a lurid picture of opposition patriots being beaten, drugged and otherwise abused, the empty charges had a particularly hollow ring to a Chief Minister with no direct responsibility for internal security and no ability to get the Governor to do anything of the sort. As Mancham told the Governor, a peer had lately said in the House of Lords that what troubled him was Britain's lack of will to protect people still friendly to her; if he were from Gibraltar or the Falkland Islands, he would be a worried man. To these, Mancham commented, the noble lord might equally well have added Seychelles. If law and order could not be preserved while the powers lay with a British governor inhibited in using them, another constitutional conference should be called: 'We

cannot just sit by and allow people to spread hatred and discon-
tentment and encourage violence with impunity.'[63]

At last Mancham was admitting in public that he doubted whether
Britain would ever grant integration anyway. His attempts to woo
African nationalist ideologues to the notion that self-determination
did not necessarily mean independence ended in final failure in
January 1973 when the OAU's Liberation Committee meeting
in Accra recognised the SPUP as an African Liberation Movement.
British benevolence was likely to be a source of weakness. Mancham
wondered aloud whether Tanzania, so committed to the SPUP,
had it in mind to annex Seychelles, just as it had joined itself to
Zanzibar; and his next editorial commented on the, for Seychelles,
unhappy fact that a British colonial régime was bound by humane
conventions which the bloodstained example of a number of the
newly-independent OAU countries showed to be irrelevant in
their own practice: 'There is no room for two Parties democracy
in Africa and those who want us to cling towards Africa cannot
deny our right to make use of some of Africa's rich experience.'[64]
The next step now, as Mancham saw it, was internal autonomy
with the Chief Minister or Prime Minister controlling security,
the news media and the civil service. René meantime was promising
grimly that if the SDP returned to power at fresh elections under
the present double-member constituencies instead of the more
rational fifteen single-member seats which the SPUP had been
seeking since 1970, then the SDP might well run out again very
soon. René pressed for the full independence which, even now,
Mancham was insisting did not necessarily follow from self-
government – a position he held on to in public till the night of
18 March 1974 when he changed that position in a broadcast for
the April elections.

In reality Mancham had already decided by mid-1973 that he
must go for independence, given Britain's unwillingness to get
off the fence on the side he favoured. Actually, as he later told
members of the House of Commons, some time in that year he
'was invited to the Foreign Office to be told in no uncertain
terms that integration was a no-go channel, and that bearing in
mind international leftist pressures and the fact that Mr René's
party was receiving increasing finance from communist sources,
it was felt that I should alter course and go for independence.'[65]
He delayed in the hope of gaining popular support for his plan

to assume control of the police, civil service and news media before making a *volte face* on independence before a shocked SDP electorate. It seems to have taken a reminder from the Governor on 15 March that British policy was to insist on elections being held on the specific independence issue to make Mancham grasp the nettle. As he put it to the astonished radio listeners, neither the United Nations nor the OAU seemed willing to look outside their own narrow ideological blinkers – they could not admit that a conservative party might actually command a majority; and in Britain the Labour Party (then in opposition but soon to be in government) was committed to ending colonial entanglements. Independent within the Commonwealth, Seychelles would be better able to keep the peace within her shores, since at present, under the British, treason did not seem to be an indictable offence.[66] The election speech by Albert René which was to be broadcast ten days later lost a sentence which the censor deemed inflammatory; by way as it were of bearing out the SDP leader himself, it seemed to carry a promise that the speaker would resort to violence if he lost this third election of his career.[67]

Nearly eight years had passed since René had told electors that the decision they were to make in the forthcoming election of 1967 was theirs alone.[68] Now, apparently, he was not so confident that they would be won over by his argument or even by his rhetoric rather than, as he might have said, being bought by small gifts from the SDP. His change of heart, and his threat, merited serious consideration, under the ruling electoral circumstances. Constituency boundaries favoured the SDP, and in Britain's eyes it was impossible to impose electoral reform without the consent of the majority party. Accordingly the SPUP won a derisory two seats on 25 April 1974 with 47.6 per cent of the poll, while the SDP carried off the other thirteen with 52.4 per cent. Stability was not brought closer. *Seychelles Weekly* showed particular prescience when it asked where was the defeated SPUP candidate for South Mahé, the thirty-four-year-old Yvon Ogilvie Berlouis, a full-time worker for the SPUP since 1974, and answered: in Dar-es-Salaam. By his own side he was credited with having been involved for some years in the armed struggle for liberation in Southern Africa.

In both human and political terms it was difficult for René and his lieutenants Berlouis, Sinon, Hodoul, Ferrari and Morel to interpret the outcome of the 1974 elections as anything other than a colonialist plot. Election-rigging, as was to appear later, came readily to some SPUP leaders themselves, for the sake of the presumed general will; but this 1974 election seemed an aberration arranged at the very instant when the Seychellois were poised to accomplish their manifest destiny of independence in the arms of the SPUP. René's party felt robbed not simply of power – as some British officials, grown cynical, wanted to believe – but of the opportunity to make basic changes of emphasis in, say, education and the balance of the economy between agriculture, tourism and fishing. College and convent still creamed off those in the society whose parents valued and could pay for education. The economic climate favoured speculators and capitalists, mostly foreigners who, it was true, would perhaps not fail to find Seychellois in high places willing to accommodate them, for a monetary consideration. In 1974, land bought for Rs 5,425,000 in 1970 – when the exchange rate was Rs 13 to £1 – was sold for Rs 12,620,000 and there was no exchange control to stop the profit leaving Seychelles.[70] Gone should have been the days, said the SPUP, when the assumption was that a Seychellois born poor, and therefore usually black, necessarily stayed poor, uneducated and often diseased for his whole life, but it was not clear that the present structure had been geared to provide people at large with much beyond subsistence.

It had always been the SPUP's complaint that Mancham saw tourism as an end in itself, not as a means to an end. After his latest electoral success, the Seychellois were expected to bask in reflected effulgence from the 'Trudeau of the East' – to identify with a lifestyle whose motif was travel, and fashion-models, and owed something to the pages of glossy magazines. The great majority of Seychellois could not afford to buy such magazines, let alone live the life depicted in them, lacking as they did access to free airline tickets. Mancham's panache seemed newsworthy to hard-pressed foreign journalists looking for a new angle on the leisure activities of international celebrities. And locally when the *Seychelles Weekly's* Christmas issue for 1975 proclaimed 'O Come Let Us Adore Him', it was perhaps not entirely clear to some, in the light of all the adoration poured forth during the year, to which saviour it referred.

Stability had nonetheless remained Britain's watchword; and

during the constitutional conference which met in London in March 1975, Mancham greatly surprised René by falling in with the Foreign and Commonwealth Office's essentially facile idea of a stabilising coalition between the SDP and the SPUP. Formally Mancham took René in, but figuratively the reverse was true for it was René who would deceive Mancham. To facilitate this *entente*, the new Assembly was increased by ten members from its existing fifteen, and there was an inflated Cabinet of twelve to accommodate a minority of SPUP ministers. Independence was set for June 1976, when a Governor-General would serve as head of state. However, when, via a delegation, the Foreign and Commonwealth Office presented itself on the spot, at Government House, near de Quincy's tomb, in December 1975, it found the two parties determined instead upon a republic. Mancham said that this decision was in no way to be interpreted as a drift away from Britain, but he was actually much influenced by the Governor-General of Australia's recent action in dismissing an elected government. Besides, his foothold upon his own increasingly uncertain tightrope was slipping. A republic would, quite simply, help to consolidate the coalition.[71]

The SDP was to provide the head of state – himself, as Executive President – while the leader of the SPUP would be his Prime Minister, constitutionally with little power compared to himself. So it was decided by the constitutional conference that met in London during January 1976. However, no one had consulted the Seychellois at large and they appeared to be horrified by the decision to get rid of the Queen. Even *L'Echo des Îles* was startled out of its customary anti-British stance to cry: '*République! Consternation! Angoisse! Colère!*' What treason was involved in such a decision – and what a strain it would impose on a situation dominated politically by the uncertain fact of this coalition.[72] Its leaders were united while pressing successfully for the return of Aldabra, Farquhar and Desroches from the British Indian Ocean Territory, and on the question of British funding after June 1976. They agreed, as their recorded deliberations show, that it was shabby to send Seychelles out into the cold post-independence world without a large capital sum for her politicians to make hay with; and they thought it an infringement of Seychellois sovereignty when Britain insisted on vetting the budetary aid she undertook to provide for the first five years, to an anticipated total of £1,700,000. Another £10,000,000 was promised in capital assistance on soft interest terms. Over such issues, the coalition was sure to agree; and Mancham could go along with the SPUP when Dr Maxime Ferrari came to Cabinet with the assurance that France would provide aid if Seychelles would revert to being at least bilingual.

Together the two political parties saw Seychelles through independence ceremonies on 29 June 1976. As Prime Minister, Mancham arrived in a white Jaguar. After reading from his book of verse to invoke his ideal Seychelles as 'a sample of the world to come', he drove away as President in the blue Rolls-Royce Corniche convertible presented to him by a British businessman and manager of pop stars, who was opening a plastics factory. The first factory opened in Seychelles had been a brewery – a common British pre-independence measure for revenue's sake, dubiously desirable in Islands where alcoholism was an age-old problem, and certainly a focus of anger for both the SPUP and the Church. Mancham left the ceremony with the hood of his grand car raised. He had declined to accede to the wish of President Idi Amin for an invitation to the celebrations, making the jocular comment that a shot aimed at the President of Uganda might hit the President of Seychelles; and it was part of his disarming technique to tell Guy Sinon, the recognised link of the SPUP with the OAU, that he appreciated the care which had been taken to ensure that after all nobody should be hurt by the bombs.

Warnings were no doubt intended to be read into this, but the public relations man in the President had nevertheless taken over from the politician. As executive head of state, Mancham travelled as much as when he had been Chief Minister. Acapulco drew him from Mahé; the small-island boy might seem to have been seduced by a celluloid vision of the good life. And it was as though, having taken over responsibility for internal security, he placed absolute confidence in the individual British professionals whom he had contracted to lead the police and train the paramilitary Special Force. Imported policemen might have been instructed, or expected to understand, that Saturday night in Seychelles was not simply party-night but also the eve of the day consecrated to political activity. The President has said that it was a fake rumour, concocted post-coup, that he ever considered postponing elections for the sake of continued stability. Albert René, for his part, claimed to have wished the next election, due in 1979, to go ahead as scheduled. The new china for Government House, now State House, reportedly bore Mancham's own initials.

Bon viveur though René was, in his own more discreet way, the SPUP's leader had not been bought over. The extensive presidential powers may have been a temptation in themselves. The SPUP's party spirit was at risk under the dampening effects of coalition, and the *People* was muzzled. In a speech at a public reception Mancham stole René's emphasis on fisheries as the coming industry – 'and Albert was furious!', said an observer. And while observers at large did not suppose that the SPUP would allow the *status quo* to outlive another election anyway, the President might possibly have stockpiled enough political ammunition against the SPUP to win. A *coup de main* might well seem a more economical and more certain way, to the radicals, of consummating what for them was their manifest destiny, than any return to ballot-boxes, except in the one-party system that the SPUP actually favoured.

The President himself had been saying so for years. Recent experience in the decolonisation of Africa sometimes suggested that the preferred moment for any coup against President Mancham by Prime Minister René would fall in June during Mancham's attendance at the Commonwealth Heads of Government Conference in London. Among anglophones in particular there was ample anxiety about René's ambitions. Government's apparant inaction in dealing with the known murderers of an Englishman was being proffered as evidence of change of direction in the local winds. Derision was expressed at any suggestion that Albert René had either been misrepresented by his own vulgar-Marxist rhetoric or changed his character now that he was Prime Minister. Over dinner in his comfortable and hospitable big house, he and his party leaders could be heard commenting on police brutality towards a thieving housemaid, with some implication that it would all have been different under a solely SPUP regime. They were merely the junior partner in government, they said, with an air of resignation. When the subject turned to the influx of foeign capital, they added that offshore sales of assets were not necessarily irrecoverable. Hints and whispers, it was later alleged, were reaching James Mancham too.

Nonetheless, to all appearances Mancham left for London seemingly unconcerned, viewing omens as Caesar had treated Calpurnia's dream and reading no famous precedent into the kiss with which, reportedly, he was bid farewell at the airport by Jacques Hodoul, sports car-driving young radical lawyer (keen, among other things that pigs should no longer travel with children in the *camions*), and a descendant of the slaver-corsair of that name. It was as though, again, the President had come to think that the tinge of violence in the SPUP was a bogey of his own creation. He seemed not to consider that men bought over with a good deal would want more, and if he knew better he still took no effective steps to address the obvious fact that the old SDP image of the SPUP was being lived out. Small-arms firing-practice was being heard. It was reported that Ogilvie Berlouis had brought firearms and training in their use back from socialist Tanzania – reportedly, some twenty Tanzanian mercenaries had slipped in too. In fact an armed coup seemed to have been in the SPUP's planning for a long time, and the new British High Commissioner, John Pugh, later claimed to have told the Foreign and Commonwealth Office in advance that the Islands were wide open to a coup, but it betrayed little interest either in the prospect or in the reality when it came. After it was over, the ex-President, now exiled, was heard to say that twenty-five men with strong sticks could have taken Seychelles. Given the state of his security forces, this was true, but perhaps more direct measures than the SDP was accustomed to could have stopped it.

When Ogilvie Berlouis's men attacked the special force's armoury in the early hours of Sunday 5 June 1977, the key was reported to have been in the absent commander's keeping. The first casualty was from among the group of self-confessed freedom-fighters, mourned at his burial as a martyr by Dr Ferrari although some contemporary verbal accounts maintained that he was shot accidently by his own side who alone had firearms. An unarmed policeman was killed with the telephone to his ear, although it was sometimes pretended that he was reaching for a gun. One of the most vocal SDP men, Davidson Chang Him, died in front of the police station next to the Anglican cathedral from what his brother, the Archdeacon and future Archbishop, recognised from the gaping exit wound in his chest as a bullet in the back. Reportedly this angered René, who had wanted no bloodshed of that sort and was remarkably successful later in convincing foreign journalists that his coup had been bloodless; but it was to be followed by other murders in Seychelles and Britain at the presumed instigation of a régime apprehensive of being overthrown by means similar to those that had brought it to power. Gérard Hoarau, President of the Seychelles National Movement, was to be shot dead at Edgware in Middlesex, England, on 29 November 1985 when his part in counter-coup activities had been revealed in public; and immediately after the coup the Islands themselves were shaken by the disappearance and presumed murder there of another SDP man, the Indian merchant Hassan Ali, who could have been suspected of involvement in a possible immediate counter-coup.

The natural prospect of such a riposte had at once encouraged and enabled the SPUP to call the nation to arms, as it said, and recruit an army, again trained with Tanzanian help; the Seychelles army was sworn to support 'the revolution', but in 1982 it lost people from its own ranks in a fracas with the Tanzanian military mentors. The police of course had always contained SPUP supporters. The deposed President had tried to rally supporters through the radio on Adnan Kashoggi's yacht but was now denied its use; when the yacht sailed, with her gold-plated bathroom fittings, it was as though to symbolise the departure of an era. The Seychelles Democratic Party's era, even so, was not devoid of political freedoms, or marked by the gross financial mismanagement that has been attributed to the working of the revolutionary régime's heavily centralised Seychelles Marketing Board. The new régime's tax haven has had its critics too.

Confined to their hotels in June 1977 by a curfew more blood-curdling in the threat than the implementation, tourists had joined the Seychellois – who were confined too – in listening on Radio Seychelles to the carefully planned steps by which Albert René – with an air of faint surprise and even, in his consummate politician's way, of slight reluctance – agreed to benefit from the overthrow of the senior partner in a constitutionally-elected government to which he had sworn allegiance less than a year before. 'You have heard on Radio Seychelles this morning that the people of Seychelles have decided to overthrow Mr Mancham's Government, and that they have asked me to form a new Government,' as he put it in a speech which introduced the fifteen years of one-party rule which were to confirm that his own ideal 'democracy' was a totalitariann one. 'It is clear', he said 'that today has been an eventful day and naturally I will not be able to tell you much.'[73]

So 5 June 1977 became Liberation Day – the day of the *coup d'état* for a real independence, according to the new régime's enhanced campaign of socialist indoctrination or, in the new unelected cabinet's word, 'education'.[74] 'Since the 5th June the Seychellois are a Revolutionary People and therefore will not sleep again,' said President René to the independence commemoration crowd at the end of the month,[75] their enthusiasm warmed by cheerleaders strategically placed, as was to happen each year with the public celebration of his birthday. It was the birthday of a local Castro, in effect, regularly re-elected under the new constitution of March 1979 with no great choice offered to voters. The 1976 constitution with its liberal Western freedoms had been suspended immediately; the party became the state; a street was renamed after Bishop Maradon; and a statue of a man in or breaking out of chains went up and was named (in Créole) '*Zomme Libre*'.

Revolutionary fervour was at once seen to involve unquestioning acceptance of presidential decrees seeking to achieve, among other things, social objectives, like an end to drunkenness and absenteeism, which colonialists had attempted to bring about by means that were less extreme. These edicts were sugared by the assurance that the ills in question derived from the capitalist example of the colonialist oppressors – meaning of course the British administrators – rather than the French founders whose successors, educated at Seychelles College and the Convent, offspring of the *grands blancs*, were liberally represented among the revolutionary régime's chief guides and beneficiaries. Some able civil servants of Chinese descent, for instance, felt insecure. At the United Nations Guy Sinon, formerly Minister of Education and now Minister for Foreign Affairs – who, like other old companions of the President such as Jacques Hodoul and newer allies like Maxime Ferrari, was to fall out with him in the 1980s – asserted Seychelles' identification with the Third World by claiming for the SPUP's imprisoned martyrs of the past much greater hardship than their mild treatment could ever have caused, with the possible exception of Guy Pool who was sentenced to twelve years in gaol for bomb-placing. And the Janus-faced element in the régime came to the fore when it decreed the reintroduction of French in the first three primary years, in the face of strong external professional advice to the contrary. The bilingualism of the élite was an enviable skill, making for capable if not necessarily resolute people, but even the zoning of schools, which the régime also decreed in order to stop advantaged children from flooding to college and convent, was not likely to bring this skill readily within the reach of the Créole-speaking masses.

Not even revolutionary decrees could raise the dead or bury the past, but they could cancel that more open society which certain British colonial overlords had sought, more than thirty years earlier, only to back off from the kind of inevitable confrontation with propertied Seychellois which, it was refreshing to reflect, had helped to turn more than one proprietor and several proprietors' sons and daughters into relative radicals. Cheap housing had been an article of faith of successive administrations since the late 1930s, and price-control had operated on essentials. Now a revolutionary régime openly hostile to merchants could easily legislate to control prices and commodities generally – causing the ultimate destruction, for instance, of the Mancham family's firm, but also great loss to taxpayers. By the financial year 1988-9, some $US32,000,000 was reckoned outstanding in advances to politically-advantaged individuals as well as to state-owned enterprises, and the *Indian Ocean Newsletter* commented that the 'artistic fuzziness of Seychelles state accounting of those days left all doors *wide open* to awkward questions and unlikely responses'.[76]

René's route was always through seas full of known reefs. By 1977 the eminently capitalistic Pirates' Arms Hotel in Victoria had been part-occupied by Eastern bloc embassies, which were much slower to recognise René than the pragmatic and slightly whimsical Western ones located in the more salubrious Victoria House. According to the new President himself, the Chinese and Russians each supposed that the other had been behind the coup, and at first were both accordingly cautious. What the Chinese would add to the amenities of the Island was soon indicated by the high wall they built around the house they bought for a chancery, and what the Russians might contribute to security was indicated by their ambassador when presenting his credentials. The Soviet Union always observed Lenin's principles of peaceful co-existence and non-interference, he said, and then in the next breath expressed resolute support for all national liberation movements, along with opposition to neo-colonialism. During the 1970s the Soviet embassy in neighbouring Mauritius had taken an active interest in elections there, and the Marxist party leader Paul Bérenger in his turn kept a fraternal eye upon his Seychellois brother. And as the Boeing 747s of British Airways, Air France and Air India climbed away from Mahé in October 1977, five months after the coup and long before tourist hotels to be taken under state control had begun falling into disrepair, there was already reason to feel that many strands in the history of Seychelles had merged after Liberation Day. But not all were mutually compatible. Certainly revolutionary principles were incompatible with freedom of speech and of political association. The SDP was underground but not necessarily defunct, its supporters willing to be conciliated but not impressed by the new régime's rhetoric, and in the event leaving the country in large numbers. While spouting democratic principles, the SPUP was already heading towards the one-party system which it dominated from May 1978 in the new guise of the Seychelles People's Progressive Front with the whole apparatus of state-owned commercial enterprises, a Seychelles People's Liberation Army, a Militia, a Presidential Bodyguard and a National Youth Service based directly on the Cuban model. Seychelles as one of the world's most attractive tax havens was a creation of 1978, reputedly with derisory financial advantage to the country. The militia of 1978, for its part, was visibly a rabble, reported the staunchly anti-communist mercenary Mike Hoare who, with covert backing from South Africa's National Intelligence Service but acting principally on behalf of the Mouvement pour la Résistance with its supporters in Seychelles as well as among exiles, was already planning his counter-coup of 1981. The militia's 1914 Mauser-type bolt-action rifles struck him as 'ideally suited to their purpose, which seems to be to terrify the native population'.[77]

The self-confessed revolutionary party was apparently run by a handful of single-minded and perhaps simple-minded Leninist if not Jacobinesque ideologues, and hardly Marxist thinkers – although they were following the established Cuban model rather than anything approaching the grotesque course of that coming apogee of undigested Leninist orthodoxy in small newly-independent island states: Grenada's irrational New Jewel Movement with its murderous pursuit of self-destruction following its armed insurrection in Grenada in 1979. Without trial, the Seychelles People's Progressive Front would gaol, exile and apparently cause the murder of its enemies, but it was to shed its own leaders more gently than New Jewel. The SPPF nationalised assets and tended to mismanage them, and from the beginning it was venturing upon what looked like nepotism in a manner that was at least never obvious under Mancham's free enterprise system. René's stepson was appointed to a lucrative revolutionary appointment. Hodoul's brother became commodore of the navy. Membership of the party with all its identification with the state was not absolutely essential to personal advancement, but it was an advantage. The régime spoke of advancement for the masses and sometimes attempted it through education, which had never, at any level, been far from political indoctrination since 1977; from 1981 till 1991 it embodied two years of socially-isolating National Youth Service. Yet still the government contained in or near its leadership representatives of groups which the colonial order had, it may be felt, pretty accurately diagnosed as being white-élitist.

Armed activists had more often been Créoles. In the Governor's office, where Mancham had held open court, sat Ogilvie Berlouis in the early days, mocking Mancham's lack of security. Promoted colonel by 1986, he was credited in that year with attempting a coup on his own account against the President, and having failed he resigned simultaneously from the army and the Cabinet, before going on in the more open atmosphere of the 1990s to form the miniature Seychelles Liberal Party. Rhetoric has its own sense of reality. René himself had sat puffing his little cigars in a small room tucked away at the back of adjacent ex-Government House, and at first did not seem to venture much into town without armed guards, whereas successive Governors with their children and dogs, and Mancham with his friends, had wandered there freely. In further contrast, and as a comment on fifteen years in the life of the people of Seychelles, when Sir James Mancham came back at last in 1992 (on a visit to discuss Seychelles' enforced return to multi-party democracy with the collapse of Marxism as a world system, and as a result of increased though very belated pressure for a return to democracy from London, Paris, Washington and Bonn) he brought a guard of about eighteen men, some of them from the British SAS.

For by then South Africa-based mercenaries – instigated yet ill-provided-for by Seychellois exiles reportedly, with the knowledge of Mancham himself, and led by Mike Hoare – had narrowly failed to take the Islands by storm in a cut-price coup. They were detected by chance at the airport on 25 November 1981 after flying in as a fifty-man Johannesburg beer-drinking club, supposedly a branch of the obscure British charity group Ye Ancient Order of Frothblowers, with dis-assembled AK-47s in their handbaggage. Tanzanian troops in their barracks withstood an amateurish haphazard attack, but three lorryloads of Tanzanian infantry fled precipitately and for ever from the main body at the airport. There the mercenaries knocked out one of two Russian-built armoured cars sent against them, but came under artillery fire. They were confident they could take the barracks at dawn, but were unwilling to risk the 20 per cent casualties this was likely to cost them. Making contact with authorities in Seychelles by phone during the shelling, Hoare thought that the presumed Minister of Defence sounded drunk and very frightened; the President sounded calm and cultivated; the head of the Mouvement pour la Résistance in Victoria refused Hoare's calls; and there was no hint of the popular rising promised by the exiles.[78] Carrying one dead comrade who had been shot accidently by his own side, the mercenaries made off back to South Africa in Air India Flight 224. The Boeing 707 had landed to refuel despite warning flares and gunfire. As Seychelles Liberal Party leader in 1992, a former Minister for Youth and Defence said that the indemnity which South Africa eventually paid for the release of six captured mercenaries gaoled under sentence of death in Seychelles was misappropriated. Ex-President Mancham believed that it was Britain or America that should have intervened militarily, as America had done in Grenada.

By then visiting parliamentarians from Moscow had admitted that the Soviet Union could help its friends overseas in the Non-Aligned Group no more, and Western goverments, who had always provided aid, were clamping down.[79] The World Bank found in Seychelles stark inequality of income, with 20 per cent of the population still beneath a very low poverty line, and inadequate expenditure in the field of education on which René pinned his public hopes for a society rejuvenated along Leninist lines. By the end of 1991, foreign currency reserves were down; even with increased export of fresh, frozen and canned fish, the trade gap was six times greater than the total value of exports. The Catholic Church was speaking out at last for democratic freedoms as the Western world generally understood them and the SDP had practised. In 1991 elections to District Councils, with their direct links to the party, had a high abstention rate. Overseas, Mancham seemed to be disputing leadership of fragmented groups of exiles with the exiled or self-exiled Dr Ferrari who had been among the first to abandon or be cast off by President René; but pressure was mounting from all the exiles. So too, and more to the point, was hostility from France as a lending agency and from the Commonwealth. In December 1991, moving adroitly before nonplussed SPPF delegates, President René, in formal response to the commitment of the Commonwealth Heads of Government at their meeting in Harare in October to promote democracy in member countries, had his party agree to return to a multi-party political system.

René's expectation of retaining control even so through the ballot-box was actually borne out in the end, after a complicated eighteen-month transition period of elections and constitution-making conducted under the eye of Commonwealth observers. He did not need to fade away quietly, as had occasionally been predicted, to his big house on La Digue once owned by the merchant and money-lender Abdool Rassool. The SPPF won tense elections in July 1992. In the more matter-of-fact Presidential and National Assembly elections of July 1993, Mancham at the head of the main group of opposition parties polled 36.29 per cent for the Presidency in an 86.5 per cent turn-out of the 50,370 registered voters – nearer 90 per cent when it is considered that some 3,000 Seychellois on the rolls were living overseas; but René was returned as President with 58.8 per cent and his SPPF won all except one of the twenty-two first-past-the-post representational seats. Mancham's Democratic Party took the last of these seats as well as four proportional representation seats with a 32.27 per cent share of the vote. One seat went to the United Opposition group of splinter parties for its 9.71 per cent, and six more seats went to the winning SPPF for its 56.55 per cent.[80]

Reconciliation, the eventual guiding principle of both major groups, had perhaps not after all been to the electoral advantage of the at first vengeful Democratic Party. Indoctrination had not been without its effect on the SPPF side. And in order that every

possible irony should be given its full flavour, one of the United
Opposition splinter parties was the Mouvement Seychellois pour
la Démocratie, led by Jacques Hodoul. In Mancham's group was
the Seychelles Liberal Party of Ogilvie Berlouis. People scattered
in principle across 115 Islands, but actually concentrated on Mahé,
were launched upon their third republic in only a modified return
to the unJacobin conviction normally strong in these Islands that
human beings cannot be made perfect by political means.

During the relatively few but crowded generations since 1770,
Seychelles in all their great natural beauty had provided a notably
benign natural environment for some individual human beings,
at all levels of society. Mahé's rugged upland terrain was likely
to promote a spare physical frame for those whose business required
them to walk the granite hills regularly. The national diet of fish
and rice was spare enough too, but when sufficient quantities
were forthcoming it promoted health. Even in what, before emancipation, would have been slave households, there might occasionally
have been heart-strengthening wine. When that free Malagassy
woman of (slave and other) property, Volamaeffa, died at her
Belombre house on 19 November 1829, she was reckoned, according to her death certificate, to be about ninety years old.
And by the late nineteenth century longevity among ex-slaves
themselves was such that one particularly aged black man was
able to get tips from British residents by giving a pantomine eye-
witness exhibition of *grand blanc* panic at the appearance of Commodore Newcome's squadron in 1794.

Psychologically, and hence politically, the atmosphere might
be far less benign in some parts of the ruling or would-be ruling
circle in Seychelles. This was particularly so because, in the 1960s
and '70s, ambition came to be strongly represented by European-
educated young *grand blanc* descendants adding a student radicalism
to their direct inheritance from forebears who may never have
ceased to blame the colonial régime for their own loss of slaves,
political predominance and the connection with France.

The radicalism of some Seychelles People's United Party leaders
might owe much to student radicalism in Paris and elsewhere in
the late 1960s, but the SPUP's intellectual roots were often deep
in landowners' own peculiar version of Seychelles' past. Interposition

of a British administrative and cultural overlay in 1810-11 had led to abolition of the slave trade by the early 1820s, and in the 1830s to abolition of slavery itself. In the trade's case, abolition was belated in terms of Law, but in both cases British law was ahead of what the French citizens of Réunion experienced. At the same time, abolition had led to embitterment that might actually pass beyond landowners' own ranks. Slaves were freed, but for many years were not directly empowered, and rarely if ever were ex-slaves to become enriched. Former slave-owners, for their part, often bequeathed resentment that lasted for generations among their own descendants and became widely diffused. Mauritians from old French families who arrived in Seychelles to do business or, well into the modern times, as members of the administration, sometimes brought more resentment from their own home island – for power in Mauritius had gone from landowners to the heirs of Indian indentured labourers, who became a numerical majority in electorial terms after being brought in originally to replace freed slaves. Independence in Mauritius was not unconnected with race-riots that caused some among the French, African and Chinese minority groups to emigrate. During the decolonising era in the region, contrasts had only been heightened, as they were for Mancham and the Seychelles Democratic Party, by developments in Réunion, which since 1946 has been an overseas *Département*, in other words an integral part of France. The Réunnionais Michel Debré was Prime Minister of France under de Gaulle.

Britain itself had been determined to leave Seychelles, as it did the rest of the world east of Suez except where strategy required some vestigial presence. Its creation of the British Indian Ocean Territory had promised to enable it to maintain this without much residual colonial responsibility; and the United States stayed on in Diego Garcia. Unwilling to recognise genuine confrontation between political parties in Seychelles, Britain had left behind there an unsustainable coalition between the two essentially antipathetic political philosophies of the modern world.

Abbreviations

AN	Archives Nationales, Paris
AR	Archives Départmentales de la Réunion
BM	British Museum
BMC	Bibliothèque Municipale de Caen
CMS	Church Missionary Society Archives, London
COCP	Colonial Office Confidential Print
MA	Mauritius Archives
MBA	Archives of the Marist Brothers, Rome
NAS	National Archives of Seychelles
PRO	Public Record Office, Kew
RBK	Archives of the Royal Botanic Gardens, Kew
RMC	Archives of the Roman Catholic Mission, Seychelles
RH	Rhodes House Archives, Oxford

NOTES

Chapter 1: 'A Key to an Ocean'

1. *The Journal of John Jourdain* (Hakluyt Society 1905).
2. AN: B743 and 44, 27 March and 14 May 1722.
3. NAS: A/1; original spelling.
4. Gaston Martin, *Histoire de l'Esclavage dans les Colonies Françaises* (Paris 1948) 115.
5. A.-A. Fauvel, *Unpublished Documents on the History of the Seychelles Islands anterior to 1810* (Victoria 1909), II.
6. Service Historique de l'Armée: MR1676; AN: de Rosily to de Castries, n.d., Colonies $C^2$171; $C^2$278, Mémoire for de Castries, n.d.
7. Grenier to Ministre de la Marine, 13 November 1770; AN: Colonies $C^2$278.
8. Service Historique de l'Armée: MR1676.
9. AN: Colonies $C^4$145.
10. Médéric-Louis-Elie Moreau de Saint-Méry, *Description topographique, physi*

que, civile, politique et historique de la partie française de l'Ile Saint Dominigue (Philadelphia 1797).

11. Madeleine Ly-Tio-Fane, 'L'Etablissement du Jardin du Roi aux Seychelles', *Journal of the Seychelles Society*, November 1968.
12. NAS: A/2.1; MA: TB/7.
13. Fauvel, *Documents*; AN: Colonies C^{4}29, C^{4}145; Ly-Tio-Fane, 'Jardin du Roi'.
14. Fauvel, *Documents*, I.
15. 'I am ill with grief at all these stupidities and this disorder.' MA: TB/7, Gillot to Souillac and Chevreau, 20 April 1785.
16. *Ibid.*, *idem* 29 March 1785.
17. *Ibid.*, *idem*, 25 March 1785.
18. *Ibid.*, *idem*, 18 January 1786.
19. *Ibid.*, *idem*, 29 March 1785.
20. *Idem*; Fauvel, *Documents*, 259.
21. MA: TB/11, D'Offay to Administrateurs de l'Ile de France, 30 November 1783.
22. MA: TB/13, Gillot's 1 December 1783.
23. MA: TB/7, Gillot's 18 January 1786 and 29 March 1785.
24. Fauvel, *Documents*.
25. MA: TB/10, Dupuy to Malavois, 10 April 1790.
26. MA: TB/23/16.
27. MA: TB/12; Jacques Moine, 'Les Seychelles et la Révolution Française', *Journal of the Seychelles Society*, November 1977.
28. 'Behold what must be laid under the eyes of the National Assembly and is, Gentlemen, truly worthy of exciting the Patriotism of Messieurs our Deputies in favour of our islands.' MA: TB/12, D'Offay to Assemblée Coloniale, 31 January 1791.
29. Maine, 'Seychelles et la Révolution'.
30. *Ibid.*
31. *Ibid.*; Lescallier's report, 7 September 1792, AN: Colonies C^{4}145.
32. Saint-Elme Le Duc, *Ile de France. Documents pour son histoire civile et militaire*, 294.
33. AN: Colonies C^{4}146-7, St Félix to Ministre, 17 August 1793; AR: L408/1,3.
34. PRO: Adm 1/2224, Newcome's 22 February 1794.
35. NAS: E/C.1, 8 June 1794.
36. PRO: Adm 51/1118; Adm 1/167, Rainier's 29 September 1794; AN: Colonies C^{4}146-7, Malartic's 25 Vendémiaire An 3.
37. PRO: Adm 51/1118, 16 May 1794.
38. AN: Colonies C^{4}145, de Quincy's 14 July 1794.
39. MA: F38A, 24 May 1794.
40. E.g. MA: TB/8, de Quincy to Léger, 2 December 1803; NAS: A/3.27, Quincy to Decaen and Léger, 1 January 1808.
41. AR: L311, de Quincy to Jacob, 10 Vendémiaire An 10. 'His age is certainly that of retirement, but his character scarcely permits him such peace.'
42. MA: TB/12, letters of 24 June and 12 September 1794; ibid., Maury and Enouf's 19 August 1794.
43. *Ibid.*, Esnouf's 23 October 1794.

44. MA: TB/29/3; PRO: Adm 1/173, Rainier to Governor of Bombay, 23 April 1803.
45. MA: TB/19; AN: Colonies C⁴148, Magellon to Ministre, 3 Vendémiaire An 10.
46. AN: Marine BB⁴158, Guieysse to Ministre, 2 Ventôse An 10.
47. PRO: Adm 51/4425; MA: F4/586.
48. Decaen to Quincy, 15 May 1807, Fauvel, *Documents*, 345-6.
49. NAS: France Morel du Boil Notarial Archives.
50. PRO: Adm 1/169, Alexander to Rainier, 20 September 1799; Saint Elm Le Duc, *Documents*, 338-9.
51. MA: TB/9, Lebouq to Quincy, 1 Vendémiaire An 8.
52. AR: L/324; MA: TB/12, Savy to President of Committee of Public Safety, 31 July 1798.
53. AR: L311; Morel du Boil Archive.
54. AR: L311.
55. AR: L324.
56. *Ibid.*
57. *Ibid.*
58. BM: Add MSS 13,881: 'Journal du Corsaire le Générale Malartic ...'.
59. Robert Surcouf, *Un Corsaire Malouin. Robert Surcouf* (Paris [1889]).
60. PRO: Adm 1/169, Rainier to Admiralty, 10 December 1799; *Moniteur*, 9 Thermidor An 9.
61. MA: F4/291, 361; F30/173; AR: L408/5; Saint-Elme Le Duc, *Documents*, 648-50.
62. C. Northcote Parkinson, *War in the Eastern Seas* (London 1954), 160.
63. MA: F4/813.
64. AR: L324; MA: F4/698.
65. AR: L408/3.
66. PRO: Adm 1/171, Waller to Rainier, 6 April 1801; E/C.1.
67. BMC: Papiers du Général Decaen, Tome 102.
68. PRO: Adm 1/173, Rainier to Governor of Bombay, 23 April 1803.
69. AN: Marine BB⁴158.
70. *Ibid.*
71. PRO: Adm 1/171, Adam to Rainier, 3 September 1801.
72. MA: F30/354.
73. AN: Marine BB⁴158.
74. PRO: Adm 1/2323, Collier to Popham, 10 September 1801.
75. *Ibid.*
76. MA: TB/8, encls Le Roy to Decaen, June 1807; ibid., Blin to Quincy, 26 July 1802.
77. NAS: E/C.1, 3 January 1803.
78. *Ibid.*; Morel du Boil Archive.
79. 'Eighty head of slaves of whom thirty male Blacks, fifteen Cupons, fifteen Negresses and twenty Negro boys and girls.' Ibid., *Acte de Vente*, May 1808.
80. Auguste Toussaint, 'Le Traffic Commercial des Seychelles de 1770 à 1810', *Journal of the Seychelles Society*, April 1965.

81. MA: TB/26; Claude Wanquet, 'Le Peuplement des Seychelles sous l'occupation française'.
82. MA: TB/8.
83. BMC: Decaen Papers, Tome 95, 'Notes et observations sur le commerce de Mozambique'.
84. Robert Chaudenson, *Le Lexique du Parler Créole de la Réunion* (Paris 1974).
85. MA: TB/8/3.
86. MA: TB/7, 14.
87. MA: TB/22/5.
88. AR: L311, de Quincy to Jacob, 10 Vendemiaire An 10.
89. MA: TB/8, de Quincy to Leger, 12 September, 4 December 1803.
90. NAS: E/C.1.
91. NAS: E/A.1.10.
92. NAS: A/2.12, E/D.1.1., MA: JJ49, for de Quincy's inventory.
93. AR: L311, Quincy to Jacob, 15 Fructidor An 10.
94. AN: AF^{iv}1214, letters to Bonaparte from Magellon Lamorlière.
95. MA: TB/8, de Quincy to Léger, 2 December 1803.
96. AR: L311, de Quincy to Jacob, 30 June 1799.
97. MA: TB/11, P.V. St Jorre to Préfet Coloniale, 14 May 1805.
98. MA: TB/8, Quincy to Léger, 28 October 1804.
99. PRO: Adm 51/1529.
100. Fauvel, *Documents*, 322-4.
101. 'Which cannot attenuate their sentiment as good Frenchmen, of which they have always and sincerely made and will make profession'. MA: TB/9, 20 October 1805.
102. AN: Colonies C^{4}123, Linois to Decaen, date indecipherable.
103. Service Historique de l'Armée: Cartes Manuscrites: Mozambiques–6.D.5.
104. PRO: Adm 1/60, encl. Bertie to Admiralty, 30 September 1808.
105. PRO: Adm 1/180.
106. AN: Colonies C^{4}129, Decaen to Ministre, 5 March 1807.
107. Fauvel, *Documents*, 200-1.
108. BMC: Decaen Papers, vol. 92, anonymous journal.
109. AN: Colonies C^{4}148, Decaen and Léger to Ministre, 7 February 1810.
110. PRO: Adm 1/61, Corbert to Bertie, 21 December 1808; BMC: Decaen Papers, vol.102; MA: TB/28, Harrison to Viret, 1 February 1829.
111. PRO: Adm 1/62, Lambert to Bertie, 5 May 1810; Adm 1/64, encls Stopford to Admiralty, 26 October 1811; Fauvel, *Documents*, 202.
112. PRO: CO167/15, encl. Farquhar to C.O., 13 January 1813; Parkinson, *War in the Eastern Seas*, 411.
113. PRO: Adm 1/64, Beaver to Stopford, 26 April 1811.
114. PRO: CO 167/9, Farquhar to C.O., 28 July 1812.
115. PRO: Adm 1/64; W.H. Smyth, *Captain Philip Beaver*, 230.
116. Fauvel, *Documents*, 204-5.

Chapter 2: The Depot of Smuggled Blacks

1. MA: TB/29, Sullivan to Colonial Secretary, 28 September 1811.

2. *Ibid.*, Sullivan's 19 May 1812.
3. *Ibid.*, Sullivan's 29 October 1811.
4. *Ibid.*, Sullivan's 23 March 1812.
5. 'It is a public functionary, it is a father of a family, it is a white-haired old man of close to sixty years who for some time has been Monsieur Sullivan's Target.' Ibid., Dumont to Farquhar, 16 March 1812.
6. *Ibid.*, Sullivan's 1 May 1812.
7. *Ibid.*, Sullivan's 1 May 1812.
8. MA: IB 23, Keating's petition, 16 March 1814.
9. PRO: CO167/20, Farquhar to Campbell, 5 January 1814 and to Keating, 10 January 1814.
10. Charles Telfair, *Some Account of the State of Slavery at Mauritius* ... (Port Louis 1830).
11. Cf correspondence concerning *Le Succès*, 1820-1: PRO: CO415/8.
12. PRO: CO167/139.
13. MA: TB/28, Lesage to Farquhar, 21 April 1813.
14. PRO: CO167/120, Farquhar to Bathurst, 10 April 1814; CO415/4, Madge to Procureur General, 6 May 1814.
15. PRO: CO167/95, 127, 140.
16. MA: TA35, Madge's 29 September 1817; PRO: CO167/127, his 22 August 1827; NAS: A/2.10, for his contract with Poiret, 21 October 1821.
17. RCM Archives, for account of Poiret; NAS: A/2.14, for details of his women and children.
18. NAS: E/C.1.
19. PRO: T71/1517, Dowland to Dick, 27 May 1873.
20. PRO: CO415/3; MA: TA35, Madge to Telfair, 15 January 1815.
21. PRO: CO167/131, CO415/6.
22. MA: TA35, Quincy to Farquhar, 20 April 1816.
23. PRO: CO167/131, Madge to Barry, 11 May 1816.
24. *Ibid.*, Madge to Smith, 16 July 1816.
25. MA: TA35, Quincy to 'Les membres composant le Gouvernement provisoire aux Seychelles', 9 May 1816.
26. *Ibid.*, fragment of a letter to Farquhar.
27. PRO: CO415/3, Smith to Farquhar, private, n.d.
28. PRO: CO167/131, Virieux to Farquhar, 27 October 1816 and correspondence June 1827 between Virieux and Commissioners of Eastern Enquiry; CO167/132, de Quincy to Prince Regent, 24 March 1817; MA: TA35, Madge to Barry, 2 September 1817, and Virieux to Madge, 11 September 1817.
29. PRO: CO415/17, Madge to Smith, 3 December 1822.
30. PRO: CO415/3, Cole to Sir Lowry Cole, 24 March 1825.
31. W.F.W. Owen, *Narrative of Voyages to Explore Africa, Arabia and Mozambique* (London 1838).
32. PRO: CO415/3, Madge to Barry, 18 May 1818.
33. MA: TA 1, Barry to Madge, 11 January 1817.
34. MA: TA 35, Madge to Barry, 25 May 1819.
35. PRO: CO167/130, Madge to Colonial Secretary, 15 October 1817.

36. PRO: CO415/3, Madge to Barry, 17 October 1817.
37. PRO: CO415/8, Molloy to Keating, 14 April 1814.
38. PRO: CO167/130, CO415/10.
39. CO415/9; MA: TA35, Madge to Barry, 24 June 1819.
40. PRO: CO415/5; CO167/56, Moorsom to Farquhar, 4 April 1821, with memorandum enclosed.
41. CO167/72, Farquhar to C.O., 21 April 1824.
42. NAS: A/2. 4; PRO: CO415/1, Commissioners to Cole, 20 April 1827, and to Hay, 21 July 1827.
43. PRO: CO167/130.
44. CO167/135, Madge to Farquhar, 2 December 1822, to Draper 26 April 1821; ibid, Moorsom to Nourse, 21 June 1823; A/2.3, 30 March 1820.
45. MA: TA 36, Madge to Chief Secretary, 10 November 1821.
46. PRO: CO167/130, Knowles to Chief Secretary, 12 September 1821.
47. MA: TA 36, Madge to Chief Secretary, 10 November 1821.
48. 'Happy in her small competence...even more than in the accord among the settlers, was in the disposition of slaves, who, satisfied with humane treatment, demonstrated zeal, devotion, and simplicity of manners that prepared them for constant docility.' Ibid, petition encl. Madge's 10 November 1821.
49. MA: TA35, Madge to Barry, 17 May 1818.
50. *Ibid*, Madge to Telfair, 15 January 1815.
51. NAS: B7, Harrison to Assistant Slave Protector, 29 October 1832.
52. NAS: B10, Wilson to Colonial Secretary, 2 May 1835.
53. MA: IC35.
54. *Ibid.*
55. NAS: B8, memo by Slave Protector, 10 December 1833; MA: TA42, Harrison to Dick, 12 May 1834; NAS: B10, Wilson to Colonial Secretary, 2 May 1835.
56. MA: TA35, Wilson to Thomas, 24 and 30 August 1833.
57. NAS: Chief Secretary to Harrison, 12 December 1832.
58. PRO: CO167/135, proclamation 3 January 1828.
59. PRO: T71/1517.
60. PRO: CO451/3, Cole's report; Théodore Frappaz, 'Souvenirs d'un jeune Marin', *Journal des Voyages, ou Archives Géographes du XIXe Siècle*, Mars 1824.
61. CO167/154, Harrison to Viret, 8 December 1830.
62. *Voyage Autour du Monde...sous le Commandement de M. Laplace...*(Paris 1833).
63. NAS: B7, Dugand *fils* to Harrison, 29 January 1833.
64. PRO: CO167/228, report by Banks encl. Smith to Russell, 17 February 1841.
65. CO167/154, Harrison to Viret, 8 December 1830; Harrison, 'The Seychelles', *Nautical Magazine*, 1839.
66. Morel du Boil Archives.
67. MA: TA4, petition encl. Keate, 10 April 1851.
68. *Compagne de Navigation de la Frégate* L'Artimèse... (Paris 1842)
69. Morel du Boil Archives.
70. Cf. Morel du Boil Archives.

Chapter 3: The Air of Seychelles

1. MA: TB11, Lislet Geoffrey, 22 April 1793.
2. MA: TA43, Mylius to Colonial Secretary, 21 August 1840, 27 January 1841; Sir Edward Belcher, *Voyage Round the World* (London 1843) II, 275.
3. MA: TA44, Mylius to Colonial Secretary, 8 December 1840, 5 January 1841.
4. TA50, medical certificate encl. Mylius, 2 November 1848.
5. TB32, Mylius to Colonial Secretary, 8 April 1839.
6. PRO: CO167/212, Mylius to Colonial Secretary, 10 April 1839.
7. Minute, *ibid.*
8. NAS: B13, Mylius to Colonial Secretary, 31 May and 21 September 1839.
9. *Ibid., idem* 7 October 1839; MA: TA50, Mylius' 15 October 1847.
10. TB53, encl. Wade to Higginson, 12 April 1854, private and confidential.
11. TA2, Mylius to Colonial Secretary, 3 February 1849; and see NAS: B31, Keate's 23 September 1850.
12. TA2, Mylius to Colonial Secretary, 13 March 1849.
13. NAS: B31, *passim*, and for Hector, *ibid.*, Mylius, 14 June 1849.
14. H.P. Thompson, *Into All Lands* (London 1951), 195.
15. MA: TA49, Mylius to Colonial Secretary, 10 January 1846; TA50, Delafontaine to Colonial Secretary, 21 October 1848.
16. TA45, Mylius to Colonial Secretary, 30 April 1843; TA48, Clement, 24 April 1845.
17. TA49, Mylius to Colonial Secretary, 5 October 1846.
18. TA49, Mylius, 2 October 1846.
19. TA49, Mylius, 3 August 1841.
20. NAS: B31, Mylius, 26 February 1849.
21. MA: TB32, Mylius, 21 September 1848.
22. NAS: B31, Ricketts to Colonial Secretary, 5 April 1853.
23. MA: TA51, encls Campbell to Colonial Secretary, 18 March 1853 and to Ricketts 4 April 1853; and Campbell's petition to Higginson, 22 April 1853.
24. PRO: CO167/366, press-cuttings encl. Hay to Grey, 10 February 1855.
25. CO167/367, encl. Hay to Grey, 26 March 1855; CO167/315, encl. Anderson to Grey, 5 October 1849.
26. MA: TA51, Campbell to Ricketts, 15 March 1853.
27. NAS: C/SS/36, Colonial Secretary to Civil Commissioner, 11 February 1841.
28. 'That would be taking the terrible words "misery to the Vanquished" too far.' RCM, transcript from Propaganda.
29. MA: TA51, Campbell to Colonial Secretary, 18 March 1853.
30. TA51, Pierre Petit's deposition, 23 June 1853.
31. NAS: C/AM/14; petition by Loizeau, 8 July 1853, MA: TA51.
32. TA52, Telfair to Wade, 30 July 1853.
33. TA53, Telfair to Higginson, 5 April 1854.

34. PRO: CO167/366, encls Hay to Grey, 10 February 1855; MA: TA53, Telfair to Wade, 5 April 1854.
35. NAS: A/2.20, Higginson to Inhabitants, 16 September 1853; MA: TA53, Telfair to Higginson, 5 April 1854.
36. TA53.
37. PRO: CO167/344, encl. Higginson to Newcastle, 14 April 1853; CO167/366, Hay to Grey, 10 February 1855.
38. MA: TA53, Wade to Colonial Secretary, 12 April 1854.
39. PRO: CO167/366, encl. Hay to Grey, 10 February 1855.
40. MA: TA53, Telfair's 3 May 1854.
41. TA54, Savy to Wade, 27 June 1854.
42. TA53, Jouanis to Ford, 31 October 1854; PRO: CO167/366, Savy to Sutherland, 16 May 1854, quoting Jouanis.
43. TA56 and TA57, letters from Loizeau and Griffiths.
44. TA58, Telfair to Dupuy, 8 March 1858.
45. TA56, Griffiths to Père Jérémie, 10 August 1856.
46. TA63, Ward to Colonial Secretary, 17 December 1864.
47. NAS: B34, Franklyn to Colonial Secretary, 8 January 1874; Stanmore, 1st Baron, *Mauritius: Records of Private and of Public Life, 1871-1874* (Edinburgh 1894), I, 208.
48. MA: TA35, Victor Parcou's statement encl. Wade to Colonial Secretary, 11 April 1854.
49. TA62, Wade to Colonial Secretary, 18 May 1863; TA35, market regulations encl. Keate's 2 August 1853.
50. PRO: CO167/427, Stevenson to C.O., 2 March 1861, and 27 May 1862, CO167/439.
51. CO167/431, Stevenson to C.O., 28 September 1861.
52. PRO: Adm127/10, Bowden to Commodore, 30 June 1865.
53. MA: TA6, Wade to Colonial Secretary, 30 July 1861.
54. PRO: CO167/708, Stewart to C.O., 30 June 1897.
55. CO530/23, Bradley's report on South Mahé for 1913.
56. RBK: Mascarene Letters 1866-1900, Ward to Hooker, 5 December 1865; MA: TA63, Ward to Colonial Secretary, 17 December 1863, and TA65, Ward's 1 July 1867.
57. TA62, Ward to Colonial Secretary, 28 February 1863.
58. *Ibid*, Ward's 16 February 1863.
59. PRO: CO167/560, Gordon to C.O., 27 May 1874 confidential; CO167/564, Phayre to C.O., 20 May 1875.
60. COCP Eastern No. 21 of 1876.
61. PRO: CO167/553, encl. Franklyn to C.O., 2 June 1873.
62. COCP Eastern No. 21 of 1876; CMS: CMA/0/6f, Tozer's 16 October 1872.
63. CMS: CMA/0/10, Chancellor's 7 April 1875.
64. *Ibid*, Chancellor's 20 September 1875.
65. *Ibid*, Chancellor's 8 December 1875.
66. *Ibid.*, Warry's letters generally; Marianne North, *Recollections of a Happy Life*, (London 1892), II, 304.
67. North, *Recollections*, II, 304; CMS: MA/01.

70. North, *Recollections*, II, 297.
71. RCM: Report to Father-General of Capuchins for year 1 September 1887-31 August 1888.
72. MA: TA9, encl. Franklyn to Colonial Secretary, 10 January 1870.
73. *Mauritius*, I, 232; PRO: CO167/535, Gordon to C.O., 21 September 1871.
74. COCP Eastern No. 21 of 1876.
75. PRO:CO167/561, encls Phayre to C.O., 28 December 1874.
76. CO167/573.
77. CO167/587, encl. Bowen to C.O., 13 January 1880.
78. CO167/581, Napier-Broome to Hicks-Beach, 16 March 1879 confidential.
79. CO167/579 and 586, encls Napier Brown's 26 March 1879 confidential and Salmon's 6 March 1879.
80. NAS: B38, Lemarchand to Havelock, 1 May 1880; B36, Salmon to Governor's private secretary, 16 August 1879.
81. PRO: CO167/589, Bowen to C.O., 24 August 1880.
82. CO167/586, petition encl. Salmon to C.O., 6 February 1879.
83. CO167/591, Havelock to C.O., 30 October 1880; C.O. to Bowen, 14 December 1880, *ibid.*
84. Minute on Broom's 21 March 1881, CO167/592.
85. CO167/596, Broome to C.O., 1 October 1881; MA: B42, Griffith to Lees, 22 July 1890, with encls at TG28.
86. CO167/596, encl. Broome to C.O., 24 October 1881 confidential
87. MA: B38, Stewart's 17 and 18 June 1881; RBK: Mascarene letters 1866-1900, Stewart to Hooker, 22 August 1881.
88. CO167/602, encls Broome to C.O., 4 September 1882.
89. Minute encl. *ibid.*
90. CO167/615, Pope-Hennessy to C.O., 15 April 1884; North, *Recollections*, II, 303; NAS: B39, report by Hodoul and Jouanis, 19 September 1883.
91. CO167/671, Brown to Jerningham, 14 October 1892.
92. CO167/650, Griffith to Pope-Hennessy, 10 June 1889; NAS: B42, Griffith to Colonial Secretary, 2 September 1889.
93. CO167/699.
94. RH: MSS. Ind. Ocn s217: Davidson's Diary 14 January 1907.
95. NAS: C/SS/74 I, Esnouff to Governor, 17 January 1891.
96. NAS: C/SS/15.
97. *Ibid.*
98. *Ibid.*
99. CO167/753.
100. CO167/754, Escott to C.O., 21 June 1902.
101. CO167/761, Escott to Cox, 1 and 7 February 1903 private; RBK: East African and Mascarene letters 1910-1914, Escott to Thiselton-Dyer, 8 August 1903.
102. NAS: C/AM/7, Escott to C.O., 16 February 1901.
103. CO167/596, encl. Broome to C.O., 1 October 1881.
104. RCM: Père Edmond's letter, August 1889.
105. RCM: Mémoire de Mgr Mouard....'
106. NAS: B41, Griffith to Pope Hennessy, 9 September 1885.
107. CO167/596.

108. RCM: Mouard's 28 February 1884.
109. RCM: Mouard to Pope Hennessy, 9 and 23 April 1886.
110. CO167/569, encl. Griffith to Lees, 14 April 1890.
111. NAS: C/SS/36 I.
112. For Sweet-Escott's views, CO167/732 and 755.
113. Davidson's secret undated memorandum, about 1913, NAS: C/AM/18.
114. RCM: Cyrus to Bishop, 29 May 1814.
115. NAS: C/AM/18, Justin de Gumy to Mackay, 5 March 1913.
116. CO530/16, encl. Davidson to C.O., 11 September 1911 confidential.
117. Henry de Monfried, *La Poursuite du 'Kaipan"* (Paris 1934), 258.
118. NAS: C/AM/18.
119. NAS: C/SS/6; PRO: CO167/175, 225, 308, 337.
120. CO530/18, encls Davidson to C.O., 2 December 1912.
121. CO530/22 and 23.
122. CO530/22.
123. CO530/16.
124. O'Brien to C.O. 23 January 1914 confidential.
125. Minute on Davidson to C.O., 6 December 1911 confidential, CO530/16.
126. O'Brien to Collins, 24 October 1917 private, CO530/32; and independent
     identification of Lanier to this author by M. Henri Dauban.
127. CO530/26, encl. O'Brien to C.O., 25 February 1915.
128. CO530/21, O'Brien to Fiddes, 20 April 1913 private.
129. NAS: C/W/1. II
130. C/W/1. I.
131. C/W/1. IV.
132. C/W/4.
133. C/SS/54.
134. O'Brien to C.O., 25 May 1914 confidential, NAS: C/AM/19.
135. NAS: Executive Council Minutes, 29 June 1934.
136. CO530/33, for typed copies of Brooke's letters; the originals are at Rhodes
     House, Oxford.
137. CO530/33, O'Brien to C.O., 22 February 1918.
138. CO530/33, O'Brien to C.O., 15 January 1915, and to Risley, 3 July 1918
     private.
139. Cf Brooke's letters.
140. 'Even supposing that his socialism were progressive, the black of this country
     is not yet mature enough to understand these ideas clearly and to profit
     from them. He will long require our tutelage which with me and many
     of my friends is far from resembling hatred against the black labouring
     people.' CO530/33, encls O'Brien to C.O., 15 January 1918 confidential.
141. CO530/46, Byrne to C.O., 9 April 1923.
142. CO530/33.
143. CO530/34, O'Brien to C.O., 2 May 1918 confidential; CO530/35, Collet's
     evidence encl. Fiennes to C.O., 30 January 1919.

Chapter 4: Seychellois and Créole

1. PRO: CO167/574, Phayre to C.O., 10 October 1877; NAS: C/SS/2.
2. NAS: B46, Escott's 18 November 1901.
3. NAS: C/SS/2.
4. NAS: B38, Stewart to Colonial Secretary, 15 July 1881.
5. CO530/45.
6. CO530/29, O'Brien to C.O. 13 May 1916 confidential, and CO530/28, 15 February 1916 confidential.
7. NAS: HK/PERs/2671; Byrne to C.O., 22 July 1926 confidential, CO530/51.
8. NAS: C/SS/37, C/AM/18; PRO: CO530/128.
9. NAS: JTB/PERS/0345 confidential.
10. CO530/34 and 36.
11. NAS: C/SS/60; PRO:CO530/44, Minute on Petrides to C.O., 14 February 1922.
12. CO530/38, Fiennes to C.O., 28 April 1920.
13. *Le Réveil Seychellois*, 31 December 1931.
14. CO530/38, Fiennes to Grindle, n.d.
15. NAS: C/AM/22.
16. CO530/42, Minute on Petrides to C.O., 24 October 1921 confidential.
17. CO530/7; CO530/10, Davidson to Stubbs, 18 August 1908 private.
18. NAS: C/SS/30, C/SS/71 II; Henri de Monfried, *La Poursuite du 'Kaipan'* (Paris 1934) 261.
19. CO530/140, Minute on De Vaux to C.O., 18 February 1928 confidential.
20. NAS: C/SS/24.
21. NAS: JTB/PERS/0345 confidential.
22. C/SS/24; PRO: CO530/145, encl. Honey to C.O., 13 July 1928, and CO530/153, 5 December 1928.
23. F.C. Cooke, *Report on the Coconut Industry* (Victoria 1958).
24. CO530/225, Honey to C.O., 19 June 1931 confidential; CO530/173; NAS: C/AM/25; PRO: CO530/301, encl. Lethem to C.O., 7 September 1934.
25. CO530/186, Stephens to C.O., 20 October 1930; CO530/188, Beamish and Stephens to Under Colonial Secretary, 13 November 1930.
26. CO530/197, Honey to C.O., 22 January 1932.
27. De Vaux to C.O., 25 July 1923.
28. CO530/271 has the original of Reid's report, published in 1933 by HMSO as *The Financial Situation of Seychelles*; Reid's private comments are in CO530/291.
29. NAS: C/SS/46.
30. *Ibid.*
31. 'Hitherto riveted at our masters' own sweet will ... no need to tell you that we are fleeced ... Secret talk among our masters is of punishing us for our "insolence" in addressing this petition to you. I have been personally warned. We await your action.' *Ibid.*
32. C/SS/12 II.
33. CO 530/380, Stephens to Beamish, 15 August 1936.

34. CO530, Minute on Grimble's 5 December 1940 confidential.
35. C/SS/2, Grimble to Dawe, 24 November 1937 private and secret.
36. C/SS/71 I and II; JTB/PERS/0345 confidential; C/SS/2, Grimble to Bevir, 25 December 1938 private.
37. CO530/405.
38. CO530/455.
39. CO530/486, encl. Grimble to C.O., 27 July 1938.
40. Grimble to Bevir, 11 July 1938 private, NAS: C/SS/54.
41. 'That would encourage them in pleasures and relaxation in which they already indulge too much ... I know the mentality of these people ... Never to have possessed anything, cannot be demoralising to a race, a people ... These blacks of this place, who have property, are they better than their ilk who have none? No, they are more turbulent, more discontented, and above all, more insolent ... a few "red skins" driven mad at not being whites.' C/SS/54, Amanda Stephens to Grimble, 6 September 1934.
42. CO530/415, Collet's 19 April and 10 May 1937.
43. CO530/339, Lethem to Bevir, 16 July 1935, extract.
44. CO530/415, memo. encl. Collet to C.O., 10 May 1937.
45. CO530/339; NAS: C/AM/28.
46. 'He who wishes to separate religion and education has ceased to think catholicly.' NAS: ED/3/2.
47. 'A fatal and culpable liberalism in the matter of education'. *Action Catholique*, October 1939.
48. MBAR: SEY 630 (1); NAS: C/SS/36 IV.
49. MBAR: SEY 630 (1).
50. *Ibid.*, Bro. Gérard's 18 May 1936.
51. NAS: ED/3/2; ED/2/12/1; C/SS/36 V; RCM: Frères Maristes: Gerard to Maradon, 2 January 1942.
52. RCM: Education: Maradon to Secretary to Government, 24 July 1939.
53. NAS: C/SS/36 IV; ED/1/1; PRO: CO530/500.
54. E.g., RCM: Maradon to Abercrombie, 11 December 1941.
55. RCM: Frères Maristes: Maradon to Michaelis, 14 November 1943. 'What a disaster this would be for the religious formation of our children.'
56. RCM: Maison Mères des Soeurs de St Joseph de Cluny: Maradon's 20 May 1939. 'I tell you that the Government is seeking to anglicise Seychelles more and more, but since this is to the detriment of religion, I must necessarily put a curb on their ambition.'

Chapter 5: *Grands Blancs* Triumphant

1. CO530/415, Grimble to Bevir, 18 August 1937 private.
2. NAS: C/W/6 I.
3. *Idem*, vols II and IV.
4. *Idem*, vols II, IX, XII; C/SS/74 II.
5. C/W/6 XII, Grimble to Nageon, 6 July 1940.
6. C/W/6 I, local memo. of 1939.
7. *Ibid*, Budget Address 21 January 1941.
8. CO530/488, 541.

9. CO530/574, Grimble to Acheson, 24 January 1941 private.
10. NAS: CRIM/2/1 I; *Le Seychellois*, 26 September 1953.
11. NAS: CON/2, Stephens to Logan, 4 January 1943 confidential.
12. CO530/574, Grimble to C.O., 5 December 1940 confidential.
13. *Ibid.*
14. Minute, *ibid.*
15. NAS: JA/PERS/0034.
16. LEGCO/2/46, Arissol to Jakeway, 15 January 1947.
17. CON/22.
18. PRO: CO530/588, C.O. to Logan, 23 July 1943; CO530/643, for Parkin-son's report.
19. *Ibid.*
20. CO530/590.
21. *Ibid.*
22. CO530/588, 637.
23. CO530/568, Smith's 30 August 1943.
24. RCM: Frères Maristes: Gérard to Maradon, 28 February and 2 March 1944.
25. E.g., NAS: ED/24; RCM: *Réglements pour les Ecoles Catholiques de la Mission des Seychelles.*
26. NAS: ED/2/5 II.
27. ED/2/24.
28. ED/2/27.
29. PRO: CO530/568, Cox's 17 November 1943.
30. NAS: SECRET, CENS/4; PRO: CO530/668.
31. CO530/619.
32. NAS: ED/2/5 II; ED/2/34 confidential.
33. *Ibid*; secret education files; and PRO: CO530/618.
34. CO530/620, Logan to Gent, 15 February 1945.
35. NAS: Secret: EDUCATION: Giles to Father McCarthy, 17 January 1946.
36. PRO: CO530/620.
37. NAS: ED/2/27.
38. PRO: CO530/668, Logan to C.O., 28 July 1945 secret.
39. NAS: ED2/27.
40. Cf. Gérard's letters to Maradon, 1940-1946, in RCM: Frères Maristes – especially that of 19 July 1946; MBAR: SEY 630 (4), Gérard's 8 July 1945.
41. 'The dear Brothers are leaving the Colony because of the unrealistic demands of the Director of Education.' MBAR: SEY 630 (4), Gérard's 11 September 1946.
42. RH: MSS Brit. Emp. S.22.
43. *Educational Reorganisation in Seychelles*, 13 August 1945; NAS: ED/2/27, ED/2/54, ED/21.
44. ED/2/34.
45. ED/2/105; ED/2/76 confidential.
46. ED/2/97 confidential; S/34/4.
47. ED/2/27A confidential; RCM: Selwyn-Clarke's letters to Maradon.
48. RCM: Collet to Carnegie Board, 13 and 22 November 1946, and to Touris, 31 January 1947.

49. NAS: TAX/4/3 IV; LEGCO/2/46.
50. LG/11, LG/3/7.
51. CD/1/12.
52. Selwyn-Clarke Papers: Selwyn-Clarke to Bailey, 18 February 1949.
53. *Ibid*, Collet to Selwyn-Clarke, 16 and 27 July 1947, and Vanniasinkam to Selwyn-Clarke, 17 December 1947.
54. NAS: LEG/6/2; LEG/6/D.
55. LEG/16 confidential.
56. LEG/6/1.
57. CON/2A secret.
58. *Ibid.*
59. *Ibid.*
60. TAX/9.
61. TAX/9; TAX/4/3B confidential.
62. TAX/4/3/B II confidential.
63. TAX/4/3/B I confidential.
64. For access to his papers I am greatly indebted to the late James Cameron.
65. NAS: CON/8.
66. *Ibid.*
67. Seychelles Planters' and Taxpayers' Archives: File 9, Committee meeting 16 December 1958. For access to these archives I am indebted to M. Gustave de Comarmond.
68. Planters' and Taxpayers' File 8.
69. NAS: TAX/4/3/B II confidential.
70. Planters' and Taxpayers' File 8.
71. Planters' and Taxpayers' File 9, Stephens to de Comarmond, 20 November 1948.
72. File 8, de Comarmond to Parsons, 27 August 1948.
73. RH: MSS Brit. Emp. S. 22.
74. Selwyn-Clarke Papers: letters from Collet.
75. Planters' and Taxpayers' File 9; Legislative Council Proceedings.
76. CON/2/A III.
77. Planters' and Taxoayers' File 9.
78. Cameron Papers; NAS: MSSC/1 II.
79. NAS: LG/5/2 II.
80. *Hansard*, 25 July 1956.
81. Court of Appeal for East Africa: Criminal Appeal 69 of 1957.
82. NAS: TAX/4/3/B II confidential; Cameron Papers.
83. TAX/4/3/B II and III confidential.
84. LEG/52/ PRO: CO530/175, 225, 308, 337.
85. RCM: Education: Maradon to Gregg, 29 June 1950.
86. NAS: LG/6/8; CON/LA IV confidential.
87. NAS: unnumbered Education Department File: Collet's 14 October 1955.
88. Executive Council Minutes, Secret, 13 September 1956; MISC/32 II; LAB/22 II.
89. CD/1/4/1; CD/10 confidential.
90. MISC/32 II.

Chapter 6: Days of Reckoning

1. Cf. J.L. Talmon, *The Origins of Totalitarian Democracy* (reprinted London 1970) 1.
2. Thorpe to C.O., 5 December 1960 secret, NAS: S/POL/1 secret; and see his 6 January 1961 secret, *ibid*; police reports are in POL/95 secret.
3. Thorpe to C.O., 7 July 1958, COLAFF/52/1 confidential.
4. CON/16 confidential, CON/22 confidential.
5. *Le Seychellois*, 10 April 1963; Lloyd to Anderson, 10 June 1963, COLAFF/63/4 confidential.
6. CON/23 secret.
7. SW/117 secret.
8. See Mancham's address in Committee Room 14, House of Commons, 21 February 1990.
9. Lloyd to Anderson, 4 March 1965, COLAFF/67/4 confidential; James R. Mancham, *Reflections and Echoes from Seychelles* (Victoria 1972).
10. Mike Hoare, *The Seychelles Affair: The legendary mercenary's dramatic account of the coup that failed* (London 1987), p.46.
11. *Le Seychellois*, 14 May, 14 August, 7 September 1960.
12. *Seychelles Weekly*, 11 July 1964.
13. *Ibid.*, 4 January 1964.
14. Cf., *People*, 25 January 1975.
15. *Seychelles Weekly*, 2 November 1963.
16. *Ibid.*, 9 November 1963.
17. *Ibid.*, 16 November 1963.
18. *Ibid.*, 10 December 1969.
19. *Seychelles Bulletin*, 14 February 1964.
20. NAS: CON/22.
21. Mancham in House of Commons Committee Room 14, 21 February 1990.
22. *People*, 28 December 1964.
23. NAS: SW/120 secret.
24. NAS: SW/120 confidential; *Seychelles Weekly*, 20 June 1964.
25. *Daily Nation*, 26 May 1964.
26. *Le Seychellois*, 12 June 1964.
27. *Ibid.*, 17 June 1964.
28. NAS: SW/120 secret.
29. *People*, 12 April 1965.
30. NAS: LEG/99.
31. SW/130 confidential.
32. Legislative Council Proceedings, 21 February 1966.
33. CON/16.
34. *Seychelles Weekly*, 15 October 1966.
35. *Ibid.*, 13 November 1965, 8 and 22 January 1966.
36. NAS: NEWS/15 confidential.
37. 'I will call it quite simply a constitution made by the English' Governing Council Minutes, 4 December 1968.
38. CON/22.

39. *Ibid.*
40. *People*, 14 June 1971.
41. *Ibid.*, 14 April 1971.
42. NAS: CON/70/1 secret.
43. ED//F/70/8; ED//E/74.
44. ED/CUD/404.
45. *Echo des Îles*, 1 February 1973.
46. *Ibid.*, 15 April, 1 May 1873.
47. Governor's Office: Personal 19/3.
48. *Le Seychellois*, 3 July 1970.
49. *Seychelles Weekly*, 5 May 1873, 24 April 1874.
50. *Ibid.*, 31 January 1970.
51. NAS: CON/56 confidential.
52. *Seychelles Weekly*, 1 February 1968.
53. NAS: CON/70/1 secret.
54. ELEC/PA/1.
55. CON/80.
56. CON/77.
57. *Ibid.*
58. *Seychelles Weekly*, 21 October 1974.
59. *Daily Express*, 19 June 1974.
60. *People*, 17 May 1972.
61. *People*, 1972-3 *passim*.
62. *Seychelles Bulletin*, 12 April 1972.
63. SDP Release No. 1.
64. *Seychelles Weekly*, 24 March 1973.
65. Cf. Mancham in Committee Room 14, 21 February 1990.
66. NAS: DG/T14/P2C confidential.
67. *Ibid.*
68. *People*, 16 May 1966.
69. *Seychelles Weekly*, 16 November 1974; *Nation*, 20 June 1977.
70. NAS: Cabinet Memorandum, 16 February 1976 secret.
71. Cabinet Minutes, secret, 13 December 1975.
72. *L'Echo des Îles*, 15 February 1976.
73. France Albert René, *Seychelles: the New Era* (Victoria 1982), p. 3.
74. *Nation*, 9 June 1977; Cabinet Memorandum, 12 August 1977 secret.
75. *Nation*, 2 July 1977.
76. *Indian Ocean Newsletter*, 1 October 1994.
77. Hoare, *Seychelles Affair*, 51.
78. *Ibid.*, 109-51.
79. *Indian Ocean Newsletter*, 13 June 1992, 27 April 1991.
80. *The Presidential and National Assembly Elections in Seychelles 20-23 July 1993: the Report of the Commonwealth Observer Group* (Commonwealth Secretariat 1993).

BIBLIOGRAPHY

PRIMARY SOURCES – MANUSCRIPT

National Archives of Seychelles

This well-organised Archives Office, as it was in the late 1970s, was the starting point for this study; for much of the time there are excellent descriptive registers needing no duplication here. In addition to the many registered series of records I was given access to material in government departments not then deposited in the Archives, according to the open principles of J.R.M. Mancham's government and later again by F.A. René's.

Through the great kindness of M. France Morel du Boil, I was able to examine his magnificent professional notarial archive of marriage and business contracts, succession inventories and family papers at large, dating from the 1790s; while for access to specific genealogies I am indebted to the Nageon de l'Estang and Chesnard de la Giraudais families, and to Mme Maryse Eichler for access to papers relating to the Jorre de St Jorre family; for the Seychelles Planters' and Taxpayers' Association archive, I thank M. Gustave de Comarmond; and for the loan of press cuttings collected by W.F. Stephens, I thank Mr Kantilal Jivan Shah.

All this original material is complemented by:

Public Record Office, Kew

Here the Colonial Office CO167 series has the Seychelles correspondence intermingled with Mauritius until separation in 1903 when CO530 takes over. The papers of the Commissioners of Eastern Enquiry at CO415 are vital too, as are the Admiralty reports from the East Indies and Cape of Good Hope Stations, and the Captains' Logs. Treasury Series T71 is valuable, relating as it does to slave-compensation.

These, the two major archives, are supplemented by:

Mauritius Archives

Here Series TB is the main source for the years of French sovereignty; it continues into the British, post-1810 era, documentation of which is then taken up by Series TA. Series IA, IB and IC deal with abolition of slavery. Series D43/2 contains letters from Seychelles 1788-1800. Series F, Guerre et Marine, and *Déclarations d'Amirauté*, contain valuable though fragmented shipping information.

Archives Départementales de La Réunion

These supplement Mauritius Archives' Seychelles holdings pre-1810, with Series L311, L324, L408 particularly; and for the same years, again, both these archives are complemented by:

Archives Nationales, Paris

Here the Series Marine and Colonies are vital; they are drawn upon for printing in Fauvel's *Documents*, though not exhaustively.

At Service Historique de l'Armée, Chateau de Vincennes, Carton 1676 in *Séries Mémoires et Reconnaissance* is valuable.

At the Ministre des Affaires Etrangères, *Séries Mémoires et Documents: Asie*, Tomes 4, 8, 11, and *Afrique* Tomes 104 and 120, relate marginally, as do *Affaires diverses politique Angleterre*, 52 and 53.

Bibliothèque Municipale de Caen

This has the papers of General Decaen, again liberally but not completely printed by Fauvel as they relate to Seychelles.

British Museum

Has the 'Journal du Corsaire le Générale Marlatic', and some of R.T. Farquhar's letters.

Church Missionary Society Archives, London

These contain a well-catalogued Seychelles collection, while at the counter-part Society for the Propagation of the Gospel vols J18, J19, J20 have some interest.

Archives of the Marist Brothers, Rome

Here the Brothers' disputes with the Bishop can be followed in SEY 621.3, 630 and 660. In more detail, this and other themes may be followed in:

Archives of the Roman Catholic Mission, Seychelles

This comprises an eclectic, uncatalogued, large and very valuable collection.

Archives of the Royal Botanic Gardens, Kew

Here is material of more than botanical interest in: Mascarene Letters 1866-1900; East African and Mascarene Letters 1901-1914; Seychelles – Agriculture etc. 1882-1919; Seychelles – Botanic Stations: Cultural Products etc. 1875-1913.

Rhodes House, Oxford

Has material relating to Seychelles, and to Charles Evariste Collet especially, in Anti-Slavery Society Papers: Brit. Emp. MSS S.22; and the Arthur Creech-Jones Papers are of interest.

Finally, under other auspices, the Selwyn-Clarke Papers were generously made available.

PRIMARY SOURCES – PRINTED

Fauvel, A.A., *Unpublished Documents on the History of the Seychelles Islands anterior to 1810....*(2 vols, Victoria, 1909).

Le Duc, Saint-Elme, *Ile de France. Documents pour servir à son Histoire civile et militaire* (reprinted Port Louis 1925).

Stanmore, 1st Baron, *Mauritius: Records of Private and of Public Life, 1871-1874* (2 vols, Edinburgh 1894).

SECONDARY SOURCES

Abel, Antoine, *Coco Sec* (Paris 1977).

————, *Une Tortue se Rappelle!* (Paris 1977).

————, *Contes et Poèmes des Seychelles* (Paris 1977).

Accouche, Samuel, *Ti anan en foi en Soungoula. Créole Stories from the Seychelles*, ed. and trans. Annegret Bollée (Cologne 1976).

Barkly, Fanny, *From the Tropics to the North Sea, including ... Five Years in the Seychelles* (London 188?).

Belcher, Sir Edward, *Narrative of a Voyage round the World, performed in Her Majesty's Ship 'Sulphur', during the Years 1836-1842....* (London 1843).

Benedict, Burton, *People of the Seychelles* (London 1966).

Benedict, Marion and Burton, *Men, Women and Money in Seychelles* (Berkeley, CA, 1982)

Bollée, Annegret, *La Créole Française des Seychelles* (Tübingen 1977).

Bradley, J.T., *The History of Seychelles* (2 vols, Victoria 1940).

Charroux, Robert, *Trésors du Monde. Enterrés, émurrés, engloutis* (Paris 1962).

Chaudenson, Robert, *Le Lexique du Parler Créole de La Réunion* (2 vols, Paris 1974).

Dayer, Louis, Les Îles Seychelles. Esquisse historique (Fribourg 1967).

Filliot, J.-M., *La Traite des Esclaves vers les Mascareignes au XVIIIe Siècle* (Paris 1974).

Frappas, Théophile, 'Souvenirs d'une jeune marin ...', *Journal des Voyages ou Archives Géographes du XIXe Siècle*, XXI, 65, 1824.

Harrison, George, 'The Seychelles', *Nautical Magazine and Naval Chronicle for 1839*.

Hoare, Mike, *The Seychelles Affair: The legendary mercenary's dramatic account of the coup that failed* (London 1986).

Jourdain, John, *The Journal of John Jourdain* (Hakluyt Society 1905).

Laplace, Cyrille Pierre Théodore, *Voyage autour du Monde par les Mers de l'Inde et de Chine sur la Corvette d'Etat 'La Favourite' pendant les Années 1830, 1831 et 1832 ....* (Paris 1833).

Laplace, Cyrille Pierre Théodore, *Compagne de Circumnavigation de la frégate 'L'Artimèse' pendant les Années 1837, 1838, 1839 et 1840 ....* (Paris 1842).

Lionnet, Guy, *Coco de Mer: The romance of a palm* (Victoria 1970).

Ly-Tio-Fane, Madeleine, 'L'Etablissement du Jardin du Roi aux Seychelles', *Journal of the Seychelles Society*, 6, November 1968.

Mancham, James R., *Reflections and Echoes From Seychelles* (Victoria 1972).

Martin, Gaston, *Histoire de l'Esclavage dans les Colonies Française* (Paris 1948).

Miller, W.G., 'Robert Farquhar in the Malay World', *Journal of the Malaysian Branch of the Royal Asiatic Society*, LI pt 2, 1978.

Moine, Jacques, 'Les Seychelles et la Révolution Française', *Journal of the Seychelles Society*, 7, November 1971.

Monfried, Henry de, *La Poursuite du 'Kaipan'* (Paris 1934).

Moreau de Saint-Méry, Médéric-Louis-Elie, *Description topographique, civile, politique et historique de la partie française de l'Isle Saint Dominique* (3 vols, Philadelphia, 1797).

North, Marianne, *Recollections of a Happy Life* (2 vols, London 1892).

Owen, W.F.W., *Narrative of Voyages to Explore the Shores of Africa, Arabia and Madagascar* (2 vols, London 1833).

Ozanne, J.A.F., *Coconuts and Créoles* (London 1936).

René, France Albert, *Seychelles: The New Era* (Victoria 1982).

St Ange, Alain, *Seychelles: What Next?* (Sydney 1991).

Scarr, Deryck, 'Whispers of Fancy: With Mr Arthur Creech-Jones in Seychelles', *Journal of Imperial and Commonwealth History*, XI, 3, May 1983.

———, *Slaving and Slavery in the Indian Ocean* (London and New York, 1998).

Smythe, Captain W.H., *The Life and Services of Captain Philip Beaver....* (London 1829).

Surcouf, Robert, *Un corsair malouin: Robert Surcouf; d'après des documents authentiques* (Paris 1889).

Talmon, J.L., *The Origins of Totalitarian Democracy* (London 1970).

Telfair, Charles, *Some Account of the State of Slavery at Mauritius, since the British Occupation in 1810; in Refutation of Anonymous Charges promulgated against Government and that Colony* (Port Louis 1830).

Thompson, H.P., *Into All lands* (London 1951).

Toussaint, Auguste, 'Le Traffic Commerciale des Seychelles de 1773 à 1810', *Journal of the Seychelles Society*, 4, 1965.

Toussaint, Auguste, 'Shipbuilding in Seychelles', *Journal of the Seychelles Society*, 6, 1966.

Waugh, Alec, *Where the Clock Chimes Twice* (London 1951).

Republic of Seychelles, *White Paper on Aggression of November 25th 1981 against the Republic of Seychelles*.

Commonwealth Secretariat, Reports of Observer Groups.

Unpublished

Stone, Ian Rodney, 'Education in Seychelles: The Government and the Missions 1839-1944', B.Phil thesis, Open University, 1977

Wanquet, Claude, 'Le Peuplement des Seychelles sous l'occupation française. Une expérience de colonisation à la fin du XVIIIe siecle' (n.p., n.d., ms. in present author's possession).

INDEX